The bar mitzvah boy pictured on the cover is not me.
No such photograph of me exists as, during the dress rehearsal, I fainted.
I would have been on the floor behind the bimah.

Some of the Dexter School track team. I am on the far right.

MATTHEW, MARK, LUKE, JOHN... *and Me*

GROWING UP JEWISH
IN A CHRISTIAN WORLD

ARTHUR D. ULLIAN

BAUHAN PUBLISHING
PETERBOROUGH, NEW HAMPSHIRE
2020

Library of Congress Cataloging-in-Publication Data

Names: Ullian, Arthur D., 1939- author.
Title: Matthew, Mark, Luke, John . . . and me : growing up Jewish in a Christian world / Arthur D. Ullian.
Description: Peterborough, New Hampshire : Bauhan Publishing, 2020. | Includes bibliographical references. |
Identifiers: LCCN 2020032467 (print) | LCCN 2020032468 (ebook) | ISBN 9780872333246 (trade paperback) | ISBN 9780872333253 (ebook)
Subjects: LCSH: Ullian, Arthur D., 1939- | Jews—United States—Biography. | Jewish businesspeople—United States—Biography. | Paralytics—United States—Biography. | Jews—United States—Social conditions—20th century. | Christianity and other religions—Judaism. | Judaism—Relations—Christianity. | Jews—Cultural assimilation—United States. | Antisemitism—History.
Classification: LCC E184.37.U45 A3 2020 (print) | LCC E184.37.U45 (ebook) | DDC 305.892/40730904—dc23
LC record available at https://lccn.loc.gov/2020032467
LC ebook record available at https://lccn.loc.gov/2020032468

Book design by Henry James and Sarah Bauhan
Cover Design by Henry James
Printed by Versa Press

Front cover images:
Stained Glass Window from Cologne Catheral, Germany. Public Domain (Wikimedia Commons),
Emotional Pinkas Synagogue wall, Alamy Stock Photo, used with permission.
Bar Mitzvah Boy ©Brett Deutsch, www.deutschphoto.com, used with permission

BAUHAN
PUBLISHING LLC
PO BOX 117 PETERBOROUGH NEW HAMPSHIRE 03458
WWW.BAUHANPUBLISHING.COM
603-567-4430

Printed in the United States of America

For my grandchildren, Otis and Seraphina,
and the generations of family to come.

May this encourage them to explore the Jewish side of their
heritage and honor its commandment to repair the world.

CONTENTS

FOREWORD

REMEMBERING A TIME OF ANTISEMITISM
AND ASSIMILATION

It is sadly true that one of the most pernicious results of prejudice is when members of a persecuted group accept the ugly stereotypes used to characterize them. As Anthony Julius has observed, "contempt for Jews, when sufficiently widespread, can foster self-contempt among Jews." It can convince Jews that unfounded, inaccurate accusations leveled against them or, by extension, against the Jewish state, are true.

Deborah Lipstadt, *Antisemitism: Here and Now*

A
s part of its fight against racism the *Boston Globe* recently featured a front page headline, "From August Halls of Prep Schools, Stories of Racism." Arthur D. Ullian's new book reminds us of past times not truly past, when antisemitism was commonplace and young Jews had no place to hide from daily exposure to "polite" antisemitism and Christian denigration of the Jewish faith at the same prep schools. This was the time of the "gentleman's agreement," when assimilation was encouraged and many young Jews found it easier to blend in rather than assert their particularity. It was the time of the "melting pot" in 1940s and 1950s America.

When I discuss this period in my classes, Jewish students have no memory of this history and find it hard to even imagine a time when Americans of many faiths and ethnicities found American culture so attractive that they changed their dress, their religion, their names and even their physical appearance to conform to American norms of beauty, culture, religion and behavior. Arthur Ullian brings those times to life with his painfully honest, sometimes funny, sometimes embarrassing but always engaging memoir.

His stories range from those about his fully assimilated mother who tries (fortunately unsuccessfully) to assimilate her son through the "best" (meaning most restrictive) schools to his own slow realization that the daily chapel he was required to attend and the Christianity that formed the cultural underpinning of the schools he went to were simply wrong, demeaning of his people and his faith, and ultimately dangerous.

Even more important for our time the memoir reveals how young Jews internalized those messages and assimilated or learned to fight as Arthur did. The book describes his years of painful struggle (often played out in hilarious encounters with his long-suffering therapists) and study to better understand the deadly impact of Christian antisemitism as depicted in the bible stories he was required to listen to every Sunday and more terrifyingly on Easter and Christmas.

This is history worth remembering in these times when antisemitic stereotypes disguised as anti-Zionism are becoming the conventional wisdom of our time and political correctness pressures young Jews to assimilate into the prevailing culture at great risk to their own identity.

In 1825 Heinrich Heine was baptized and declared he had converted from Judaism because conversion was his "entry ticket into European Culture." Arthur's book reminds us that abandoning our identity, our love of our people, and our connection to Zionism and Israel is too high a price to pay for admission to a movement that claims to value every nationality and minority identity but has only contempt for our people.

In the end, Arthur's lifelong search leads to an understanding of the progress the Church has made as well as its failures. More importantly he comes to a new appreciation of the beauty and majesty of Jewish traditions and texts, and the importance of his own Jewishness and its ability to bring meaning and purpose to his life.

—**Barry Shrage**
Professor of the Practice, Hornstein Jewish Leadership Program,
Brandeis University and President, Combined Jewish Philanthropies of
Greater Boston, 1987–2018

PREFACE

Historians are rarely demographers, so it is likely that the history you studied in school included little information on population size for any given region or time period. Numbers available for early populations are estimates by and large, but even the estimates tell a story. A cursory look at Jewish population growth from the first century to the present suggests that something doesn't add up.

In the first century, Jews apparently comprised approximately 7.5 percent of the population of the known world—perhaps seven to eight million Jews in a total population of one hundred million.[i] But that turns out to be roughly the same number of Jews living in the world in 1882. After that, our numbers more than doubled by 1939—the start of World War II (and the year I was born). The well-documented

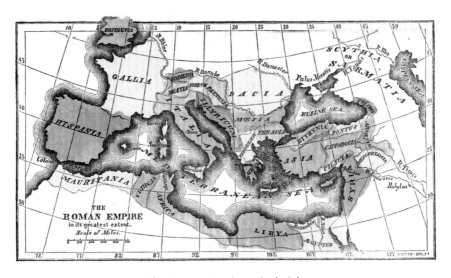

The Roman Empire at its height

atrocities of World War II slashed our population by six million, after which it doubled again, to approximately 14.4 million today.[ii]

Had our numbers increased at the rate of the general population, Jews would number 135 million strong today (equal to one-third the population of the United States).[iii] Instead, there are only 14.4 million Jews living in a world of 7.5 billion people. In 2020, we are an infinitesimal percentage of the world's population.

What happened? Why the dramatic ups and downs? Where are the rest of us?

Introduction

If you're a young boy growing up Baptist in Macon, Georgia, or Birmingham, Alabama, it's understood that you will receive a rifle for your tenth birthday and that one Sunday morning—after church—you'll don camouflage gear, jump in your Dodge Ram, and go off hunting ducks or deer with your father and older brothers.

Whereas, if you're a Jewish boy growing up in the suburbs of New York or Boston, your Sunday mornings will be spent in Hebrew School, and your physical activity is more likely to involve tennis, skiing, or soccer. The case you carry around will contain not a Winchester 22, but a violin. You'll be programmed to aim for the best university you can get into, followed by medical, law, or business school, and one day, you'll probably leave your office early for a weekly appointment with your psychiatrist.

Are these stereotypes? Absolutely.

But I have to admit I *was* that Jewish boy, I did play the violin, and I spent many of my adult years in therapy, filling many of those fifty-minute sessions with revisiting my boyhood and adolescence and coming to the realization that much of my personality has been shaped by encounters with that oldest form of stereotyping—antisemitism.

From fifth to twelfth grade, I went to school with boys who were the sons, grandsons, and great-grandsons of Boston's oldest, wealthiest, and most prominent families. Many were descended from America's first families, those who arrived on the Mayflower. Their culture alternately confused and amused me, and, in response, I stereotyped them then, and am probably doing it now—but, hopefully, mixed with equal parts of affection and admiration. You'll have to be the judge.

Psychologists have discovered that the act of stereotyping others is hardwired into our brains as a survival mechanism when we confront people from outside our own "tribe." It's apparently part of the fight-or-flight response, when you must quickly assess potential danger. But this is a response that can be reprogrammed as we learn to appreciate, both emotionally and intellectually, that stereotypes are often exaggerated or just not true at all.

In the course of this book, I have examined the various ways in which Jews have been stereotyped through the centuries, where these misrepresentations originated, how they were continually reinforced by Christian thinkers, Christian writers, and Christian culture—and the horrific results that ensued for generations of Jews. While attending mandatory chapel at school, I encountered the accusations hurled at the Jews by the authors of the New Testament Gospels and the deep historical animosity Christians seemed to have for us. In class, I heard those accusations repeated in different forms: Jews only care about money and conspire to control international finance. Jews poisoned the wells of Europe and caused the Black Plague. Jews murdered Christian children and used their blood for ritual purposes. Worst of all, Jews were responsible for the death of Jesus. Greed. Conspiracy. Infanticide. Deicide. Accusations we have paid for in blood for centuries.

However, I often think back to a conversation with a Catholic priest who told me that shifting the blame to the Jews for killing Christ was a political choice by the Gospel writers, and that the Jews had nothing to do with that event. From that conversation, I literally felt a weight I had been carrying around subconsciously for years lift from my shoulders and from my spirit. My immediate reaction was that, if my school friends understood that the accusations against Jews had been entirely invented, they might feel that same relief and be freed from the burden of hatred.

This memoir records my journey of many years during which I read everything I could find to show that the claims against us simply could not have happened. My hope is that by discovering the actual history behind the Gospels, my Christian readers will experience the same sense of relief.

Nelson Mandela articulated this notion in his autobiography:

> *A man who takes away another man's freedom is a prisoner of hatred. He is locked behind the bars of prejudice and narrow-mindedness. I am not truly free if I take away someone else's freedom, just as surely as I am not free when my freedom is taken from me. The oppressed and the oppressor alike are robbed of their humanity.* [iv]

A hundred years earlier, Abraham Lincoln said much the same thing:

> *As I would not be a slave, so I would not be a master.*[v]

The hatred learned in the Church by those who isolated, expelled, tortured, and massacred us down the centuries must surely have robbed them of their humanity and taken a huge psychic toll on them. The hater essentially locks himself up in a ghetto of negativity that consumes all his emotional energy and potential creativity, and eventually has the effect of separating him from the wider community. Even Christians who live moral lives of acceptance and kindness can find themselves categorized with those who would harm and oppress, and thus experience some of the weight of guilt. I assume that many of the boys I went to school with would fall into this category—good men who privately feel uncomfortable when they hear an antisemitic joke at a party or see on the news that a hate crime has been perpetrated against a synagogue in their community.

Jesus grew up as a Jew, preaching many variations of the central commandment that all Jews are tasked to live our lives by every day: *tikkun olam*—Repair the World. Another version of this commandment, found in the Talmud, says to us: "If you save one life, you save the world entire."

I hope that readers of this book will accept it as my own act of *tikkun olam*.

Chapter 1

APPARENTLY, MY FAMILY MURDERED THEIR GOD . . .

My story starts in elementary school, where, even as a little kid, I always knew when it was Wednesday. I knew because every Wednesday, from fifth grade on at three o'clock sharp, every boy in my class would abruptly close his book, change into a tuxedo (we're talking about 1950 here), stuff his school clothes into his locker, file out, climb onto the school bus, and disappear.

Every boy but me, that is.

Those Wednesdays were my first experience of social exclusion. I never knew until much later where my classmates were going or why I wasn't asked to go along. I only knew that suddenly, without warning, I was the only one left in the building, a ten-year-old kid alone with the janitor.

Where do you guys go every week? I never had the nerve to ask.

I had recently arrived as a new fifth-grader and I assumed I wasn't picked because I had missed some important piece of information everyone else was in on—like a secret handshake that everyone seemed to know but me. Or maybe I wasn't good enough at whatever it was they were going to do—like at a neighborhood pickup ball game, where everybody stands around while two self-appointed captains choose up sides and everyone prays not to be the last one standing. Anyway, I wasn't picked, so I went home.

I don't remember how I discovered where my classmates went, but the answer turned out to be simple. I was the only Jew in a prestigious WASP (White Anglo-Saxon Protestant) private school in

ULLIAN

Brookline, Massachusetts, and Miss Hall, the dance instructor of choice in the WASP community, thought that since Jews wouldn't be attending any of the debutante cotillions that awaited my classmates, why bother instructing me in proper dress, proper cotillion manners, and the foxtrot?

My mother had been determined to enroll me in this upper echelon school, where I was relegated to be the first and only Jew admitted to date. I don't imagine she was thinking of me when she made that decision.

Being the only Jew was bad enough, but it was soon obvious that my fellow students were all related to each other too. The clue was the shared names. There was a slew of Cabots sprinkled throughout the grades, with Cabot appearing as a first, last, or middle name. Same for Thorndike, Forbes, Lowell, and Lawrence. There would be a Peter Lowell Thorndike Abbott III, who, naturally, was related to John Thorndike Forbes II. I was certainly not a second or a third; I couldn't be, because in my Jewish tradition we don't name our babies after living family members.

On the contrary, I was a newcomer in the most profound sense: a first-generation American. My father, a well-dressed businessman with a terrific sense of humor, had come to this country as a two-year-old in the late 1890s from a village called Mogilev, in the part of Russia known as Belarus. Like tens of thousands of other Jews, his family—and my mother's as well—had emigrated to escape the repeated pogroms (targeted massacres) inflicted by the local Christian population with the tacit approval of the authorities, along with the rampant poverty caused by the isolation of Jews from mainstream Russian society.

If my mother was going to send me to a school like that, maybe she should have thought ahead and named me something like "Efraim Mendelssohn Uliano II." That way, as they called out those graceful names, brimming with legacy, at awards day or graduation, mine wouldn't have fallen so flat. Arthur David Ullian. Not much ring there.

Eventually, I discovered that many of my classmates were named after streets, cities, and towns: Berkeley, Boylston, Coolidge, Fuller, Appleton, Binney, Peabody, or Lowell. I thought this was quite an odd thing to do, until I realized that they weren't named after the streets, cities, or towns, but having settled here in the seventeenth and eighteenth centuries (while my family was being expelled from one country or another), they had modestly named those streets, cities, and towns after themselves.

I read once that there was a street in Naples named *Via Scannaguidei,* literally "Kill-the-Jew Street," not exactly something a Jewish boy could be proud of. I went looking for it years later when I was travelling in Italy, but it's no longer named that. Someone changed it some years ago, perhaps thinking it revealed a bit too much about the city's past.

In any case, I didn't know what I was doing at that school, and I never dared to question my parents' decision. But I liked to imagine that I could summon up the nerve to ask the headmaster. In my fantasy, his answer would be something like:

"You know, Arthur, I've been thinking the same thing: What *are* you doing here? You don't know our hymns. You barely know the Lord's Prayer. I've been watching you, Arthur, and you get as far as 'Our Father, who art in Heaven,' and then you start mumbling because you don't know the rest. And when we say, 'Let us pray,' you just bend your head ever so slightly. Don't you see that all *our* boys put their arms on the back of the pew in front of them and then put their heads down on their arms? And furthermore, Arthur, you don't have a town or a city, let alone a street, named for your family. How *did* you get admitted here?"

I never confessed to my parents that anything was wrong at school, and they never suspected, though I can remember throwing up many mornings before we got in the car to go. To some degree, I never even admitted to myself that something didn't feel right.

But the thought that I was fooling everyone, that they would eventually find out I didn't really belong, lingered throughout my school years, overshadowing my childhood, adolescence, and beyond. The feeling never disappeared, because my environment never changed. I kept on moving in the same direction, associating with the same people, and burrowing deeper and deeper into a society that wasn't really my own. Through all those years, from childhood to young adulthood, I often felt deep down that I was merely tolerated, and made it through the discomfort of that feeling by acting as much as possible like the other boys, fooling and joking around. Of course, it's likely that every adolescent everywhere feels something similar, due to the lack of confidence and insecurity of the young, but when you actually *are* different from your peers in some significant way, the effect is magnified. Going along to get along is no substitute for the genuine belonging that everyone longs for.

From this private elementary school, everyone moved on in seventh grade to even fancier, bigger name New England prep schools, all dressed in our identical uniforms of gray flannel slacks, blue blazers, button-down oxford shirts, school ties, and penny loafers. And once again, I found myself in an environment where I was the only Jew, although at this school perhaps half a dozen Jews had attended since its founding in 1798. Since I was a member of the class of 1957, I guess that works out to one Jew every quarter of a century.

At this school, we were expected to attend chapel, which was described in the admission packet as "nondenominational." I looked around for a Star of David,

Me at age 9 with my violin

but found only crosses. Apparently, what they meant by nondenominational was that all Protestant denominations were represented, and the few Catholic boys were more or less accepted. The guest ministers who were invited to lead these services on Wednesday mornings spoke from a pulpit so high that they could look down on the boys in the pews of the little stone chapel and read to us from the New Testament about how my "tribe" had murdered Christ, how we betrayed him, spat on him, desecrated our own temple out of greed, and massacred innocent children. The message was hard to miss: Jews were the Antichrist—a people to be feared and shunned.

In all the hours I spent in that chapel, I never heard one good thing about a Jew in the Gospels or any other part of the New Testament. I remember the Good Samaritan story they kept bringing up, but where was the Good Jew story? The Samaritan story is a parable about a couple of robbers who beat up some guy, steal his stuff, and leave him lying on the road to die. A priest and a Levite happen to walk by, and upon seeing this guy on the ground, cross to the other side of the street, heartlessly ignoring his plight. Now a priest and a Levite are not just your run-of-the-mill Jews. Levites are the family (one of the twelve tribes) associated with study and teaching of ethics, and a priest would be considered a community leader as well. That these particular Jews would pass by someone who was suffering suggests that things with the Jews were rotten from the top down.

The story goes on: Then a Samaritan happens by, and he picks the man up and brings him someplace to be cared for. The minister then explains that the point Jesus was making in this parable was the importance of loving thy neighbor.

What's new about that? I wanted to ask that minister up there on his pulpit. *That's right out of the Old Testament, which we call the Hebrew Bible.* I heard this all the time in temple: "Love thy neighbor as thyself, and love thy God with all thy heart and mind and soul." The New Testament just repeats what Jews have been preaching for five thousand years.

Why were we so hated? I wanted to know. My grandmother always gave the same unsatisfactory answer when I asked her about it: "Antisemitism, oy, it's been going on forever," she would say in her Yiddish accent.

"But why?" I would ask again. "Here, take a cookie," she would reply, as if to say, "don't ask me any more questions about this."

Those school years were very difficult. Not that I was overtly picked on. My classmates were, and some still are, my friends. Nobody ignored me or made fun of me. But there was an invisible line I couldn't cross. Any activity outside of school was understood to be out of bounds for me. Socializing with my classmates in their homes or invitations to join their family activities simply never happened. I wasn't invited to their parties—I didn't even know there *were* any parties. Their parents were invariably polite to me when we were introduced on campus; they always managed a pleasant smile, but that was as far as it went.

But combined with the messages I heard preached in chapel, it was all too much. I felt like a spotlight was shining right on me, as if I were constantly on display in front of the whole school as the living example of those evildoers the minister was trashing. What was I supposed to do, just sit there in my pew? I didn't know what to do.

The lead-up to Easter week was the worst. The readings from the New Testament during this holy week all involved the Passion Story, and it was here that every vile misdeed one could imagine was committed by the Jews of Judea, culminating with that most unforgiveable misdeed of all: deicide—the killing of God. Did we Jews really do all that? I wished I knew. I urgently needed to be able to say, *No, it's not so!*

Even as a kid, I found some of the accusations a little far-fetched. In the first place, if Jesus was God, how would you be able to kill him? A clue was given to me some forty years later, when a Catholic priest I traveled with to Israel on an interdenominational study tour mentioned that blaming the Jews for crucifying Christ was a purely political act. Now this was a perspective I hadn't heard before, and not only did it make sense, but I felt that some of the weight of guilt I had been carrying around since I was a kid was lifted off me. We were standing on Mount Scopus, overlooking the Dome of the Rock, Al-Aqsa, the mosque the Arabs built six hundred years after the destruction of the First Temple, and the same spot where Abraham made preparations to sacrifice his son Isaac. It was also from this spot overlooking Jerusalem that the Roman general Titus directed the destruction of Jerusalem and the Second Temple in 70 CE. This place, with its great significance in Jewish history, made the priest's explanation that much more powerful for me as we discussed the crime that has been the chief source of our people's suffering for two thousand years.

In 1962, the Second Vatican Council, convened by Pope John XXIII, went as far as to remove some of the blame from Jews living

View of the Temple Mount from Mount Scopus, Jerusalem

after the time of the Crucifixion. Those alive at that time, though, must still be considered guilty and must still carry that guilt.

My response then, not too different from the one I'd had at school, was "How exactly could we have carried this off?" Couldn't the Son of God, who was capable of performing miracles like walking on water, feeding thousands of people with one loaf of bread and two fish, curing the blind and the lame, and raising Lazarus from the dead prevent himself from being captured and crucified? The priest's statement, if true, suggested that all Jews, living and dead, could be absolved from the responsibility for Christ's death—*including* those living at the time of the crucifixion.

It was just what I needed to hear. The priest's passing comment on Mount Scopus launched me on a lifelong mission to study and understand Roman, Jewish, and Church history, to find the answers my grandmother could never give me.

So many of the accusations contained in the Gospels, I have since found, are inaccurate and misleading, including the "Good Samaritan" parable. The Samaritans were not so good, quite the opposite. In Raoul McLaughlin's book, *The Roman Empire and the Silk Routes*, he notes that the warlike Samaritans were constantly attacking the Empire. They were so notoriously aggressive that the Emperor rejected their peace terms because: ". . . he knew their race to be untrustworthy [and] wanted to utterly annihilate them."[1] I can almost imagine the Gospel writers getting together to write the story, and one of them saying, "Let's really make the Jews look bad by casting these terrorists as the good guys!" It would be like writing a parable about "the Good Talibans"—maybe the last people you'd call on if you needed help on the road at night.

Chapter 2

BE IT NEVER SO HUMBLE . . .

Both my childhood homes were located on the tops of hills where there were no other Jews. This was not so easy to manage in Newton, Massachusetts, where there were and are still lots of Jews, lots of temples, and lots of Chinese restaurants. I couldn't have explained it as a child, but I later realized that my mother was a determined social climber, suffering from an extreme case of assimilation disorder (thank you, shrink #1), and who, quite simply, felt she was better than everyone else. A friend of mine once told me about her aunt, who had Alzheimer's disease. My friend's father would joke that the one good thing about Alzheimer's was that it made his sister forget she was better than everybody else. Well, my mother never forgot to her dying day.

I eventually figured out that the reason she sent me to these exclusive schools for blue-blooded WASP boys was that she thought it would move her higher up the social ladder she was trying to climb. She never realized that the White Anglo-Saxon Protestants had their own social ladder and it wasn't available to her, either by sale or rent. She couldn't buy a house in their exclusive neighborhoods, so maybe living on top of a hill was as high as she could expect to go.

Our first hilltop house was in a predominantly Catholic neighborhood. The other kids were kind of tough and not particularly friendly, but they were the only game in town, and I often biked down to the flat area of the hill where they hung out. One guy, Johnny McAllister, bigger and tougher than the rest, often chased me around, occasionally punching me in the shoulder with his middle knuckle protruding. He threw me to the ground once, straddling me and putting his knees on my upper arms to pin me, then pressing his fingers over my mouth with such force that the imprint of his hand lasted for days. I had no idea how I had provoked him, but made it my point to stay away from him after that. Based on what I was hearing at school, I guessed he was after me for killing Christ. Strangest of all was that, occasionally, when we were playing, a group of kids would run away, yelling "no woojes allowed!" and leave me standing alone in the street. Just before we moved out of that neighborhood, one of those kids told me that "wooj" was Jew, sounded backwards. How did those little kids even know I was Jewish, and why did they feel the need to be so hostile?

All this was taking place in the 1940s and early 1950s. It was a time when, by tacit agreement among Realtors and home-sellers, Jews couldn't buy homes in the exclusive suburbs and Back Bay Boston neighborhoods where many of my school friends lived. Nor could we join their country clubs or register at certain hotels. Keeping us out must have required a certain amount of sophisticated detective work, and it was rare that anyone slipped through, as my wife and I found out many years later. We offered the asking price for a house in one such neighborhood, but the broker must've smelled a rat because after several days he called to say how "terribly, terribly sorry" he was, "but a higher offer has been received and accepted by the owners."

"Sure, twenty bucks higher," I told my wife.

I figured out how they did this during prep school, this knowing who the Jews were. I learned on one of the rare occasions I found myself in a classmate's home. There, on the corner of his mother's writing desk, was a small black book with red lettering and three thin red stripes drawn smartly at the top and the bottom of the cover. Very discreet, very tasteful. This little black book was the *Social Register*, which I was sure every one of their mothers proudly displayed on her own antique desk where she sat to write thank-you notes and dinner party invitations on creamy stationery, engraved with her monogram or family crest.

They referred to the *Register* for the names and addresses of those prominent families they expected to associate with. There was a summer edition as well, in which summer homes were listed, along with yacht club affiliations, including the name and size of the yacht. The *Social Register* dates back to the late 1800s. If you weren't in it, you were out.

In Palm Beach, Florida, where my parents would sometimes take us for school vacations, the oldest and most elegant hotel, and the only hotel on the beach, The Breakers, was off limits to Jews. How they knew you were Jewish when you called to make a reservation, even with no detectable accent, was a mystery. If your name was "Goldstein" or "Shapiro," that was easy enough to pick out, and clearly an Eastern European accent wouldn't even get you as far as the reservation line. But what about our name, which ends in "ian," and is usually associated with Armenians? They don't like Armenians either? I thought I had the answer: they simply consulted the *Social Register*. I may have been the only Jew in Palm Beach, and a kid to boot, who knew the secret.

We needed our own places, so eventually a Jewish hotel-chain operator from Boston saw an opportunity and decided to build our own version of The Breakers. And maybe, just to spite Breakers-builder Henry Flagler, he bought Flagler's palatial marble home, Whitehall, which stood directly opposite the hotel on the Intracoastal Waterway side. (Palm Beach is a very narrow, long island, bounded by the Intracoastal on one side and the ocean on the other.) Somehow this Jewish developer got a zoning permit to build a fourteen-story building right behind the Flagler palace and attach the two structures, utilizing the original front door as the hotel's grand entrance. The original iron gates surrounding the new hotel broadcast the message, "riff-raff keep out." In the final *coup de grâce*, he called the hotel "The Whitehall."

Flagler would have flipped over in his grave to see so many Jews prancing around, the women dressed in mink stoles even when the temperature hit eighty degrees, everyone dining on gourmet matzoh ball soup, chopped liver, and gefilte fish, and all this going on in his elegant marble home, which no Jew had ever sullied before. Dinner was served in his grand dining room with its floor-to-ceiling windows overlooking the Intracoastal, where guests ate to the music of the Ruby Newman band and violin players strolled from table to table dressed in white dinner jackets. It was all meant to mirror the style of The Breakers, I heard, but across the island they didn't have the great Jewish food. Those guests were probably served something more like the bland prep school fare they were used to, and instead of Ruby Newman they had Lester Lanin.

At our next hilltop residence in Newton I didn't need to worry about anyone beating me up, because only one elderly couple in their eighties shared the hill with us. That hill was so steep I had to walk my bicycle up, and in the winter we needed chains on the tires to get home; even with chains it was often impossible. In a snowstorm, my father would often have to abandon the car at the bottom and walk up. Convenient? No. Exclusive? Yes—and that was exactly what my mother wanted.

She believed that R. M. Bradley, the broker, chose her as the purchaser of this house because he recognized in her all those fine qualities required to live in such an exclusive prize. The clincher was that she was able to tell him her son attended the same hotsy-totsy prep school as his son. In reality, the old Yankees knew that since there was so much land up there, a developer would eventually buy it all and build spec houses, selling them to any Moishe, Abe, or Saul who showed up with a check. They were right, and within ten years lots of Jews were living on the hill and the bloom was off this rose.

My mother was difficult and not always easy to take, but somehow there were lots of strong and delightful memories as well. My father had a record player the size of a dresser, which not only played records, but recorded them as well. Every other Sunday my paternal aunt and uncles would come over for dinner, followed by wonderful concerts in the living room with almost everyone participating. My Uncle Sam and Aunt Anna Sherman were usually the stars of these family shows; both had near-professional voices and Anna played the piano beautifully.

My father would slip a blank glass record into the recording machine, and in a booming voice that sounded like a radio announcer he would introduce the concert:

"We are all here today, Sunday, January the twenty-third, nineteen hundred and forty-three, extremely honored to present the distinguished tenor from Worcester, Massachusetts, Samuel Uliano, accompanied by world-renowned soprano Anna Shermano. Today, they will perform for you 'Eli, Eli' in the original Hebrew!"

Then the two of them would start off, making up most of the Hebrew words, swaying back and forth in unison, almost crying as they reached the poignant moments in the song—the whole performance ending with a standing ovation from all the relatives gathered in our living room.

Then my father would call on me and ask if I would treat everyone to my rendition of "Baa, Baa, Black Sheep," followed by my older sister—quite an accomplished pianist herself—playing Beethoven's "Moonlight Sonata." As I got older, I would bring out my violin and my mother would accompany me. (I kept those records all these years, and just recently had them converted to CDs with all the scratches removed. It's bittersweet to listen to them now and hear the voices of people I loved who have been gone for so long.)

There was never any question that ours was a Jewish home, complete with traditional Jewish cooking, Jewish expressions, and Jewish joking around. The only thing that was missing was a mother who never quite got the hang of behaving like a stereotypical "Jewish mother"—one whose every thought is for her children. In retrospect, I would have appreciated just a little bit more of that.

29

Chapter 3

WADING IN DEEPER

I t took me a few weeks of getting dropped off and picked up at school to see that something besides our last name was different here. Then it struck me. We drove up each day in our big new Buick, while my classmates arrived in old Ford station wagons with wood trim on the sides, or older sedans painted in sedate colors—sometimes with thin red racing stripes along their length (to match the stripes on the *Social Register*?). Some of their cars had subtle monograms on the doors, and many sported college or club decals on the rear window. Most of their cars had license plates with no more than four numbers, some with the year their father had graduated from Harvard or Yale—like 1927. Our license plate, on the other hand, was six random numbers signifying nothing, other than the fact that we hadn't come over on the Mayflower.

Dammit, Mom! I wanted to say. *Why didn't you do a little homework before you sent me here, and at least find out what kind of car we're supposed to drive, and where you order the monograms and decals?* You needed to know the basics, I thought, if you were trying to barge into their society; you couldn't simply mail in an application to one of those fancy schools. We looked like a bunch of know-nothing immigrants right off the boat. There I was, a first-generation American, and they had been here for centuries. Their furniture had been here longer than we had.

Actually, to be honest, the car part wasn't her fault. We *had* to buy Buicks. Everyone in the family had to buy Buicks because my Uncle

Murray owned a big Buick dealership in Chelsea, and on the back of every car he sold he stuck a small, raised chrome sign that read "by Ullian," This was about as far as you could get from the understated elegance the Yankees had perfected over the course of three hundred years.

There were plenty of other things that set me apart as well. When I boarded at prep school, my father would occasionally come to visit in the afternoon and would always stop at the G&G Delicatessen on Blue Hill Avenue (a previously old Jewish Boston neighborhood) to bring me a hot pastrami sandwich with a kosher half-sour pickle, a cream soda, and some chocolate-covered Halvah. He would drive up to the front porch of my dorm, Robbins House, in the enormous Buick, cigar in his mouth, wearing his gray fedora with pinched indents like the one Harry Truman sported.

Now that I think of it, my father looked a bit like Harry Truman, complete with the wire-rim glasses.

The wood-paneled walls of our dormitory, oiled and polished for more than a hundred years, had never been assaulted by a pastrami sandwich and a half-sour pickle, and seemed to suck it all in, leaving the dorm to smell like a Jewish delicatessen.

I smell something funny, I imagined each student coming through the front door would exclaim.

I do too.

And then a mob of them would follow the scent up the stairs, down the hall, and stop in front of my room only to discover me sitting on the edge of my bed, secretly scarfing down my alien sandwich and garlic-riddled pickle.

Life at school in the eighth grade grew more intense as the cotillions and the parties got closer and my classmates prepared for their older sisters' and cousins' coming-out events. My Bar Mitzvah was also looming closer, but lucky them—all they had to do was learn the foxtrot. I had to learn Hebrew and read it from a four-hundred-year-old Torah scroll while holding a sterling silver place keeper with its pointy finger on the end. And I had to accomplish this in front of an entire temple packed with friends and relatives, all waiting for me to screw up.

A week before my big day there was a dress rehearsal in the temple. I was on the *bimah* (altar), standing behind the massive pulpit, wearing my *yarmulke* and *tallit* (skullcap and prayer shawl), and when I looked out into the cavernous sanctuary where the principal was seated, I got dizzy and, boom, I hit the floor.

"Where did he go?" the principal yelled as he ran up the stairs onto the *bimah* to see what had happened. He found me sprawled out behind the pulpit, my *tallit* covering my face, my *yarmulke* askew, as he frantically tried to find a pulse.

When I recovered and finally got home, I ran up to my room. How was I going to get up there behind that pulpit the following Saturday and survive? In addition to my Torah reading, I would have to make a speech in English, discussing the meaning of the Torah portion I was about to deliver. The English part was not the problem, as I had already written it out with the help of my Bar Mitzvah tutor and had practiced it many times in front of the mirror over my bureau. But my Hebrew was weak.

The Torah scroll doesn't even include the vowels that usually appear under the Hebrew letters, something I am sure is intended to drive Jewish kids crazy. Try to learn English without any vowels! The scribes must have thought it was too much extra work to add the dots, and figured that if you had paid attention in Hebrew school, you would know the words and wouldn't need the dots.

Well, I didn't know the words, and it was making me very anxious. Couldn't I just fake it like Sid Caesar in a TV shtick, where he would mimic a foreign language, making it all up but injecting a few English words here and there so the audience would understand what he was talking about? The word endings just needed to sound guttural, like someone clearing his throat. After all, this was a Reformed (modern, liberal) temple; most of the congregants even ate lobster.

Converting to a foxtrot religion with country clubs and tennis courts sounded pretty appealing to me at that moment.

Somehow, I made it through the service without fainting, and only one cousin found fault: "Pretty good, Arthur, but there were a few mistakes."

So here, take back your fountain pen, I wanted to say to the critic. I had made it through, and that was good enough for me.

Surely Christianity is far simpler. In the middle of the first century, when Paul and his followers were beginning to convert pagans to his new religion, he knew it had to be accessible, so he made it "Jewish light." He kept the Ten Commandments, for instance, but circumcision was out. How could you possibly expect a guy more than eight days old to sign up for that?

Keeping a Kosher home, which required two sets of pots and pans, two sets of dishes, two sets of everything just to keep the *milchig* (dairy) and the *fleishig* (meat) separate, was too expensive and too complicated. So that was out.

Studying and reading the Torah, debating the meaning of every word, phrase, and paragraph, understanding the hundreds of laws governing daily life and trying to keep those laws . . . it was way too much homework and most pagans were illiterate anyway. So those things were out too.

And why not be able to achieve salvation and a terrific afterlife just by accepting Jesus, who so considerately died for your sins?

While you're at it, Paul, make the Christian holidays coincide with the familiar Roman ones, like assigning Christmas to December 25, the date Julius Caesar had already declared a holiday in 46 BCE to mark the winter solstice, complete with the lighting of candles. (The Romans were off by a few days; the solstice is actually December 21.)

After the Bar Mitzvah, the tradition was to host a brunch in the temple's social hall and invite everyone attending the service, even those who didn't know the Bar Mitzvah boy. (That was a clever way to get people to come to temple on Saturday morning, kind of like the Salvation Army, who invite the homeless to a worship service and, if they sit through it, give you a cup of soup and sandwich.) But you had to go all out at an *Oneg Shabbat* (delight of the Sabbath); a huge spread was expected. There would be every kind of bagel, three kinds of cream cheese, hand-cut belly lox, an enormous whitefish, sablefish, green salads, egg salads, herring, and everything you would ever want from Katz's fifteen-foot-long refrigerated deli case (if you weren't paying). Then there was Danish and *rugelach* (pastry roll-ups with cinnamon and nuts or apricot jam) for dessert.

Later that night, you'd have a big catered party at your home, where you served more of the traditional Jewish gourmet foods: knishes, kishke, kugel, chopped liver, shrimp cocktail (remember, we weren't kosher), and more.

And that was it. Done! I was now a man at thirteen.

All during this time, I heard only scraps of information about the cotillions that were beginning to take place. My classmates had to be aware I was never invited, and I imagine they were embarrassed to talk about these parties in front of me. But in my fantasies, they resembled what I thought went on in Masonic temples—dry ice pumping smoke into the air, back-lit with colored spotlights, and secret rituals taking place.

What I eventually gathered was that each beautiful blond, debutante, dressed in a long white gown, would walk down the center aisle of an elegant banquet hall on the arm of her father. She would be trailed by her escort, one of my classmates, who had been practicing this ritual since the fourth grade and now was lending his arm to the girl's proud mother.

Arrayed in front of them, in my imagination, was a grand stage, carpeted in red, with four or five old grandes dames seated in chairs fit for Queen Elizabeth or, better still, Queen Victoria, dressed in faded, fifty-year-old debutant gowns, which were shortened as these stewards of society shrank in size. As each debutante approached, the old ladies would rise, smile approvingly, and tenderly touch the hand of the white-gloved debutant.

A year or two later, the coming-out parties began, and I assumed they had to be a whole lot more fun than our knish parties, but I really didn't know since Miss Hall had been correct to assume I would never be invited. She would have been shocked to discover that I did crash a few with friends who also hadn't been invited but knew about the events through the preppy grapevine. These parties were held at local country clubs and included big-name bands, dancing, and open bars, but almost nothing to eat. Apparently, the idea was that with enough to drink, you didn't miss the food.

One party stands out. My friend Rabbit (I still don't know where that nickname came from) heard of a party he hadn't been invited to. He was spending the weekend at my home (boarders could leave campus if they were staying with students who lived in the area). This particular party was being held in one of the most exclusive tennis and cricket clubs in the world—so exclusive, Jews were barely allowed to drive on the same street, let alone enter the club.

"We can crash it, but I'll need a tux," Rabbit whispered to me after dinner.

"My father has an old one and he won't mind because he won't know," I whispered back.

We got dressed and off we went. We must have been sixteen or seventeen at the time, because I remember that we drove ourselves in one of my parents' cars. It was my first time at one of these things, and even without the advantage of being prepped by Miss Hall on how to be a model guest, I felt certain I could wing it. I thought that getting in would be the toughest part, but to my surprise it was easy. The nice thing about WASPs is that they are far too polite to inquire if you have an invitation. They greet you with a pleasant smile, and you're in.

Was that a Jew we just let in? I imagined the two women greeters saying to each other. My paranoia was running wild as I anticipated the tap on the shoulder asking me to leave. That would have done it. I'd never be able to show my face at school again. Everyone else belonged to the same clubs or attended the same church, so they looked familiar to each other. But of course, they didn't know me from Adam. Thankfully, the tap never came. After a while I began to relax and breathe normally again. I followed Rabbit to the bar, ordering what he ordered.

That club was and still is so well fenced you can't see any part of it from the street. Once inside, I found that it was not splashy, but stately and comfortable. I noticed all this while trying not to look around as if I had just gotten off a bus from Milwaukee. I took my drink and walked toward the grand covered balcony, a structure furnished in old wicker that was covered in traditional green-and-white striped fabric, looking like it came right out of the Newport Tennis Casino. Here on the balcony was obviously where members could sit overlooking the impeccably groomed grass courts, drinking martinis and watching impeccably groomed members play in their dress whites.

This party was nothing like any Bar Mitzvah I'd ever been to. There was lots of liquor and precious little to eat (Jewish parties are exactly the reverse). Rabbit got smashed and eventually collapsed in the circular driveway right by the front door. Getting up, he tried leaning against the front wall to steady himself, and then proceeded to throw up all over my father's tuxedo.

I began to notice that there was a distinctly Yankee look, made even more prominent by the outfits they wore. (Southerners call all Northerners Yankees, but Yankees are what New Englanders call the descendants of the earliest immigrants to America—the English-born Pilgrims and Puritans of Mayflower and Plymouth Rock fame.) But it wasn't only the clothing they wore. I tried it all—the pink shirts, polo shirts with up-turned collar, the nearly transparent framed glasses, even the slightly English-sounding Harvard "lock-jaw" accent. There wasn't much more I could do to replicate the look. It was the healthy, glowing, tanned complexions and classically formed bodies, nothing like the ones I saw slathered with Coppertone around the swimming pool at the Fontainebleau in Miami. There was no way I was ever going to look like Michelangelo's well-muscled David, standing in the piazza in Florence; nor was any Jewish guy I ever knew. Actually, the real David in the Bible was probably a scrawny little Jew like the rest of us.

My classmates' fathers not only looked more athletic than my father, but they also looked younger, no matter what their age. Some seemed to have a slight limp, perhaps from an old hockey or football injury, which only enhanced their rugged image. They all played a solid game of tennis, sailed in the summer, skied in winter, and enjoyed telling what they thought were hilarious stories about Salty or Poopsy or Bunny falling off the porch after one too many. A lot of my friends' parents seemed to have one of those funny nicknames. For the longest time I thought they were talking about their dogs.

Once, in art class, we looked at a slide of Leonardo da Vinci's *The Last Supper* and discussed all the arty stuff, like the angles of the walls showing perspective, the symbolic meaning of the scene in the

The Last Supper, da Vinci, ca. 1495–1496

Detail of the head of Judas from
The Last Supper

windows in the background, how Jesus is placed at the center—all those details that take up class time. But my attention was drawn to something else. What struck me was that Jesus and the apostles looked exactly like my classmates, which is to say they had light skin and straight, thin noses, some even slightly turned up, which happened to be the preferred style for young Jewish girls getting nose jobs in the 1950s. All except Judas. He was the apostle who betrayed Jesus for thirty pieces of silver and is seen sitting two seats to the left of Jesus, clutching his money pouch. Judas's complexion is decidedly darker than the rest, and from my vantage point in the classroom, I would swear that his nose looked Jewish.

I was thinking of a question I could ask the teacher (to make him think I was a serious student). But the question that popped into my head made me start to laugh so hard that, trying to hold it in, I couldn't have asked it if I'd wanted to:

Sir, I think Leonardo may have got it all wrong. After all, Jesus and all the apostles were Jews, but they don't look Jewish to me, unless da Vinci was making the point that when you get baptized and became a Christian, you get a new nose as a bonus. Is that right, sir?

Later, I heard this very issue addressed on National Public Radio, confirming my schoolboy thoughts. Robert Wallace, in his book *The World of Leonardo, 1452–1519*, found that da Vinci had spent a lot of time looking for models of young men with faces that exhibited innocence and beauty, but when it came time to find a model for Judas, he found just the right man imprisoned in a Roman dungeon. This person had a dark complexion, scars, and unruly hair covering part of his face: all in all, a sinister-looking fellow you wouldn't want to meet on a dark street.[2]

Anyway, what I had thought was so funny about the painting vanished as my teacher continued: "As you look at the painting carefully, the apostles aren't eating; they're all talking excitedly, gesturing and pointing. Does anyone know why?"

No one raised their hand, so he said, "Jesus had just told the apostles that one of them would betray him."

I held my breath, waiting for what I knew was coming. Again, I was the villain in the room. And I thought art class was supposed to be fun.

I had heard these words in chapel and now I was hearing them in art class too. Painted in 1498, *The Last Supper* has been viewed by millions of people. It is one of the most famous artworks in history, and everyone is reminded of the original slur against the Jews contained in Matthew 26:21 (King James Version used throughout this book): "Verily I say unto you, one of you will betray me." The same words are repeated in the communion section of the mass as well: "On the night Our Lord was betrayed . . . He took bread."

No matter what class I went to, there seemed to be some evil Jew lurking in the curriculum.

Chapter 4

MY INTRODUCTION TO THE NEW TESTAMENT

Now the chief priests, and elders, and all the council,
sought false witness against Jesus, to put him to death.

Matthew 26:59

In the dark and obviously Semitic features of Judas, as depicted in da Vinci's "Last Supper," to this verse from Matthew 26:59, I can recognize the fault line that began to break apart the world for centuries of Jews.

These priests, elders, and the council referred to in the verse were all Jews, according to the minister as he read to us from Matthew in chapel. There was not too much subtlety there. Our chief priests and elders were scheming and figuring out how to get rid of Jesus. Matthew made us sound like a bunch of no-good bastards eager to kill the son of God.

The unease I felt at the country club, or when I arrived for the first time in the school's U-shaped driveway, was nothing compared to this. The school chapel stood on the top of a small hill at the end of the campus—a perfect replica of an English country church, typical of many New England prep schools. These schools were founded by wealthy, old Protestant families, and our chapel must have been Episcopalian, the American offshoot of the Church of England.

Even though I went there every Wednesday morning from the seventh grade on, my recollection of the interior is blurry because of my anxiety about being there. I vaguely remember a large stained-glass window with images of military men from every branch, and a plain white cross standing on a table under the window. I have a faint memory of a raised pulpit with an ascending curved stairway, but I'm only guessing now. The only thing I can describe for certain is the floor.

My classmates and I all filed in, sitting with our friends, none of whom seemed to be taking it very seriously. Chapel was just another opportunity to horse around, and my classmates all seemed ready with ideas on how best to annoy other boys sitting next to or in front of them. The most popular prank was to place a prayer book on the seat in front of you after everyone rose for a hymn or prayer, opening the book slightly so it would stand up. When the kid sat down again, he would land on the book's sharp edge and let out an embarrassing scream. It didn't take long before you learned to survey the area with your hand before sitting down. Flicking the ear of the kid in front of you was also a good one, especially when the sanctuary was quiet, causing another embarrassing moment for the victim.

"Then did they spit in his face and buffeted him; and others smote him with the palms of their hands," the minister continued reading from Matthew. Another glowing example of how rotten we are. If I hadn't been Jewish myself, just hearing these words read all the time from the holy Bible could have turned me into a real good antisemite.

We learned that the Jews conspired to put Jesus to death. We learned how in the morning we Jews tied him up and turned him over to Pontius Pilate for trial. At the trial, the Jews were solidly against him and wanted him out of the way. Pilate offered to spare one of three men condemned that day, pleading with the Jews to spare this gentle person who called himself Jesus Christ. But we wouldn't hear of it. We wanted him dead, and so we all started yelling:

"Crucify him, crucify him!"

Pilate's wife became very upset and wanted to spare Jesus's life, and Pilate himself washed his hands of the whole affair, saying, "I am innocent of the blood of this just person: see ye to it."

"Then answered all the people, and said, 'His blood be on us, and on our children.'"

That did it! His blood is on me, and that means no dancing school and no cotillions either. I didn't even have a girlfriend yet, and already my children and grandchildren were cursed.

At this point in the reading I sensed that everyone was looking at me as I slumped lower and lower in my pew. The fun of being part of those boyish pranks evaporated. My muscles tightened, and my eyes were glued to the floor as I sat there, frozen. No wonder the floor, with its worn wooden planks, is the thing I remember best.

When I finally escaped into the fresh air, feeling desperately alone, I would distract myself by thinking how funny it would have been if I had stood up and run out of the chapel waving my hands, yelling, "I did it, I did it!" like in a Perry Mason TV show where the brilliant defense attorney gets the guilty guy to break down and admit his crime.

The crucifixion story was read at Easter, but Christmas wasn't a whole lot better. The Gospels, the first books of the New Testament, relate the life of Jesus from birth to resurrection. In the Gospels, the Jews are introduced as the villains of the story right away in the first few pages.

"When Herod the king had heard these things, he was troubled, and all Jerusalem with him," a guest minister read from Matthew.

The Jewish king then tries to trick the three wise men into revealing where Jesus lives in order to kill him. But Joseph has a dream and the Holy Ghost or an angel tells him to get out of there right away, because Herod is after his child. So, Joseph, Mary, and baby Jesus travel to Egypt and do not return until the angel tells Joseph that Herod is dead.

The minister continued: "Then Herod, when he saw that he was mocked of the wise men, was exceeding wroth, and sent forth, and slew all the children that were in Bethlehem, and in all the coasts thereof, from two years old and under, according to the time which he had diligently inquired of the wise men."

"Weeping, and great mourning" was heard, and children could not be comforted, as an army of Jews slaughtered innocent children. (Although these would have been Jewish children being killed, Christians in later centuries interpreted this as Jewish men slaughtering Christian children. We know this because this "massacre of the innocents" is a recurring theme in religious painting and church architecture for the next fifteen hundred years, and

Pilate Washing His Hands, Preti, 1663

this would not have been the case had they thought Christians were the perpetrators.

Nevertheless, that story had a familiar ring. Every Jew knows the story of the ten plagues visited by God upon the Egyptians; it's an important part of the Passover seder that we celebrate each year. Death of the firstborn was the last of the plagues, the most terrible one, designed to convince the Pharaoh to let our people go from slavery. The firstborn of the Egyptians would be slain by the angel of death, and in our story too, mourning and weeping could be heard among the Egyptians.

So, what was this Gospel all about? Matthew certainly made it as exciting as a page-turning novel. A child is born, a jealous king plots to kill him, then the father hears from a secret source that the child is in danger and they all run away to a distant land and hide.

That's a gripping story line; I wonder what comes next, a reader would naturally think. It would have been a lot more entertaining if the story didn't have the Jews killing the little babies. All they needed to add was, "Any resemblance to real races, living or dead, is purely coincidental."

Traveling through Europe many years later, I saw art depicting this "massacre of the innocents" in cathedrals in Pisa, Siena, and Notre Dame Cathedral, and there are probably more examples in churches and museums throughout Europe and America. It's a popular theme depicting the grizzly scene where an army of Jews is seen stabbing and slaughtering little children. This would certainly stir up a mob to beat and kill Jews in revenge for these (allegedly) Christian babies. Because of Gospel stories like this, Jews became sitting ducks, waiting to be slaughtered by true believers for the next two millennia.

Only much later, when I began to study the history of these events, did I discover all the inconsistencies in that story. Just by looking at the relevant dates, it becomes clear that the Gospel accounts of this massacre were a complete fabrication—more like recruitment propaganda than historical fact. Even the date and location of Christ's birth are uncertain. As recently as 2012, Pope Benedict XVI, in the last installment of his trilogy, "Jesus of Nazareth,"[3] questioned the supposed date of the birth of Christ, believing it to be off by a few years. The Apostles John and Mark report that Jesus was born in the Galilee, the northernmost part of Judea. Luke and Matthew, however, claim that he was born in Bethlehem, south of Jerusalem. Bethlehem became the accepted birthplace because Luke includes mention of a general census that required Joseph and Mary to travel to Bethlehem to be counted. During the time of this census, Christ was born. But historical records indicate that the census didn't take place until 6 CE, six years after his supposed birth and ten years after the death of King Herod.

Matthew's claim that Christ was born while Herod was king (Matthew 2:1) is clearly wrong because Herod died in 4 BCE. This king Herod was referred to as Herod the Great; the other Herod is

Agrippa II, who wasn't born until 27 CE. There is also no reference to any order to kill young boys by any historian of the time. Yet this would have been such an enormous and unusual event that it certainly would have been referenced by historians.

At school, I could see that Christmas was a happy time for Christians. They put up trees strung with colored lights, threw parties, served baked hams for Christmas dinner, and sang lovely carols. We Jews have nine skinny candles, eight to represent each day of a miracle that was said to have taken place, plus one to light the others, and we eat potato latkes made with cooking oil to represent the oil used to keep the eternal light in the temple burning. Jews like to eat, so every holiday is an opportunity to enjoy traditional foods specific to the celebration. Nevertheless, to imagine that latkes fried in oil represents lamp oil that lasted eight days is a bit of a stretch. On the other hand, I have found that eating grated potatoes and onions soaked in oil can definitely give you a stomachache that lasts eight days.

The night before Christmas vacation there was caroling in the common room of my dorm, where all the boarders would congregate before going in to dinner. I would bring out my violin and play along. Everyone seemed to enjoy the violin accompaniment and I liked it too, as it kept me from having to sing the words "and Christ is born," and Jesus this and Jesus that. Thinking about it now reminds me of the paradox of simultaneously being comfortable among my friends and yet feeling like such an outsider.

Once, I tried to slip in "I have a little dreidel, I made it out of clay," the popular Hanukkah song, thinking there might be another secret Jew I could flush out as he reflexively started to sing along. But no such luck; I was the only one.

One Christmas Eve, I went with a group of friends who lived on Boston's landmark Beacon Hill to sing carols in front of the eighteenth-century townhouses surrounding the cobbled-stoned Louisburg Square. The whole scene was right out of a cornball movie: snowflakes falling on gas-lit lamps, everyone wearing red-and-white scarves and knitted hats with pom-poms on top, singing "Silent Night" and "O Come All Ye Faithful." The townhouses were all open and carolers were invited in for hot cider and cookies. The husbands, in their double-breasted yacht club insignia blazers, and the wives, in their tartan plaid satin skirts, greeted us at the door. Everyone seemed to know everyone else.

"Hello, Gardner . . . do I know your friend?"

"Oh, this is Arthur Ullian, a school chum."

"Well, Mr. Jullian, thank you for coming, and a very Merry Christmas to you. Do you live on Beacon Hill?"

"No, I live in Newton."

"Oh! Well, it's aawwfully nice to meet you anyway."

During the years I boarded at school, in addition to Wednesday chapel, we were required to attend a real church on Sunday—and they had a faculty member stationed at each of the nearby churches to take attendance. I sampled every denomination: Catholic— very heavy; Episcopalian—very elegant, beautiful choir, and lots of incense; Congregational—less ornate, with a simpler service. The architecture of the Congregational church struck me as the nicest: white painted wood inside and out, a simple cross at the end with no crucified image of Jesus, simple windows, a red carpet down the center aisle, and the pews on either side capped with freshly varnished wood, like you would find in a proper vintage sailboat.

At the beginning of the school year I would walk with my friend Peter to the Congregational church up the street. We would quickly run up to the balcony, where no one could see us, and we'd cut up and do stupid things like throw spitballs down on our friends below. We eventually got caught, so that ended that.

Peter was my good friend, having attended the same feeder school, and we shared an appetite for fooling around. He was the only schoolmate who invited me to his home, which was on Marlborough Street in the Back Bay section of Boston. It was an early nineteenth-century brownstone, and this was long before those elegant buildings were divided into apartments and condos, so his family owned the whole four-story building. Peter invited me to his summer house too, located on the rocks overlooking the ocean in Rockport, on Boston's north shore. I liked his parents, and I think of him often as I drive down his family-named street in Cambridge. He died prematurely of cancer, and I was touched that his mother asked me to say a few words at his funeral at the landmark Trinity Church in Copley Square. Peter and I had kept in touch, and before he was diagnosed with cancer, we went sailing in Buzzards Bay on my boat with his new wife, whom I liked very much and who, perhaps not surprisingly, was Jewish.

After we got caught fooling around in the balcony, the fun part of the church experience ended, and without the fun I found I didn't like it much, especially the way the minister would end each prayer with, "We ask this in the name of Jesus Christ, our Lord." Occasionally, I would pretend to go to church, spending two minutes there and then sneaking back to my dorm, hoping no one would see me and remember that I wasn't a Christian. I would hide in my room, waiting for my friends to return, then seamlessly slip in with them as they assembled in the common room while waiting to go in to Sunday dinner.

We sat at long tables with our dorm masters stationed at the end to keep order. We were served by student waiters, all of us rotating through so that eventually everyone did that job. I think that's how it went; I can't remember exactly. But there is one thing I can't forget. It was a Sunday when a tall skinny teacher, armed with his clipboard containing the church attendance sheets, asked:

"Forbes, where did you go today? And you, Cabot?" Each had a quick and easy answer. Then he came to me.

"Where were you, Ullian?"

I don't remember exactly what I answered, but I do know that those were more of the excruciating moments in which I felt all eyes laser-focused on me. I can still feel my stomach churn with the urgent desire to disappear under the table.

What I should have said, with the same easy manor as Forbes and Cabot, was:

I went to Temple Mishkan Tefila, sir. Jews worship on Saturday, which is our Sabbath. As it says in both the Old and New Testaments, "on the seventh day, He rested." So why do all of you rest on the first day? Saturday was your Sabbath too, until Constantine decreed that it would be held on Sunday. He also changed the date of Easter to the week after Passover, explaining that "Christians must have nothing in common with that detestable Jewish crowd." [4]

Then I would have finished with, *When are you going to realize I am Jewish? Did you know that right outside the ghetto in Rome, where the Church locked us up for three hundred years, there's a small church with Hebrew lettering chiseled into the stone over the door—a church where we were forced to sit every Sunday and listen to your sermons in the hope that we would convert? Is that what you're trying to do to me here?*

If I could have said all that, maybe I would have saved thousands of dollars and hundreds of hours of shrink time. And I probably would have enjoyed school a heck of a lot more. Instead, I silenced myself once again.

Constantine was the first Christian emperor of the Roman Empire, and he eventually converted all of Rome to Christianity, some by force. But the Jews refused to convert, so in response, Constantine promulgated laws designed to diminish and segregate the Jews from the rest of Roman society.

Constantine was no saint, as becomes evident from reading about him. He murdered both his son and wife and was the first in a long line of Christian rulers and popes to create laws that increasingly threatened the ability of Jews to survive. These laws dehumanized Jews to the extent that it became acceptable to persecute and murder them—a practice that continued through the next sixteen centuries. In fact, Constantine set the precedent for torturing and executing people just on the basis of their religion or beliefs; the practice was unknown before the fourth century, when even conquered people were permitted to keep their own religion.

In converting to Christianity, Constantine followed in the footsteps of his mother, St. Helen. She is responsible for building the Church of the Nativity, on the spot where she assumed Christ was born, the Church of the Holy Sepulchre, where she assumed the crucifixion took place, and the church on the Mount of Olives facing the gate through which Jewish tradition predicted the Messiah would enter Jerusalem. At some point while she was in Jerusalem looking for sites important in the life of Jesus, she tracked down a Jew who supposedly knew where the actual cross of Jesus was hidden. Around this event, a myth developed that Jews had hidden the cross because they understood its power. "The Jews thought they had defeated Christianity by killing Christ, but through the finding of the cross and nails . . . Christianity had come to life again [and] they [the Jews] were defeated." [5]

Under Constantine's rule, as Jerusalem was Christianized, a chasm opened that influenced events throughout the west for the next seventeen centuries. Jews were forbidden to enter the city, except on the ninth day of the month of Av to mourn the destruction of the temple. Constantine also built the Lateran church in Rome, in front of which he erected a colossal statue of himself. Today, only his big feet remain. I went to see the church while I was in Rome because of its importance in Jewish history. It was here that the Lateran Council would meet over the centuries and decree laws against Jews—laws that required us to wear identifying patches, laws excluding us from professions by which we could make a living, laws stripping our citizenship with all the attending rights we had enjoyed under Roman law since Julius Caesar. The church that stands on that spot in Rome today was rebuilt in the middle ages on the foundation of the original. A replica of the original statue stands in front of the church.

By the end of the fourth century, succeeding emperors completed the Christianization of Rome and continued violent responses to

Jews and other groups that opposed it. It was at this time that St. Augustine, bishop of Hippo (354–430 CE), emerged as an influential Christian thinker and prolific writer. He preached that the harsh treatment of the Jews was not harsh enough.[6]

Façade of the Lateran church in Rome with remains of the statue of Constantine

After a while, the teacher with the clipboard stopped asking me which church I had attended. But by then I had spent enough time flipping through the King James Bible that I had internalized a healthy dose of the anti-Jewish accusations in the New Testament. Even as a schoolboy, I was struck by the constant attempts by the Gospel writers to link Jesus to our Hebrew Bible prophets in order to prove that the coming of the Messiah had been foretold, and that Jesus was specifically the one prophesied to come.

One of the first things I learned about was Jesus's family tree, apparently going back forty-two generations—all the way back to Abraham, his supposed ancestor.

Are you kidding me, how did they figure that out?

My father and his two brothers all had the same birthday, January 22, but in different years.

"How can that be?" I asked my father once.

"They had no records," he replied. "No one from our little *shtetl* (village) had any idea of 'English' dates. They had no time for such details; they were just trying to stay alive. Some U.S. immigration officer at Ellis Island must have asked my parents for the month, day, and year of their children's birth, and they just made up an answer. So, we all celebrate January 22. Anyway," my father went on, "one birthday party for everybody is cheaper than three, and we didn't have enough money for even one. I might be one or one-and-a-half years older or younger than I think I am."

In 1785, the Inquisition of Spain was about to appoint Dom J. Antonio Llorente as commissioner of the tribunal of the Holy Office of the Inquisition in the city of Logrogno and was told that "it was necessary for him to prove that his ancestors, as far back as the third generation, had never suffered any punishment by the Holy Office, and that they were not descended from Jews, Moors, or heretics." The Holy Office then figured out that you had to look at a person's relatives going back four hundred years in order to prove that there were no heretics, Moors, or Jews, so they would need to examine the lives of "4,064 persons, the number calculated from the ordinary term of human life." They finally settled on proving that the name of no ancestor "was found inscribed on the registers of the Inquisition."[7]

So, if the Spaniards couldn't determine ancestry in the fifteenth century, and it's not even that easy in the twenty-first century with the help of the internet, how would it have been remotely possible in the first century to trace back three thousand years and determine that Jesus was a direct descendent of Abraham? It's ridiculous.

What was also obvious from my introduction to the New Testament was the attempt by Matthew, Mark, Luke, and John to prove that not only was Christianity the new and legitimate religion, the substitute for Judaism, but that Christians were now to be considered the "chosen people." They also set out to prove that the Old Testament had prophesied the coming of the Messiah, come down to earth through the womb of a virgin, and fertilized by God through the Holy Ghost. To believe all that, no wonder you have to call it a "mystery."

Jesus made some prophecies that did turn out to be true, like the destruction of the temple. As Jesus prophesied: "Not one stone here will be left upon another, which will not be torn down." But the mystery of how he got that right was solved when I realized that the Gospels were written well after the death of Jesus, and well after the Romans destroyed the temple in 70 CE. And sure enough, not one stone was left upon another. You can see that when you go to Jerusalem.

The virgin birth prophecy takes a little more reading to understand, and once you do understand you have to hand it to Matthew for having the chutzpah to change the few words in the Torah (the Five Books of Moses in the Hebrew Bible) necessary to pull off that prophecy. Matthew found something from the Prophet Isaiah that he thought no one would catch. Change the word for "young woman" to the word for "virgin" and you have it. I looked at the passage in the King James Version of the New Testament and compared it to the same passage in the Hebrew Bible. The original passage from Isaiah says: "Behold the young woman is with child, and she will bear a son, and you shall call his name Immanu'el."

Matthew then changes a couple of words and adds a little something at the end to make it clear: "Behold, a virgin shall be with child, and shall bring forth a son, and they shall call his name Emmanuel, God with us."

I remember I once made a mistake in French class by using the French word for "meat" instead of the word for "meet" in my translation and was made to stay after class to write the words in French and in English on the blackboard one hundred times. But Matthew's mistranslation was not a mistake one could honestly make, because the Hebrew words for young woman and virgin are completely different.

The Gospel writers must have thought, "Oh, who's going to know? We'll burn their books later anyhow." And they did just that. On Rosh Hashanah, September 9, 1553, the pope decreed that the Talmud and other Hebrew books be taken from Jewish homes and synagogues, brought to the Campo di Fiori in Rome, piled high in the square, and set on fire. The Holy Office of the Inquisition had condemned the Talmud as blasphemous. Similar book burnings occurred in the other Papal States, and the Talmud was included in the first *Index of Forbidden Books.*

The other problem with using this passage from Isaiah is one of timing: it refers to a military crisis that took place 732 years before Christ was born. Judea, as described in the Book of Isaiah, was under attack from two great armies, and in this prophecy, Isaiah was assuring the King of Judea that he would triumph, Judea would survive, and the victory would take place very soon. When he goes on to say that the child's name will be Emmanuel, it is like saying (metaphorically) that God will watch over you, and when the child gets older the "land whose two kings you dread shall be abandoned."

So, this prophecy has nothing to do with Jesus. And how, may I ask, was Mary supposed to remain a virgin for 732 years?

Every Christmas, I look forward to going with friends to Boston Symphony Hall to hear the Handel and Haydn Society perform Handel's *Messiah*, a magnificent and powerful piece with its stirring "Hallelujah" chorus, which everyone in the audience knows very well. Some orchestras offer a special sing-along performance. In the first part of her recitative, the alto sings:

Behold, a virgin shall conceive and bear a Son, and shall call his name Emmanuel, God with us.

With what I know now, how am I going to keep myself from nudging some perfect stranger in the seat next to me and whispering in her ear, *Did you know that this Emmanuel has nothing to do with your baby Jesus?*

Actually, Jews whispering into Christian ears was against the law for most of the years after Constantine. They didn't want us to infect them with our ideas, so they did everything possible to keep us apart. We would be required to wear badges or special hats so they would know to keep their distance. They forbade us from having contact with Christians and warned that if we tried to convert a Christian, we would be executed. Apparently, they were worried that Christians did not have enough knowledge of their own religion to get into a fair debate with a Jew, so King Louis IX of France offered a creative solution:

"The best way to argue with a Jew is to stab him in the stomach." And this is the man for whom Saint Louis, Missouri, is named? What would you have to do to be disqualified from sainthood?

Chapter 5

MISAPPROPRIATING OUR RELIGION

I always thought that Judaism and Christianity were close cousins. People always refer to our shared values, our Judeo-Christian ethics focusing on "the dignity of human life, our holy texts, our mutual adherence to the Abrahamic covenant of common decency and support of traditional family." The term "Judeo-Christian" dates from the mid-nineteenth century. This is how Wikipedia, the common cultural denominator of the internet, states it. Both religions include the concept of one God, both accept the Ten Commandments, and, on top of that, Jesus was a Jew and a circumcised one at that (Luke 1:59). So was Paul, formerly Saul of Tarsus (Acts 16:3).

I must admit, as I traveled around Europe, I checked out all the little penises I found on the images of baby Jesus on church sculptures, paintings, and stained-glass windows, and also on the Jewish cherubim (baby angels) flying around on ceiling frescoes. (You laugh, but who else would they be? Roman angels? Everyone portrayed in the paintings and windows was Jewish. I occasionally climbed on chairs just to check. Now that I think about it, someone watching me might have thought I was a weird pedophile.

So, with all that similarity, why aren't Jews and Christians best buddies? Where did all the anger and hostility come from?

It turns out that the reason Paul and the Gospel writers needed to usurp and appropriate large chunks of Judaism because in Rome at the time, only two bona fide religions were accepted: Hellenism and Judaism, as both had a long history. The rest were considered mystic cults.[8]

So, for this new Christian religion to qualify as a real religion and not merely a cult by Roman definition, the Gospel writers positioned it as a logical extension of Judaism . . . and moreover, as the perfection of Judaism. They took the term "chosen people," applied it to themselves, and claimed Jews went astray when we first desecrated the temple and then refused to accept Jesus as divine. To legitimize Christianity, they had to demonize Jews. Christian growth and success came at a terrible cost to us.

In this paradigm, the New Testament would naturally have to supplant the Old. So, early Christian writers appropriated Jewish history as their history, beginning with Abraham, and by mistranslating some passages in the Old Testament and slightly altering others, they created the impression that our Hebrew Bible prophesied the coming of Jesus as the Messiah, and that the life and teachings of Christ were the true fulfillment of the Old Testament prophets.

The Church and the Synagogue,
Cathedral of Strasbourg

I saw a frieze in the Cathedral of Strasbourg that demonstrates this paradigm. The Church, portrayed as a woman, stands strong and straight on the left, whereas the Synagogue, portrayed as the woman to the right, wears a blindfold and carries a broken staff. She bends her head down and away in shame, apparently unable to look the figure of Christianity in the eye. This is a common representation, often seen at the portals of churches throughout Europe. There is another one at Notre Dame.

Once Paul saw that the Jews were not going to convert to the new religion, he began preaching to the Romans. He accused the Jews of losing sight of God, of falling out of God's favor, of no longer being worthy. Keep them miserable, he stated, but do not slay them all, for we will need them when Jesus returns at the second coming "to provide the converted remnant which was to be the final crown of the church." [9]

Cyprian, an early Church father in the third century, wrote several volumes entitled "Testimonies against the Jews," in which he analyzed the Old Testament, cherry-picking passages that illustrated how the Jews had lost their way and could no longer expect to inherit the kingdom of God.

A century later, Augustine wrote his well-known text, *City of God*. In Book XVIII, Chapter 46, "Of the Birth of Our Savior," he lays out the fatal formula for dealing with Jews because they had not accepted Jesus as the Messiah, and, expanding on the message of St. Paul, states that they must suffer, they must become a living example of what happens to a people who do not accept Christ. But they should not all be slain; some must remain as living witnesses at the time of the second coming to see how wrong they had been. St. Augustine argued that Jews blindly read the scriptures without understanding their true meaning. The Church did not really want to share the scriptures with the Jews, so they eventually appropriated them all from the very beginning, with "Abraham as the father of many nations, of whom only one, and that themselves, was chosen." Other early Christians made the same claim to Jewish history, referring to the Hebrew leaders as "our ancestors," even claiming Moses as proof of Christianity's long history. [10]

Back when Christianity had only a few followers, potential converts had to be convinced that Jews and Jewish law were anathema. In addition to the Gospels of Matthew, Mark, Luke, and John, writings of the other early Church thinkers–Paul, Justin, Tertullian, Hippolytus, Cyprian, and Oregon—form the basis of the next two thousand years of antisemitism.

The Book of Isaiah in the Hebrew Bible is often used to show that the coming of the new Christian religion was foretold, and why the Jews would eventually be scattered and doomed. In *The City of God,* Augustine points to the following passage from Isaiah to make his argument:

> *"Though the number of the children of Israel be as the sand of the sea, the remnant shall be saved" [Isaiah 10:22 and Romans 9:27–28]. But the rest are blinded, of whom it was predicted, "Let their table be made before them a trap, and retribution, and a stumbling-block. Let their eyes be darkened lest they see, and bow down their back alway" [Psalm 69:22–23 and Romans 9:9–10].*

But just as with the prophecy of the virgin birth, this passage has nothing to do with Jesus or with the Jews not accepting Jesus as the Messiah. Isaiah was again referring to a war that had raged in Judea more than seven hundred years before Christ's birth, and was only assuring the Jews that they would defeat this enemy.

Some of the changes Christians made to the Hebrew Bible to prove that their beliefs derived from the earlier text stray pretty far from Jewish beliefs. For example, Christians believe in the concept of heaven, and if one accepts Jesus as the savior and redeemer, they believe that you go to heaven—in spirit, if not in body, as your skeleton remains in the same place and does not move once you are buried. Christians believe that the soul makes the journey.

But what exactly is the soul? Some Christians initially thought it was located in the heart, and later located it in the brain. In the King James Version of the Old Testament, they point to the Hebrew word *nefesh,* which can mean breath, life, throat, or neck, but does not mean soul. Baker's *Evangelical Dictionary* states that "soul" appears 755 times in the Old Testament, but I'm sorry, Mr. Baker, *nefesh* doesn't mean "soul." As biblical scholar Robert Alter said in a December 20, 2018, interview in the *New York Times Magazine* section, translating *nefesh* as "soul" doesn't make a lot of sense in many of the places in the Bible where the word is used. He gives the example of Jonah, who exclaims something like, "I am drowning; the water is up to my *nefesh*." Here the word has to mean "neck."

I laughed when I read this, thinking what a 9-1-1 operator would say when I yelled, *Help! My friend is drowning! The water is almost up to his* nefesh!

Call me back when it gets up to his pupik (belly button).

In addition to his fateful order to make the Jews suffer, Augustine concocted a theory condoning the use of violence when used to achieve "spiritual ends." Such action he terms a "just war," which later became the justification for raising large armies aimed at expanding Christianity and converting entire populations. These "just wars" turned out to be bloody, savage massacres of Jews, Muslims, heretics, and pagans all over the world.

Most Jews of the time paid little attention to these early Christian writers, as their memory of Jesus was nonexistent, but small groups of Christians persisted to create a following. Their big break came in the fourth century with the conversion of the Roman Emperor Constantine, who used the might of his army and the moral authority of a state religion to impose severe restrictions on the Jews. Canon law written to restrict Jewish rights and behavior flowed naturally into secular law as the Church and the state became one.

The conversion of Constantine is another popular theme in Christian art. He is often portrayed in a manner similar to Michelangelo's famous Sistine Chapel image of God appearing from a cloud to touch and animate the figure of Adam. Another such painting by Raphael hangs in the Vatican Museum.

Popular art—painting, sculpture, stained glass, music, and architecture—depicted the stories of the New Testament and functioned much as social media does today. This art, seen in churches and palaces, had enormous power to influence thought and move ideas through largely illiterate communities. Constantine's attitude toward the Jews was the beginning of policies and beliefs that have prevented the number of Jews in the world from growing much beyond the population living in the first century. The Church and its followers successfully fulfilled the pronouncements of St. Augustine and St. Paul: Make them suffer, but do not slay them all.

Chapter 6

"I AIN'T NO JUDAS"

John Martorano, known as "The Executioner" by his buddies in the notorious Winter Hill gang headed up by Whitey Bulger, confessed to twenty murders. When interviewed on the television show *60 Minutes* he shamelessly boasted, just to make sure everyone would know he wasn't such a bad guy after all, "I'll go along with a lot of things, but I ain't no Judas, not no informant."

Martorano explained that the nuns and priests had taught him Judas was the lowest, most vile person in history.

The very name "Judas" is another stereotype we have been forced to live with. It's the familiar story about the Jew who betrays Jesus to the Roman soldiers with a kiss . . . for money. This is yet another humiliating accusation of how we Jews are always ready to betray anyone for a few coins, even our dearest friends. Since I first heard the story in chapel at school, my ears have been attuned to hear that name, "Judas." And it's amazing how often I heard it as a boy and still do, casually used to describe someone who cannot be trusted. For instance, there is an old Alfred Hitchcock film called *Foreign Correspondent*. In it, the authorities want the correspondent to turn in the father of the girl he hopes to marry; he knows her father to be a German spy. The correspondent replies, "What do you want me to do, play Judas?"

The name is also used as a warning: "Be careful, he could be a Judas." It's the same way the name "Shylock" is used to describe a heartless, greedy bastard.

While negotiating the peace agreement following World War I, the U.S. Congress and some of the biggest American bankers didn't want to forgive the war debts piled up by France and Britain, even though they had sacrificed many more lives than we had. For that, the British called us "Uncle Shylock." (None of those bankers were Jewish, by the way.) And at a Senate confirmation hearing to confirm Eugene Meyer as chairman of the Federal Reserve in 1930, Senator Brookhart of Iowa testified against Meyer, calling him a "Judas Iscariot . . . one who has worked the Shylock game for the interests of big business." [11]

When I first read the Judas story in the Gospels, it was hard for me to understand why the Roman authorities needed Judas to point Jesus out in the first place. Jesus had recently made a big entrance into Je-

rusalem, with huge crowds laying down palm fronds on the road and singing hosannas. (That grand entrance is celebrated on Palm Sunday, one week before Easter, when you see everyone coming out of church carrying palm fronds.) In addition to the big commotion he created as he entered the city, the Gospels tell us that Jesus went into the temple and created another huge public scene by turning over the tables of the money changers.

So, I would like to know why, with all that ruckus, and with the Jewish police

Crowds welcoming Jesus as he enters Jerusalem, Duccio (ca. 1308-1311)

Judas identifying Jesus with a kiss, with a mob of angry-looking Jews with sticks trying to get at Jesus. Giotto (ca. 1304-1306)

and the Roman police around through all of it, did they need someone to identify him with a kiss? You can't establish the big entrance and then not have people know who he was. Did John Wilkes Booth need someone to kiss Abraham Lincoln so he would know who to shoot? Did Brutus need someone to kiss Caesar?

"Another thing about the name Judas," I told my shrink. "You know there were eleven other apostles at the Last Supper, and none of them had names that make you think of a Jew. There was Bartholomew, Thaddeus, Philip, Peter, Matthew, and a couple of Jameses, but only Judas had a name that actually sounds like the word 'Jew.' I'm not no Phil; I'm not no Bart." That would have worked out a lot better for us.

The continual resurrecting of the betrayal by Judas has had disastrous consequences for Jews. In 1492, the Jews of Spain begged King Ferdinand not to expel them and offered him thirty thousand ducats to reverse his decree. The thirty thousand might have persuaded the king, especially coupled with his concern that the expulsion would have a negative effect on the economy. But the Grand Inquisitor Torquemada, a major Jew-hater, persuaded the King otherwise:

"Judas Iscariot sold Christ for 30 pieces of silver; Your Highness is about to sell Him for 30,000 ducats. Here He is; take Him and sell Him"; And he left a crucifix on the table, signifying that Christ would have wanted the Jews expelled to avenge his crucifixion.[12]

My wife and I went to a Catholic wedding recently, and the taking of Communion was offered as part of the nuptial mass. It's not a requirement, but this couple chose to include it. I had not witnessed this before, so I was curious. After the altar boy prepares a table up front with wine and wafers, the congregants line up and the priest says: "On the night that he was betrayed our Lord Jesus Christ took bread."

"You know, we're the ones who betrayed their Lord . . . that's who he's talking about," I whispered to my wife. "And now we're supposed to go to this wedding reception and eat and dance, even though we've already been found guilty? Remember not to kiss anyone!"

I didn't really want to go to this wedding reception. *Maybe they'll seat us at the betrayers' table,* I thought, reverting to my old prep-school habit of making a joke out of some uncomfortable situation.

I also wondered to myself, *What's this "Christ took bread" on Passover all about?* How come the Gospel writers didn't know what Jews ate on Passover? It's curious how practicing Christians rely only on their own reading of scripture and rarely know anything about the Jewish context of Jesus's experience—from Passover seders to his use of parables as a teaching method. Because of their lack of context, Christians miss the fuller understanding of Jesus's life and message.

In any case, if this Last Supper were a Passover seder, there would not have been any bread on the table—just a stack of Manischewitz matzoh beneath an embroidered matzoh cover one of the apostles got from his grandmother.

Chapter 7

JEWISH LIFE BEFORE CONSTANTINE

While conventional wisdom says that Jews were always persecuted and shunned, life prior to Constantine's conversion in
the fourth century was actually no worse for Jews than for anyone
else. The old argument has it that antisemitism in one form or another has been around forever, and the rise of Christianity was not
responsible for it. Even most Jews I know believe this, but there is
little evidence to support that view.

To the contrary, there is considerable evidence that the Jews enjoyed freedom of religion and citizenship and lived much like everyone else, alongside everyone else. It was only the Christian writers
who portrayed the Jewish people as morally inferior and interpreted
their existence as little more than place-holders for God's law until
Christ arrived.

Another aspect of antisemitism involves the belief that Jews are
clannish and keep only to ourselves. Not only were we *not* inclined
to stay to ourselves, we did in the early centuries exactly what we do
now—assimilated. We change our names now and we changed our
names back then. We wanted to wear what they were wearing, we
wanted to live in nice homes, we wanted to make a living just like
others did, we wanted to play the same games. We just did not (and
some still do not) want to eat pork.

There was probably some version of this old joke floating around
in those early years before Christ: "A son invites his parents over
for dinner to see his new apartment, but they never show up. In the

morning, the son calls his mother: "Ma, where were you?"

"We were downstairs in the lobby," she answers.

"So why didn't you come up?" he asks.

"We forgot your new name."

The first real contact between Rome and Judea occurred around 160 BCE, when Judah Maccabee repelled an attack by the Greek army led by Antiochus IV. Fearing that Judea was vulnerable to another attack, Maccabee wanted to negotiate a mutual protection agreement with Rome, as Greece was their common enemy. Judah sent his ambassadors, Jason Ben Eleazar and Eupolemus Ben Johanan, to meet with the Roman senators in the Forum. They told the assembled senators how the formidable army of Antiochus IV had attacked Jerusalem and the Maccabees had trapped the Greeks on a narrow pass as they trudged uphill toward the city.

Could these ambassadors actually have been comedians Carl Reiner and Mel Brooks, the original 2000 Year Old Man? Speaking to the senators, the ambassadors sarcastically referred to Antiochus Epiphanes (meaning "The Great," a self-bestowed title), as "Antiochus Epimanes" (meaning "Madman"). The senators burst into laughter, enjoying this little play on words.

This might have been the first Jewish joke ever heard in Rome. But the ambassadors weren't quite through, and followed it up with another jab (as Alan King or Jackie Mason might do to keep the laughs coming), relating how Antiochus had erected a colossal statue of Zeus inside the temple, and what do you know? Zeus was the spitting image of Antiochus himself.

The Roman senators were convinced, and they voted to become allies of Judea, entering into a mutual protection alliance, the terms of which were memorialized on bronze tablets that the ambassadors carried back to Jerusalem. The tablets have been lost, but the agreement is recorded in the First Book of Maccabees (17–29):

May all go well with the Romans and with the nation of

the Jews at sea and on land forever, and may sword and enemy be far from them. If war comes first to Rome or to any of their allies in all their dominion, the nation of the Jews shall act as their allies wholeheartedly, as the occasion may indicate to them. To the enemy that makes war they shall not give or supply grain, arms, money, or ships, just as Rome has decided; and they shall keep their obligations without receiving any return. In the same way, if war comes first to the nation of the Jews, the Romans shall willingly act as their allies, as the occasion may indicate to them. And to their enemies there shall not be given grain, arms, money, or ships, just as Rome has decided; and they shall keep these obligations and do so without deceit. Thus, on these terms the Romans make a treaty with the Jewish people.

For Rome to recognize Judea as a nation was as important then as it was in 1948, when the United Nations voted to recognize Israel as a nation. It certainly doesn't sound to me like we were on the outs with Rome, as popular culture today suggests.

When I was in Israel one year after the Six-Day War, and drove up that same winding road to Jerusalem, I saw the burnt-out Arab tanks and equipment the Israeli army had destroyed and left by the road as a reminder of how Israeli forces pushed back the Arab invasion after the U.N. granted Israel statehood. This was the very same pass where the Jews stopped the mighty Greek army twenty-two hundred years earlier.

And they claim this isn't Jewish land.

In contrast to the Christians who came after them, Romans acted in friendship toward the Jews and demonstrated their respect for Jewish law that forbade the worship of idols by covering their stanchions adorned with images of Roman gods as they marched through Judea.

When we had a choice in the matter, we never held ourselves aloof from other cultures or kept to ourselves as "accused," but just the reverse, both politically and individually. Most of us assimilated with gusto as far back as Alexander the Great, who, on his way to conquering the world, made peace with Judea in 333 BCE, granting Jews their right to live in freedom under Jewish laws and customs. Judea became a colony of the Greek Empire, but retained its freedom and self-determination.

But for the Jews, this sudden exposure to Greek culture was a shock, as up until this time they had rarely traveled outside their own territory in the Middle East and were unfamiliar with other societies. Jewish law and social structure were quite sophisticated, and Jewish intellectual development was similar to and equal to that of the Greeks. But the Greeks had something extra to offer that was rather appealing—hedonism. Who could resist a culture of hedonism with its material comforts, rich food and wine, high fashion, and a belief in extravagance as a demonstration of social standing?

How interesting is that? Extravagance? What could be more Jewish? People used to make fun of Jews for having wall-to-wall carpeting, wearing mink stoles in Florida, and driving Cadillacs. My father used to joke that if you wanted to find out who was Jewish in the neighborhood, peek in their living room windows: if they have wall-to-wall, they're probably one of us. But now we don't have to be ashamed anymore; it's just our adopted Greek culture from twenty-three hundred years ago coming through!

We changed our names to Greek-sounding names as well, and some of us even bore the pain of reverse circumcision, just to be able to work out and participate in the games without looking different, since in Greek, *gymnos* (gymnasium) means exercising nude. So, don't tell me Jews have always tried to keep ourselves apart, and that our customs and different behavior are why people are compelled to hate us.

Go try getting your own reverse circumcision.

The Jews had a strong nation and a set of laws that guaranteed freedom and civil rights, which lasted more than four hundred years until 70 CE, when Jerusalem was destroyed by the Romans. However, Jews lived in freedom for another 250 years within the Roman Empire until the rise of Christianity under Constantine, which erased that freedom for the next seventeen hundred years.

It's important to understand that this First Jewish War was a revolt by the Jews of Judea as a result of the oppressive Roman rule over the colonies. It is also important to note that even though this was a long and bloody war for the Romans, they did not use this war in any way to initiate "a universal religious persecution" against the Jews.[13] Every country bordering on the Mediterranean, including Spain, was under the control of Rome at this time; Judea was no different.

Rome's wars of conquest were intended to increase its riches and to keep its colonies under control and make them trading partners. Basically an equal opportunity employer of slaves, their treatment of captives was equally cruel toward all the defeated, to provide an example of what happened if you attacked Rome. Some prisoners were brought back as slaves, some used as gladiators, women were forced into prostitution, and others were sentenced to a life in the galley ships of war. For Rome and other powers at the time—Greece, Macedonia, etc.—this was how they kept their empires growing economically. War was considered a good and honorable business, that made the victor wealthy; it was not motivated by racism, ideology, or the need to proselytize to another culture. The defeated population was invited to join the empire—to become citizens and to prosper.

There had been a number of wars between Pompey and Caesar, between Antony and Cassius, and Octavian and Antony in mid first century BCE. Although the Jews were not part of these internal conflicts, their lives were affected by them. Crassus, who was the third member of the triumvirate that included Julius Caesar and Pompey, plundered the temple in Jerusalem while he was proconsul of Syria. This act triggered a revolt in Judea, resulting in thirty thousand Jews being sold into slavery as punishment. It was during all this internal conflict within Rome that Herod convinced Antony and Octavian, the new rulers in Rome, that he would serve Rome best and they should appoint him king of Judea.

There were many Jews who violently opposed Herod, particularly in the Galilee, where bands of Jewish citizens battled with the Roman soldiers stationed there to defend Herod's rule. Similar clashes occurred in Jerusalem, led by the last of the Maccabean dynasty, but these were quickly and ruthlessly put down by the Roman army, which outnumbered the rebels. The historian Josephus relates that even Herod was appalled by the Roman fury.

Following this revolt, Herod tried to lessen this internal strife and bring some peace to the country by encouraging commerce, building a magnificent temple on the Temple Mount, and strengthening the defenses. The Jews hated him nevertheless. Although Herod is referred to in the Gospels as "King of the Jews," he was not really Jewish; nor was he elected or appointed by the Jews. He was a descendent of the Idumean royal family, who, along with the rest of the Idumeans, were forcibly converted over a hundred years earlier when Judea captured their country. This policy of forced conversion under Johanan Hyrcan was condemned by the Jews and was the last and only time Jews engaged in that policy.

Because Herod was detested by the Jews, and feared that they would revolt against him, he built Masada as a fortress in the middle of the desert as a place to escape to in an emergency. He was not a particularly nice guy. He executed his wife, two of his sons, his relatives and friends, and anyone who opposed him. Herod contracted cancer, but even as he lay dying, he ordered some rebels to be burned alive. Herod divided his kingdom among his remaining three sons, giving the eldest control of Judea. But the Jews objected to Herod appointing his own family and broke out again in revolt. His son, Archelaus, was as cruel as his father and massacred three thousand people in the temple court, per Josephus. He reigned for ten years and finally, by 6 CE, the Roman emperor agreed to an appeal by the Jews of Judea to get rid of the hated Herod. This marked the end of semi-independent rule in Judea, as Rome now decided to appoint a procurator (governor) under the direct authority of the emperor.

One of the early procurators was Pontius Pilate, who sentenced Jesus to death. Pilate ruled for ten years and was called back to Rome in 36 CE after many complaints against him. He infuriated the population by desecrating the temple with silver images and stealing the temple treasures to build an aqueduct, all of which resulted in outright rebellion, particularly in the Galilee. The Roman Army stationed there crucified the rebels, who could be seen everywhere hanging in agony. (Crucifixion was the usual method of execution in the Roman colonies; Jesus was not the only Jew to suffer on the cross.) Disorder grew and the soldiers became more aggressive, killing at the slightest provocation. The zealots rioted, and fanatics prophesied the end of the world and the coming of the Messiah, and were ready to follow anyone who claimed to be the Messiah. There was a widespread feeling of desperation, and this was the environment into which Jesus emerged, began to preach, and was eventually crucified himself.

The English historian Cecil Roth tells us:

> *The whole moral responsibility for Jesus' death [was imposed] on the Jews. . . . Jewish scholars and others have urged that the trial before the Sanhedrin [the Jewish Court] never took place; that the passages which refer to it do not compare with what we know from other sources of the procedure and competence of this court; that Jesus had done nothing to break Jewish law, let alone invoke capital punishment; and that the episode is a fiction—Jesus had simply fallen afoul of the Romans who regarded him as a political agitator.*[14]

An enormous amount of this information about Jewish life before Constantine comes from the discovery of the Jewish catacombs in

Rome and other populated cities throughout the Roman Empire. Many of these catacombs were discovered during the Middle Ages, but the Jewish catacombs were not fully investigated until the early 1900s. The very idea of using catacombs was actually a Jewish practice, beginning with Abraham, who buried his wife in a cave he purchased for the purpose. With no natural caves in Rome, Jews built catacombs by digging into the rock underground to approximate the caves of Judaea. The Romans, in contrast, cremated their dead upon pyres and placed the ashes in above-ground chambers. Later, the early Christians followed our practice and built their own catacombs, in part to emphasize the idea that Christianity was the inevitable replacement of Judaism.

Mussolini repeatedly referred to the Jews as "newcomers" and "strangers" in Italy, but his own residence, the Villa Torlonia, was built on top of an ancient Jewish cemetery dating back to the first century. So, who, exactly, was the newcomer?

The majority of the names found on Jewish tombstones during these early centuries are Greek. Esther became Aster and Jonathan became Jonatas, and other last names, like Tulios, Aurelios, Julianos, and Samul, were Hellenized as well. Some prominent Italian families living in Rome today can trace their heritage to these early Roman Jewish families: de Pomis, de Rossis, and Piatellis.

The Pontifical Commission for Sacred Archaeology was responsible for the preservation of both Jewish and Christian catacombs until the end of the 1970s. Unfortunately, while the commission preserved the Christian sites, it entirely ignored the sacred Jewish catacombs, and made it practically impossible for anyone, including scholars, to gain entrance to the Jewish sites. Again, this policy had the effect of suppressing any historical evidence of a robust and successful Jewish community prior to Constantine.

Around 1973, conversations were initiated between the Italian government and the Catholic Church concerning rights to the catacombs, which had been in the sole possession of the Vatican since

1929. Realizing that they would soon lose control of these sites, the Pontifical Commission for Sacred Archaeology cleaned out the Jewish catacombs, removing all evidence: the ancient tombstones as well as the bodily remains—the bones, the skulls. Even today the tombstones remain the property of the Vatican, but the Jewish Museum, located in the main synagogue in Rome on Lungotevere dei Cenci, maintains plaster copies of these missing tombstones.

The inscriptions on the early stones were written in Greek, the language spoken by most literate people in the Empire, and bear the same phrases we see carved into stones today: "Shalom," "Shalom in Israel," and "May he (or she) Rest in Peace." These stones repeat the very words found on what are believed to be the tombs of Abraham and Sarah, discovered south of Jerusalem in Hebron. The Christians later adopted this inscription: "Requiescat in Pace" or "R.I.P." The drawings on the gravestones are familiar symbols as well: the *shofar* (ram's horn) blown at the Rosh Hashanah service, the *lulav* and *etrog,* which represent the branch and fruit used in the *Sukkot* or harvest ritual, and the seven-armed candelabra representing the seven days of creation.

The inscriptions from the catacombs also reveal the names of Roman synagogues and their officers and provide us with a living memory of the Jews of two thousand years ago. For example, there was the scribe Marcus Quintus Alexus, whose job was to read the Torah and lead services. He also hand-inscribed a complete Torah for the Synagogue of the Augustesians, of which he was a long-time member. His tombstone indicates that he was an archon of the synagogue, a member of its governing board. Marcus was clearly an important person who enjoyed great respect in the community.

Then we find Eirina Parthenike, who was the beloved wife of Clodius, a successful man who was a father and benefactor of the Campesian Synagogue. Then we have Menophilos, married for thirty-five years, who loved his grandchildren, "lived well as a Jew," and was the father of his synagogue, the Calcaresians. He may well have been in the pottery manufacturing business since that synagogue was located in the neighborhood where pottery was made. He clearly made a nice living and gave generously. Rufinus, age sixty-nine when he died, enlisted in the Roman army and was a fine soldier. Another ancestor tragically died at age thirty-five. Her name was Eusebis and she was the beloved wife of Gelasius, who was born in Caesarea, a large city in Judea below Haifa. And found on the stone of Leo Leontius: "Friends I await you here."

Leo, I think, must be a distant cousin. He reminds me of my father, who wrote on a municipal bond that he knew I would redeem many years after his death:

"Are you still thinking of me?"

I am, Dad.

In all this early information, there is simply no reference to persecution or anything approaching the miserable lives we were made to live once Christianity took hold with the inauguration of Constantine. It was then, in the fourth century, that any semblance of Roman citizenship or Roman justice for Jews was thrown aside.

The question of whether there was anti-Jewish behavior prior to Christianity has long been debated among researchers, but the historical evidence of institutionalized hatred of Jews prior to Christianity seems nonexistent. (The term "antisemitic" was not widely popularized until 1879, and was likely used to make Jews seem even more foreign.) Leon Poliakov, a scholar and prolific writer on antisemitism, finds that prior to the birth of Christ there are "scarcely any examples of popular outbursts against the Jews [except in Alexandria]. The masses were not concerned with them and harbored no special prejudice against them." [15]

The New Testament, on the other hand, repeatedly makes this claim. "Paul departed from Athens, and came to Corinth and found a certain Jew named Aquila born in Pontus, lately come from Italy, with his wife Priscilla; because that Claudius had commanded all Jews to depart from Rome and came unto them" (Acts 18:2).

Not true! There is no historian living at the time who affirms Paul's claim. The historian Josephus (born Yosef ben Matityahu), who carefully recorded Jewish events in the first century CE, does not refer to any expulsion. Neither does the senator and Roman historian Tacitus. The historian and biographer of Roman rulers Suetonius says that "only Jews who rioted were expelled." [16] The third-century historian Cassius Dio asserts that Claudius did not expel the Jews because their numbers had become too great for expulsion, but, while permitting them to continue to observe their traditional way of life, he forbade them to hold meetings. [17]

The general absence of anti-Jewish sentiment is further demonstrated by the treatment of the Jews of Rome during and after the war ending in 70 CE with the destruction of the Second Temple. One would think that such a war would have engendered considerable hostility toward Jewish citizens living in Rome, much as that experienced by the Japanese Americans during World War II. But no such thing happened and it "seems in no way to have affected the status of the Jews in Rome itself." [18] Further, after the temple was destroyed, "the privilege of which they [Jews] had enjoyed in both the city and throughout the Empire was not diminished." The only significant change was the transformation of the temple tax, which the Jews had paid annually, into a poll tax called *Fiscus Judaicus*, which instead went to supporting a Roman temple. The taxes were very small; Leon estimates them to be about a dollar a year in purchasing power.

Vespasian did not intend this tax as a special penalty directed against the Jews. Rather, it was meant to replenish the treasury, which had been depleted as a result of Nero's extravagance and civil wars. The tax was later eliminated by the Emperor Julian in 361 and the tax roll itself was burned so that the tax would not be re-imposed." [19] (The Emperor Julian was the nephew of Constantine. He rejected Christianity and restored the rights of Jews, but, tragically for the Jews, he died two years later.)

"Getting to know our history certainly is an eye-opener," I started to tell my shrink one morning. "Christian writers, both in the New Testament and in histories, make us look like a bunch of beggars with no influence anywhere. We read in Latin class about the Roman conquest of Gaul: '*Gallia est Omnis Divisa in Partes Tres*' (All Gaul is divided into three parts), the first sentence of Caesar's *Gallic Wars*. But there is not a word about the Jewish war, though it was of equal if not greater importance to Rome and was commemorated by more edifices than any other Roman conquest. I'm not saying I'm proud of that, but it does make the point—don't you think?"

I told him about the Arch of Titus in the Forum, which was dedicated to the Roman general who defeated the Jews in 70 CE, along with the Coliseum, built in record speed by Jewish prisoners of that war and other slaves, and dedicated to Titus and the Emperor Vespasian, his father. And the largest museum built at the time was constructed to display the treasures taken from Jerusalem. The Jewish nation was strong and powerful, though no history book tells us that. But we were not as powerful as the Roman army, and in hindsight we shouldn't have taken them on.

(As I think about that session now, I wonder what he was writing down in his notebook. Probably, *Oh, God, another history lesson. I never heard of a case like this in medical school. Well, I may as well relax and learn a little something while I'm collecting his fee.*)

I must admit, I never learned anything either in prep school or college about the role Jews played in the ancient Roman or Greek empires. It's true that the victors write the history. And it was to the advantage of Church historians to portray Jews as beggars, thieves, a rootless people, living in disgrace, in order to create an example of what happens to those who refuse to accept the divinity of Christ. The Church went so far to prove this point that it removed the remains of our relatives and tombstones from the catacombs. Even in death we were made invisible.

What we know about the period before Christ comes largely from the writings of Josephus and other historians of the time. The Egyptians, for example, retold the Passover story from their own perspective—quite different from the Jewish version in the Book of Exodus. In Exodus, the Jews are the heroes and the Egyptians the cruel oppressors, whereas in the Egyptian version, they threw the Israelites out of Egypt because the Jews were lepers and corrupt to boot. An Egyptian historian of the second century BCE, Manetho, wrote of the Jews: "The King caused all the sick to be gathered together, in number, it is said, 80,000, and imprisoned them in quarries on the east bank of the Nile in order that they might labor there along with other Egyptian captives: there were among them illustrious priests also tainted with leprosy." [20]

Tacitus, the Roman historian of the late first century, expanded on Manetho's view: "The Jews reveal a stubborn attachment to one another, and active commiseration, which contrasts with their implacable hatred for the rest of mankind. They sit apart at meals, they sleep apart . . . they are singularly prone to debauchery, [and] they abstain from intercourse with foreign women." [21]

This opinion from Tacitus is often used to justify the claim that antisemitism was widespread long before Christianity took hold. But you have to look at what really went on in Rome in the wake of their widespread military expansion and the resulting absorption of many foreigners into the culture. People from the various countries who were defeated by the Roman army and who migrated to Rome were referred to as "tribes" and most often became citizens with the ability to vote. There was no ethnic discrimination. The diversity in Rome at the time, similar to the diversity in the United States of America, led to more tolerance of others. The Jews who voluntarily migrated to Rome after Judea became part of the Roman Empire became citizens like all the others Rome had defeated. Jews were treated no differently.

But later, the Emperor Hadrian (117–138 CE) became alarmed at religious expression that he thought would undermine his secular authority. To counter that, he strengthened Rome's pagan belief system and restored the Pantheon, a temple dedicated to the Roman gods. He feared these new cults, and to prevent the further rise of their influence, he made punishable by death any non-traditional religious practice. For Jews, this included study of the Torah, celebrations of festivals, and circumcision.

But just as the brutal regime of Antiochus three hundred years before had provoked Judah Maccabee to rebel, Hadrian's laws provoked the Jewish leader Simon bar Kochba. This time, rebellion proved to be a tragic mistake. In 132 CE, Bar Kochba led an open revolt against the emperor. The Romans showed no mercy, destroying Jerusalem and salting the earth so crops could not grow, reducing the possibility that the city would be rebuilt. This event led to the final diaspora (dispersal) of the Jews. Ironically, Hadrian died six years after the revolt, and his successor, Antoninus Pius (138–161 CE), immediately revoked Hadrian's laws.

Following this Second Revolt, there were just a few disruptions in Jewish life over the next 250 years, during which a succession of rulers reaffirmed Caesar's liberal civil policies. In the year 212 CE, the Emperor Caracalla decreed that all free people in the empire be granted citizenship. The baths Caracalla built in 212 CE, on the Viale della Terme di Caracalla, were larger than the four baths already existing in Rome. They were open to all free citizens, even the poorest, representing the Roman emphasis on civil rights following the death of Hadrian.

My wife and I went to see a performance of *Aida* (with elephants, no less) in the ruins of these baths. Knowing the history of ancient Rome as I do now, I could have given a lecture during intermission, explaining how the pre-Christian emperors like Caracalla acted the way good Christians should, granting all citizens the freedom to practice their religion.

The Jewish community in Rome was most likely formed before 100 BCE, but it wasn't until 63 BCE that the Jewish population expanded rapidly. This population spurt was not completely coincidental; it resulted from the successful invasion and capture of Judea by Pompey. Pompey's motivation was not racial, but purely political, as he was looking for a victory to counter Caesar's success in Gaul in order to position himself to become emperor.

Judea was a perfect target, since the Jews, already involved in a civil war between the Pharisees and the Sadducees, were very vulnerable. The former were descendants of the Hasidim who claimed that it was religious faith that saved the Jewish nation from the Greek army, while the latter claimed it was national power. The Sadducees were considered part of the wealthy establishment, in contrast to the Pharisees, who were generally poor.

"This part of the history becomes a little complicated, and involves a feud between two brothers," I tried to explain to my shrink. "It's like a Shakespearean tragedy, both in its complexity and in the fatal result, which was the capture of Judea by the Roman army.

"When Judah Maccabee died, his brother Jonathan became the leader, and when he died, leadership passed to their nephew Johanan Hyrcan in 135 BCE. He strengthened the army, expanded the state, increased commerce, and made the country even more able to resist Syrian aggression. However, during his reign, two political parties emerged, the Pharisees, who were opposed to the policies of expansion, and the Sadducees, who were allied with the goals of the Hyrcan government. Conflict centered on Johanan's conquest of Idumea and the forced conversion of the people. This policy was condemned, and it was the first, last, and only time Jews ever engaged in conversion of another people."

For the next few years, the parties fought, until finally, Queen Salome, wife of Aristobulus the first, intervened and governed peacefully with the aid of the Pharisees. With Salome's death, her son Hyrcan II, who had been a high priest, ascended to the throne, and the struggle between the two political-religious groups flared up again. Hyrcan's brother, Aristobulus II, led an army against him, but

Hyrcan gave up almost without a fight and pledged to live in peace with Aristobulus as king and high priest.

But there was a man living in Jerusalem by the name of Antipather, whose parents were Idumean nobility, which would naturally give rise to questions about Antipather's loyalty to the Jews. Antipather, the father of Herod, saw an opportunity to gain power and went about convincing Hyrcan that his brother Aristobulus had usurped the throne that was rightfully his. With the help of Arab neighbors, Hyrcan attacked Jerusalem and civil war broke out again.

But this time a larger power existed outside of Judea. Pompey, the Roman general, was trying to compete with Julius Caesar, who was making great gains in the west against Gaul. Pompey saw an opportunity to make a name for himself by capturing Judea. Pretending to be a mediator between the two Jewish factions, Pompey attacked Jerusalem on Yom Kippur in 63 BCE, and because of the holiness of the day, the Jews did not defend themselves. The Romans marched in with very little resistance, taking Aristobulus prisoner.

Pompey was ambitious and wanted to be Emperor. With his private army, as James Watt says in his book, *Mortal Republic*, Pompey hoped to impress the Senate with his victories. "In a little more than three years, Pompey would defeat Mithridates. . . . [He would] conquer large swaths of Asia Minor and all of Syria [and Judea]. . . . He offered favorable alliances to local kings and cities that left them particularly well disposed toward him. Pompey now enjoyed a network of friendly sovereigns. . . ."

Wow, I thought to myself, *two thousand years later the Egyptians tried the very same tactic and attacked Israel on Yom Kippur in 1973, but this time the Jews were not going to lose their nation and furiously fought back against the Syrian and Egyptian armies. There is so much history repeating here.* Upon graduation today, young Israeli army recruits climb to the top of Masada and pledge that Judea shall not fall again. [22]

The victorious Pompey paraded through the Roman forum, displaying the fallen King Aristobulus, thousands of Jewish prisoners, and Judea's treasures. Aristobulus's family was allowed to live as part of the Roman aristocracy, though he himself remained in prison. The Jewish prisoners were sold as slaves, but were bought out of slavery by free Jews, which is required under Jewish law. In a year or two, practically all were free.

Under Roman rule, conquered nations were permitted autonomy in maintaining their traditions and cultures, becoming citizens and prospering alongside Romans. Conversion was not an issue for Romans. It wasn't until Pompey captured the east, including Syria and Egypt, that Rome began to engage in international trade, which naturally brought many merchants to the capital, including Jewish merchants, increasing the Jewish population and influence in Rome.

Tension within the ruling triumvirate—Caesar, Pompey, and Crassus—came to a head in 49 BCE, sparking a great civil war. Eager to defeat Pompey, Caesar freed Aristobulus from prison and convinced the king to form a large army to defeat Pompey and take back Jerusalem for the Jews. Pompey, however, heard about this plan and secretly had Aristobulus poisoned.

Now, into the middle of this turmoil, comes an early version of the Combined Jewish Philanthropies, or, as it is called nationally, the United Jewish Appeal, collecting money to provide financial support for Judea.

Somehow it was learned that Floccus, the Roman ambassador to Asia whose portfolio included Judea, had embezzled some of the money that was intended to go to the temple in Jerusalem. (Sending money to Jerusalem was a right Caesar had granted the Jews ten years earlier.) Charges were brought against Floccus, who was a friend of Pompey and therefore an enemy of Caesar. Caesar wanted to embarrass Pompey and moved the trial close to Octavian's Portico, which the Jews would have to pass under as they went to the forum from their homes in Trastevere.

Floccus hired Cicero to be his lawyer and deflect attention from the accusation of misappropriating funds. In framing his defense, Cicero broadened the scope of the case to question the basic right of the Jews to send money out of the country at all. Floccus claimed that all he was doing was withholding the funds because he disagreed with Caesar's earlier decree. Cicero's defense ultimately persuaded the jury, and Floccus was acquitted, but the right to transfer funds to the temple in Jerusalem was maintained. Nevertheless, some early Christian writers use Cicero's words from the trial as evidence of early antisemitism.

The Jewish community of Rome was centered on this small island in the middle of the Tiber River, conveniently located across from the forum. The Ponte Quattro Capi, the bridge of the four-faced Roman god Janus, connected the left bank of the Tiber to the island, and is the only Roman bridge that survives intact from the classical period. The statue of Janus at the end of the bridge was meant to invoke the power of the god to protect the entrances to the city.

When my wife and I were there in Rome, I took that journey, pretending I was with my ancient cousins, walking from our homes over the bridge and into the forum. I know that we wouldn't have talked about freedom or citizenship, as we were all citizens then, enjoying life along with everyone else. It would never have entered our minds that all this happiness and freedom was soon to come to an end as Rome became a Christian nation.

Rome was ruled by emperors, yes, but retained the institutions of a Democratic republic. There was no precedent in the ancient world for eliminating freedom of religion or freedom of speech, and laws to protect those human rights had been in place for close to a thousand years. But it would all be taken away and the long period of unimaginable oppression would begin.

And I have to ask the question the Church refuses to answer: Why?

Christians themselves fared reasonably well under Roman rule except for some isolated incidents, including the brief period when Christians were famously fed to the lions (249–251 CE) under the emperor Decius. But the emperor finally realized that this practice interfered with the efficient functioning of the army, as many soldiers were Christians. [23] So, it is true that for various reasons, early Christians were persecuted by some very cruel emperors. But Jews learn that, as we read from the Haggadah each year during Passover, having been oppressed and having suffered as slaves, we can therefore never seek to enslave or oppress others.

Jesus understood that lesson, and repeated it in his Sermon on the Mount. But, sadly, that lesson, which Jesus made the centerpiece of his life and his preaching, was never learned by Church leaders or by those who professed to worship Jesus as the son of God through all the subsequent centuries.

But before it all went wrong, before the years of persecution began, Transtiberim (Trastevere) was a bustling community of Jews and other immigrants working in various occupations at the center of government and commerce. Many worked on the docks, loading and unloading cargo that arrived from Ostia, a large port on the Mediterranean not far from Rome, where ships from Africa and Egypt brought foods and other goods for sale. From Ostia, they would be transported in small boats up the Tiber River into Rome. Ostia also had a large Jewish community involved in trade, and their synagogue, Ostia Antica, is nicely preserved. The Jews of Rome, together with their Gentile neighbors, made their living as tailors, tentmakers, craftsmen, and proprietors of little shops selling all kinds of wares and produce. The shops in the forum were usually small, with one right next to the other along the street, some with back entrances for deliveries. They probably were very much like the shops in the Old City in Jerusalem today. The wealthier Jews were physicians and jewelers, importers and exporters of grain and other commodities, manufacturers of pottery, leather goods, and olive oil, and held other skilled occupations. Far from being persecuted, they lived, worked, and thrived alongside their gentile neighbors.

So, the idea that Jews have always been persecuted because of their strange customs, their different appearance, their proclivity for keeping to themselves, and all the other characteristics the Church has asserted, has been accepted as historically true. But look at the map of the Roman Empire at its height (in the preface of this book). It extended from Britain down through Europe, the Middle East into Africa, Arabia, and to the east, to Armenia, encompassing a wide swath of the cultures of the ancient world. To suggest that the cultural characteristics of the Jews, among all this diversity stood out as weird or unacceptable is just ridiculous.

This is as absurd a statement as the one made by the president of Iran, Mohammed Ahmadinejad in a speech to the students and faculty at Columbia University in September 2007: "In Iran, we don't have homosexuals, as you do in your country."

At that, the entire audience laughed and booed.

This should have been the response to the assertion from the Church that Jews were persecuted long before Christianity, thus absolving themselves of their sin of unending persecution. But the tragedy is that no one laughed, and another slanderous statement has become Gospel truth, making it acceptable to point the world's finger at Jews for their innate pernicious behavior. And this in turn has led to the demonization of an entire people over time, right into the present day, when anti-Zionism is coming from both the left and the right. This is a dangerous mixture.

Whatever happened to "You shall not bear false witness," one of the commandments required, according to Jesus, for salvation? Isn't it time for the Church, in the name of Jesus, to renounce the lie that Jews have been persecuted forever?

Enough blood has been spilled.

Chapter 8

"THANKS FOR ALLOWING US TO USE YOUR COUNTRY . . ."

Massachusetts State Senate President Billy Bulger (1978–96), a first-generation son of Irish immigrants, once joked to me that he often opened legislative sessions by turning to William L. Saltonstall, seated in the assembly, and saying, "Thank you, Senator, for allowing us to use your country for a while."

The Saltonstall family has been in this country since 1630 and, along with their fellow Yankees, built it into what it is today for the rest of us to enjoy. Perhaps we're not giving them enough credit for taking that perilous sea journey from England in a tiny 150-foot leaky boat, 102 of them with forty in crew, crammed together with all their worldly possessions for a trip that took eight months. When they reached Plymouth, there was nothing here but a bunch of wild turkeys and natives whom they would have to befriend if they were to survive their first winter. So, when the rest of us came over—Italians, Irish, Jews, Poles, Chinese, and others—they had it all nicely set up for us. The beds were made, the war of independence was won, and they had written a great constitution that provided us with freedom of religion, speech, assembly, and all the other great things that were missing in the old country.

In addition, they were smart businessmen, innovative, ambitious, and determined to build a thriving economy. In the 1830s, Francis Cabot Lowell started the textile industry in Waltham, Massachusetts, replicating the English weaving technology and introducing modern manufacturing methods, i.e., bringing raw materials in one door and shipping the finished goods out another, all within one building. To do the really hard work, they invited over the Irish, most of whom were only too glad to escape the potato famine. Thousands of Irish immigrated as the textile industry expanded, and the factory owners were happy to find work for their children too, as they could use their little fingers to tie knots and get under the weaving machines. Then, as the population grew and the infrastructure needed to expand, Italian stone masons were needed to construct buildings and lay new roads. The Chinese were welcomed by the railroad magnates to do the back-breaking work of laying tracks across the country. Enormous wealth was amassed by these businessmen, who eventually gave their dollars and their names to universities such as Stanford, Brown, Carnegie, and Rockefeller.

I don't think anyone ever invited the Jews. We didn't exactly have a useful skill set. The Jews of Russia and Poland lived in *shtetls*, and because of local discrimination were not able to engage in normal commerce. Consequently, the talents we developed weren't of much use, unless you needed a bunch of rabbinic scholars who could debate all day long the meaning of one or two words from the Torah. Or you might find a good kosher butcher or a matchmaker. I think we just came uninvited, settled in New York, and eventually found our way to other cities in the Northeast and beyond. What we did have going for us, unlike many of the immigrants who preceded us, is that we were the "People of the Book." Even the lowliest peasants among Jewish émigrés were literate. Our culture has always deeply valued education for our children, and that proved to be a huge advantage whenever we relocated to a new country, including America.

The fact that there was religious freedom here in America, with the prospect of full citizenship, was a whole new experience. This ideal of equality was brought by the English Pilgrims to the new world, since they themselves had been marginalized and oppressed in England. But I believe that, in their minds, Jews were different from the subsequent waves of immigrants who shared their Christian religion. Feelings about Jews in America were certainly influenced by the historical European stereotypes based on our portrayal in the scriptures, literature, and art. Ben Bernanke, the former U.S. Federal Reserve chairman, who grew up in a small town in the South in the 1950s, mentions in his memoir that other kids used to ask him to show them his "horns."

There are other kinds of stereotypes that even sophisticated people believe. The notions that Jews are shrewd businessmen (though you probably wouldn't want one as a partner), and that Jews are loud, pushy, and aggressive, and will always bargain to get the best price on everything are just a few of those damaging stereotypes. Polls taken in America during the early years of the twentieth century revealed that more than half the population held extremely negative views about Jews. Polls taken within the last few years suggest that one-third of Americans believe Jews are more loyal to Israel than to America.

Like thousands of other immigrants, my paternal grandparents and their three children settled in the West End of Boston near the site of the Boston Garden (a sports arena, not flower beds). Within a single generation, their descendants were doing well enough to move out of the city to the nearby suburbs of Newton and Brookline, a migration that began in the 1920s and '30s. The immigrant generation saw that their children were well educated and that they themselves could speak proper "American," even when that meant working during the day and going to school at night. They gravitated to real estate, jewelry, food services, and other retail businesses that could be grown from small peddling operations. Their children and grandchildren, with the benefit of college educations, quickly moved into the professions. For Jews, the goal in the early part of the twentieth century was to succeed and assimilate seamlessly into American society.

Many of the boys I went to school with were descendants of those first American industrialists. When you asked what someone's father did, generally the answer was "investments." I later learned that was code for managing the old family money. As a rule, Yankees never talked about their wealth or possessions. The Yankees didn't need to show off; their money came from newspaper publishing, textile mills, banking, law, shipbuilding, and railroads. Who could compete with that kind of lineage and capital?

Later, when I got into business myself, I realized that many of my classmates' names were those of the partners in Boston's major law firms. There was a Choate, a Hall, a Grey, a Goodwin, and a Procter. One of my schoolmates was even named after my favorite toothpaste, which I thought was kind of crazy until I realized it was the name of a huge pharmaceutical company, obviously owned by his family.

It was understood that, along with Irish and Italians, Jews would not be hired by the prestigious law firms or the major hospitals in Boston, New York, and other large cities, so, beginning in the 1930s, we started our own. Can't interview at Ropes & Gray? Go to Mintz, Levin, Glovsky. Can't be admitted to the residents' program at Massachusetts General or Peter Bent Brigham hospitals? Beth Israel will be glad to have you. The Jewish community also built and supported universities like Brandeis, established in 1948, complete with a football field. Jewish professors and bright students could now be admitted to a good university when the "quotas" (widely applied admission limits for Jews) were reached at Harvard, Princeton, Yale, and the other Ivies.

A friend who attended Brandeis in the early years told me that, after several years had gone by without the school ever coming close to winning a football game, some bright faculty member had the idea that they should recruit some big, strong (i.e., Gentile) football players from high schools around Boston and give them scholarships. Sure enough, Brandeis started to win, which was great, except that those new recruits would tend to beat up the Jewish students who happened to be in the locker room when the football team returned from practice. (Punishment for killing Christ?) Well, that ended Brandeis football. In 1960, they tore down the goalposts and turned the field into something else. Most of the Jews I know aren't into team sports so much, although they're pretty good at collecting baseball cards and knowing the statistics of every player going back to the 1920s. I have a friend, a scientist at the National Institutes of Health, who was on his high school varsity math team in Brooklyn. I myself joined the track team in prep school, thinking that learning how to run fast might come in handy one day.

Sports aside, there remains the eternal Yankee question: Where do you summer?

It seemed to me that all the kids at school vacationed at summer homes that had been in their families for generations, located in places that were impossible to find on maps, because they *weren't* on the maps. Some even owned private islands in Penobscot Bay, Maine, or the Bahamas. The kids were cautioned never to divulge the names or locations of these communities to outsiders. I, on the other hand, didn't learn that lesson and readily blurted out our secret places: Hull in the summer, which is really just Nantasket Beach, and Eden Roc, our winter hideout in Miami, where the "k" was left off in the hope that people would confuse it with the Eden Roc in Antibes, France.

My wife, Dora (you'll meet her soon), and I visited one of these hidden islands in Maine while cruising in Penobscot Bay one summer. Following directions that I had been given, we rowed to a small floating dock built between some rocks to give it protection. My friend met us at the dock and took our line. As we walked up the well-worn path to the "camp," he told me it was rare for these private islands to be sold to someone outside the family, but for one reason or another he had been able to purchase this one. It struck me then how much I felt like an outsider and how secretive the old Yankees were—so secretive I didn't even know there were secrets.

That camp, as they called it, contained several primitive wooden buildings. There was a cookhouse, connected to a large common room where the family would gather to eat and play games, which were stacked in boxes on large bookcases, alongside jigsaw puzzles and old toys. There were ping-pong and pool tables and model boats made by their uncles and cousins, which they would race in the bay. A great stone fireplace with a huge timber mantle anchored the end of the room.

"This is where all the cousins get together and practice all summer for our annual end-of-summer skits," he told me. "And here are the posters advertising the skit, listing the actors. Some of these go back to the late '30s."

I couldn't help but feel jealous: so many friends, such a big active, happy family. The summer camps I went to were nothing like this. Mine were highly regimented, with counselors blowing their whistles at every opportunity. For me, summer camp was two consecutive thirty-day sentences.

But on their island, a series of rustic wooden buildings was nestled among century-old pines. Here is where their families would spend their days setting out lobster traps, fishing, sailing, playing tennis on a crudely maintained court surrounded by chicken wire nailed to old wooden posts. A couple of nicely weathered Adirondack chairs were placed on the side for anyone who wanted to watch. There was no electricity and the water came from a well.

Once, at a class reunion, one of my classmates told me that the reason he never invited me to his home is that his grandmother didn't think I would feel comfortable there. Then he added, half-joking, that his mother used to say, "If you let in one, you get them all."

He was right about that. They had the loveliest, most unspoiled spots in New England . . . and they were all restricted.

You still run into one of these Yankee grandmothers occasionally. I remember not so many years ago, we went to visit a friend at his home in a seaside town, a home with its own dock in the harbor and a tennis court. We entered by a winding dirt road leading to their compound, which included two houses, a barn, and a boatshed to store their small boats over the winter.

The boat shed was full of the tools you need to make small repairs and discarded parts you never want to throw away. There were plenty of extra lines hung on nails; a collection of oars, some varnished, others painted, and an old wooden flat-bottom skiff, its green and white paint partly peeling away. Moldy life jackets lined the walls and a mast and rolled-up sails rested on the rafters above.

It had a dirt floor, exactly what you want in a boat shed, so in the winter there's plenty of moisture to keep the wooden boats from drying out. In the corner was a workbench filled with screws, cleats, shackles, and other hardware you need to repair a sailboat. Under the table were some old red gas containers and cans of boat paint. (Reading all this, my friend and editor Leslie pointed out the irony of me feeling so different from these Yanks, yet shamelessly fawning over every little rusty screw, faded piece of canvas, and moldy, un-wearable life jacket they own.)

Oh, you're so right. My immersion in WASP culture was so complete that I never realized until recently what a paradox I was caught in. In talking about my school days I've always avoided using the trite phrase, "Some of my best friends were Christians," but it strikes me now that I didn't have any *other* kind of friends.

Anyway, this compound was my dream house. I would have loved to spend summers with lots of cousins organizing football and tennis games, rowing my skiff across the harbor in my grownup life jacket to sailing school at the yacht club, where we'd learn how to race as well. The entrance to the compound was located off a country road, accessible only after receiving explicit directions: "Just follow the long road, and where it bends, you'll see a huge maple tree; you can't miss it. Then exactly one quarter of a mile farther on the right there is a faded red mailbox, marked number 205. I must apologize, the numbers are very small and the 5 looks more like a 3." We must have driven up and down that road half a dozen times, getting out of the car to get a closer look at every red mailbox.

This community and its yacht club were off limits to Jews, and my guess is that these areas opened up only after the price of real estate (and the taxes) rose so dramatically that the multiple heirs could no longer afford to keep them. Some wanted to break the restrictive code, even selling to some "nobody," as long as they could get the asking price.

We sat down in my friend's living room, overlooking the harbor, with his wife and grandmother.

"Do you have children?" the grandmother asked my wife.

"Yes, we have one son," my wife replied.

"And where is he at school?"

"Solomon Schechter," my wife answered.

"Solomon Schechter? I have never heard of that school," she said, trying, but failing, to pronounce it correctly. The "hech" in Schechter is a hard sound to get out; you make it as if you are clearing your throat. Maybe you have to be born into it, as lots of Yiddish words are hard to pronounce. It's like trying to ask a songbird to make the guttural sound of a crow. We have tried for years to teach our friend Steve how to pronounce *kvetch* (complain), but even after being practically a member of our family for two decades, he can't get it right.

"It's a Jewish day school," my wife explained to the grandmother.

"Oh," she replied, now trying to think of what to say. "Yes . . . my gastroenterologist is Jewish."

The topic then quickly changed to something less awkward. We have to hand it to our Jewish doctors and dentists for giving these old Yanks a pleasant answer when they can't think of anything polite to say about the Jews.

In some respects, we *were* different from the parents and grandparents of the kids I went to school with, and I imagine those differences kept being reinforced by the literature they read (including the Bible) and the stories they traded about Jewish acquaintances. Basically, they just didn't know us and perhaps didn't really want to. Stereotypes have a way of erasing the fullness of the life and culture of a group of people and replacing those details with distasteful images that are easy to distance oneself from.

Chapter 9

STEREOTYPED IN THE ARTS

When my classmates studied English literature, history, and other subjects suited to group discussion, we would sit around large, oblong conference tables. We read Chaucer, Byron, Dante, Dickens, and others, but spent most of our time studying Shakespeare—his language, poetry, character relationships, and plot intrigue. It all held my attention as we read *Macbeth* and *Julius Caesar*.

But then came *The Merchant of Venice*. I hadn't read but a few pages when my eyes suddenly landed on the word "Jew." Then, those familiar anxious feelings would start to spread through my body as I fortified myself for more horrific tales of how evil the Jews were.

Though the name of the play is *The Merchant of Venice*, the only thing anyone remembers about this play is the Jew, Shylock, who makes a loan to the merchant Antonio. Antonio comes across as a kind Christian who is willing to lend his friend money without interest, but, not having the cash, ends up having to borrow it from the Jewish moneylender. Because Shylock didn't want to lend him the money, Antonio is so desperate that he agrees to secure the loan with a pound of his flesh as his bond. He is depending on his ships arriving in port to provide the money necessary to repay Shylock. But the ships run into trouble, and now the Christian is stuck.

No one believes Shylock will actually take the pound of flesh, and Antonio's friends even offer Shylock three times the amount owed to let the merchant off. But the Jew, apparently with no conscience, refuses even ten times the amount owed. A trial then takes place and it is decided by the judge (the character Portia in disguise) that he can take the pound of flesh, but that no blood can be shed in the taking, nor can Shylock take even one ounce more or less than exactly one pound, or he will be executed and all his estate forfeited.

Shylock quickly backpedals, but the duke rules that because of Shylock's threat to kill or at least maim the merchant with the flesh-cutting, all his estate will be taken anyway, with half going to the merchant. The merchant, again out of Christian love, agrees to give it back to Shylock with the condition that when Shylock dies, the money goes to his son-in-law (a Christian), and further, Shylock's life will be spared if he converts to Christianity.

Everyone agrees to the deal, and everyone is happy. But I didn't like the whole thing.

We talked about this play for what seemed to be an eternity. I felt I was the center of the drama—a living, breathing Shylock sitting right there at the table, disguised as a schoolboy in my navy-blue blazer.

Give me your pound of flesh right now! My true identity was finally revealed.

It was difficult to see any redeeming feature in Shylock. He represented the basic greedy Jew, as Shakespeare suggested that money was our sole interest in life. After all, didn't we desecrate the temple with our money-changing tables that Jesus overturned? Our school chaplain had told us all about that. Now, when somebody says "money changers," I know what they mean. They mean me.

It certainly would have been easier to condemn Shylock than to find a credible defense for his behavior, but his famous soliloquy hints that he might have some redeeming feature—that he is a human being the same way Christians are.

"Hath not a Jew eyes? Hath not a Jew hands, organs, dimensions, senses, affections, passions? . . . If you prick us, do we not bleed? If you tickle us, do we not laugh?"

There was a question on the exam later, something like "Defend and discuss one of the characters in *The Merchant of Venice*." I tried to concoct a defense for Shylock using this well-known speech, but it must not have been terribly convincing; the teacher wasn't impressed and my grade reflected that view. But I had the fleeting feeling that, for once, I had tried to stand up for the Jews.

How was I to defend Shylock, and why was it my responsibility in the first place? Do I argue with William Shakespeare, the great playwright of *Julius Caesar*, various King Henrys, *King Lear*, and the other history plays, which all seemed to me to be accurate accounts? What was my choice other than to see Shylock as a typical Jew, with all the stereotypical characteristics: the hooked nose, shifty eyes, greed for money, tendency to take advantage of others, and all the negative attributes I must have subconsciously absorbed, as did my non-Jewish classmates?

One day in class, I happened to glance over at Peter's book, which was open to the page we were discussing, and there in the margin he had written, "Swarthy Jew." I didn't exactly understand what "swarthy" meant, but I knew it wasn't flattering, and most likely was a negative description of a dark-skinned person. I was surprised he had written that, and it obviously bothered me more than I realized, as I still remember it to this day. Peter had never said anything to me that was offensive or hurtful. I considered him my friend, and not wanting to chance losing his friendship, I never asked him what he meant.

The Merchant of Venice struck at the very core of how I felt I was viewed at school. All Jews were usurers, heartless moneylenders charging interest at exorbitant rates. "He 'Jewed' me down," was such a common expression that it was often used even when I was around to hear it. None of my fellow students really meant anything insulting or prejudiced. Some didn't even associate the verb with the religion: to "joo" someone down simply meant to drive a hard bargain. For many, it was just an expression, like saying "God bless you" after somebody sneezes.

"You know Arthur was right there."

"I know, oops."

I was more embarrassed than they were when this happened, and always pretended I hadn't heard. I had a Jewish friend who used to kid with his non-Jewish friends, saying "He 'Presbyterianed' me down" when describing a purchase. I loved that, especially that he had the balls to say it. I certainly didn't.

I don't like to admit this, but it was pretty common, when leaving the gym after whatever sport you were into, that if you wanted a Coke from the machine in the vestibule you would ask someone if you could borrow a nickel (this was 1955). When I loaned a nickel, I never had the nerve to ask for it back. I figured that if I did, they would think of me as Shylock.

No wonder I was in therapy for years.

Usurers, Wall Streeters, stockbroker types–this is who we are in the minds of many. But what about J. P. Morgan, Astor Trust Co., Chase National Bank, First National Bank of Boston, State Street Bank, and the Rockefeller holdings, to name a few? Now *there* was a bunch of hard bargainers.

Recently, I was talking about business with a casual acquaintance, and in a most off-the-cuff manner I mentioned how I had been screwed by a business associate. "Is he Jewish?" he asked. His response took me so much by surprise that I couldn't collect my thoughts fast enough to say: "No."

But he happened to have guessed correctly.

Who really demanded the pound of flesh? Well, it turns out it wasn't us Shylocks. Shakespeare picked up the story from an event that occurred ten years before he wrote the play. In the real story, it's the Christian who demands the pound of flesh from the Jew.

I spent an entire therapy session telling my shrink the real story. The idea of taking a pound of flesh as a bond or guarantee had actually been around a long time, going back to the thirteenth century.[24] The earliest version of this tale had nothing to do with a Jew. It was about a slave who makes a contract with another person and guarantees it with a pound of the debtor's flesh. The same warning was given by the official adjudicating the slave's case as was given to Shylock: "If you take any more or less than a pound, you'll be hanged."

There is another story, repeated so closely by Shakespeare that you could almost call it plagiarism. It has to do with Sir Francis Drake looting Santo Domingo in 1586, an event that occurred ten years before publication of *The Merchant of Venice*.[25]

Drake, a pirate and a slave trader (before being knighted), was on an expedition around South America sponsored by Queen Elizabeth. As he passed by Santo Domingo, he couldn't resist raiding the island, and while he was at it, he happened to destroy a property owned by a Christian merchant by the name of Secchi. That property was insured by a Jew by the name of Sampson Ceneda.

Secchi called on Ceneda to report the loss, but the Jew assumed Secchi was taking advantage of the raid to make a claim on his own property. He said to the Christian, "I'll lay you a pound of flesh it's a lie," kind of like saying, "I'll lay my life on it." The Christian took the bet and demanded a contract, which they both signed.

When the Jew heard that the property was in fact destroyed, he told the Christian he was prepared to cover the damage. But the Christian said, "No! I want the pound of flesh, just as it is written in the contract. I can take the pound of flesh from that part of [your] body which is not necessary to mention."[26]

From that part of the body which is not necessary to mention? I think I know what that means, I thought to myself. *Thank God Shakespeare didn't include that little tidbit in his play. It's bad enough to kill their God, but to lop off their private parts, that's beyond terrible. It makes me shiver to think about it.*

The Jew appealed to the governor of Rome, who in turn asked the pope to intervene. The pope instructed the Christian Secchi to "take a knife therefore and cut a pound of flesh from any part you please of the Jew's body. We would advise you, however, to be careful; for if you cut but a scruple or a grain more or less than you are due, you shall certainly be hanged."

The Christian immediately agreed to a cash settlement, but the pope turned around and asked the Christian under what authority he had placed such a wager, because the Jew was the property of the state and the Christian would have been taking somebody else's property. In addition, the Jew had no authority to give away any part of his body, which was not his own to dispose of.

"Now that's a twist I never heard of," I said to my shrink. "They took all our rights away and they *own* our bodies too? What is that all about? This took me a little more research to understand, but here it is," I told my shrink. "You'll never believe it!"

It started with the First Crusade in 1096, during which thousands of Jews were slaughtered in France and Germany by Christian soldiers marching off to liberate Jerusalem from the Muslims. One of the leaders of that Crusade, Godfrey Bouillon, who later became the Christian ruler of Jerusalem, "vowed that he would not set out for the crusade until he had avenged the Crucifixion by spilling the blood of the Jews . . . that he would not tolerate that even one man calling himself a Jew should continue to live." [27]

This declaration gave everyone else permission to kill and rob Jews, making it extremely dangerous for Jews to make a living on the roads as peddlers. They needed protection, which was offered them by the lords and dukes of the city states for a fee, kind of like buying protection from the Mafia. They would contract with Jews for a set period of time, generally five years, allowing them to go about their businesses and lend money, but they had to give a large percentage of their profits to the lord in return. He owned the Jew for the duration of the contract and could rent his Jews out, sell them, pawn them, or cancel the contract all together and evict them from the territory at any time. So, the papal ruling in the Secchi-Ceneda case was correct, as it would naturally follow that the Christian had no right to take property belonging to the Duke, and the Jew had no right to give it in an act of suicide. [28]

98

STEREOTYPED IN THE ARTS

I guess Shakespeare figured that his play would go over better if the roles of the Christian and Jew were reversed. There was no chance he would offend any Jews in the audience because there wouldn't be any. Jews had all been expelled from England in 1290, three hundred years earlier.

Even with no Jew in sight, it was common for people in England to use the word "Jew" in a pejorative sense to mean moneylender, or just a person who was untrustworthy. There was no need to prompt the Christian audience to enjoy mocking the Jewish moneylender Shylock.

So, when the Royal Shakespeare Company came to Boston to perform *The Merchant of Venice*, I was ready. I called the theater and talked to the person who was putting together the playbill. "Do you know what the real story is behind the pound of flesh?" The woman on the phone must've thought she had a real kook on the line.

"No, I don't."

And I told her the story. To my surprise she didn't hang up, but seemed quite interested. I gave her the source, and she put it on the theater website. I really wanted to see it printed in the playbill, but she said it was too late.

"Anyhow, it's amazing what it does for your self-confidence when you know a thing or two about a thing or two. I wish I was back at school with that ammunition. What I would have liked to say around those oblong tables, and in chapel too," I said to my shrink as I left.

Having heard the money-changing story time and time again in chapel, I knew just where this moneylender/money-changer stereotype of the Jew came from: right from the Gospels of the New Testament. I had experienced similar squirmy, uncomfortable feelings when we discussed *The Merchant of Venice* in class as I had in chapel when the minister would describe how outraged Jesus was when he came into the temple, took one look around, and was appalled to see how we had desecrated our own place of worship.

We had cleansed the temple after the Greeks desecrated it, which is what the Hanukkah story is all about, and now Jesus has to do it for us. Matthew, Mark, Luke, and John all tell the same story:

> *Jesus then went into the Temple and drove out all those who were selling and buying there; he upset the tables of the money-changers and the seats of the dove-sellers. He said to them, "According to scripture, my house will be called a house of prayer; but you are turning it into a den of robbers. (Matthew 21:13.")*

It doesn't take a lot of research to see that this whole money-changing story is a fiction, invented to show that we were capable of desecrating our own temple and destroying our own religion.

Actually, the money-changing tables and the sellers of doves and other animals for sacrifice were never located within the temple, other than one day in the year that was nowhere near Passover. The tables and the merchants selling sacrifices always did their business in the Court of the Gentiles, outside the temple walls. Animal sacrifice was common among ancient religions. For Jews, it entailed the giving of edible food purchased for the priests. Sacrifice could only occur at the temple, so after it was destroyed, the practice ceased. Gentiles as well regularly offered sacrifices, which were referred to as "vow offerings and free will offerings." In *Antiquities* and *The Jewish War*, Josephus mentions this, and provides names of kings and princes who offered sacrifices in the temple.[29]

When I was in Israel after the 1967 war, I went up to the Temple Mount, where the golden-domed mosque of Al-Aqsa now stands and where the temple once stood. What is striking is the expanse of the Temple Mount, which is a rectangular shape the size of twenty football fields, according to our guide. The temple was at the northern end, separated by a wall from a much larger area called the Court of the Gentiles. This is where both Jewish and non-Jewish visitors to Jerusalem would enter. The west, south, and east sides are where the

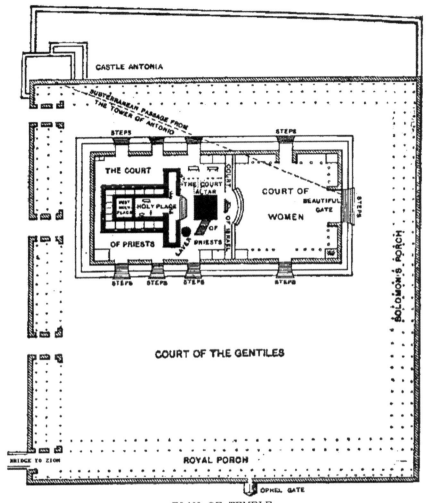

PLAN OF TEMPLE

Note that the Court of the Gentiles, where currency conversion took place, is outside the sacred sections of the temple.

money changers would set up their tables to exchange travelers' coins into the currency of Judea. Cash and other valuables the tourists didn't want to carry around with them could be locked up in secure vaults below the temple, guarded by the temple police. There was a pergola—a roof along these three sides supported by columns—to protect the money changers and merchants from the hot sun and the elements. The design is well described by the historian Josephus and by others, and has been confirmed by archaeological digs.

Exchanging money was as essential for world travel then as it is now, and was practiced universally throughout the entire Greco-Roman world. There was nothing sinister or evil about the money changers' function, nor was the temple desecrated by them and therefore in need of cleansing by Jesus. The Court of the Gentiles was never part of the temple that was considered hallowed ground. Its function was for conducting business, which was how it was designed and built in the first place.

However, the Gospel writers, relating the life of Jesus after the temple had been destroyed, obviously did not know much about how the Temple Mount had functioned or about activities in the court of the Gentiles in particular. Today, through archaeological digs, we do know how daily life unfolded there.

In talking with Christian friends, I find that they tend to agree the money changing took place in the Court of the Gentiles, but still consider the court to be part of the temple, and thus think of it as "hallowed ground." But, as I have pointed out before, Jews only consider cemeteries and places like Auschwitz, where human remains are buried, to be hallowed ground.

These friends also make the point that Jesus's act of overturning the money-changing tables made the Jews so angry that they wanted to see him executed. Again, no! The greater likelihood is that Jesus never actually committed this act of overturning the tables, because banking and money changing in Roman temples was a long-standing and common practice throughout the Roman world—a necessary practice that society could not function without.

In *Ancient History Encyclopedia*, Victor Labate tells us that traders traveling through the empire from one country to another with coins, letters of exchange, and other items would deposit their money and valuables in the basements of the pagan (and Jewish) temples—

as did all the local citizens. The temples were simply the safest locations available, as they were always occupied with "devout workers and priests and regularly patrolled by soldiers." [30]

The development "of commerce throughout the Mediterranean and the expansion of trade with foreign markets, between the third century BCE and the third century CE, led to the growth of banking in a Roman world." Money changers were referred to as *mensarii*, from the Latin word *mensa* (bank or table). In order to maintain a functioning economy, which included dealing with foreign currency, money-changers needed to be sophisticated and were required to be licensed by the state or to belong to special guilds in order to be able to certify to the legitimacy of the exchange rate. Just as it is today, banking needed to be publicly regarded as honest and legitimate in order to function properly.

The bankers dealt with poor citizens to help them resolve their problems of indebtedness, and were also responsible for the circulation of money, extending of credit, resolution of non-performing loans, commerce, trade, and the creation of wealth. Given that 7½ to 8 percent of the first-century population was Jewish, it was likely that many Jews were bankers. Only later did the Catholic Church decide that lending money and functioning as a banker was a sin. It is clear that the justification for that decision came from the Gospel story of Jesus in the temple.

This intentionally misleading accusation that the Jews desecrated the temple, requiring Jesus to cleanse it, is obviously false, but it did provide a reason why Jews might want to execute Jesus. And it became the basis for the persistent stereotype that Jews are only interested in money, so much so that we would desecrate our holiest place.

The whole business of Shylock and the other stories portraying Jews as greedy moneylenders is actually based on a pretty shaky foundation. The "Scarlet U" for usury, which Jews have been forced to wear for centuries, is both inaccurate and undeserved. Time to remove it.

Chapter 10

BACK IN HISTORY CLASS

"Who killed Christ?" the teacher asked.

"The Romans?" a classmate sitting across from me quickly answered.

"And who else?" he asks.

Oh, my God, what now? I held my breath, staring down at my notes, waiting for one of my friends to say, *You mean, Arthur?*

That's what I feared someone would blurt out, though no one said anything. However, that teacher of ours, thinking we needed to know this because it might be on the exam, said, in his most assertive tone and phony English accent: "The Jews! The Jews! The Jews! The Jews!" The repeated words were ringing in my ears.

Why did he need to say it over and over? Didn't he see me sitting right there and think that it might be inappropriate (let alone unkind) to single me out in class? I had heard this accusation in chapel, which was bad enough, but right there in class, where everyone couldn't resist looking at me to see my reaction? I needed some defense, some argument, but I had nothing. I had been sucker-punched in the stomach and couldn't open my mouth. Years later, after I had done a lot of research, I could have responded. By that time, with school far in my past, I could only take out my anger and frustration on my therapist. But sitting in history class that day, my only thought was, *this has to be wrong.*

The former president of Israel's Supreme Court, Justice Haim Cohen, retiring in 1981 after serving on the bench for twenty years, published a compelling legal argument concluding that it could not have been the Jews who killed Christ, but had to have been the Romans, based on their respective laws. He questioned by what legal authority the Jewish Sanhedrin could have convicted and executed Jesus, and under what laws the Roman court could have carried this out. According to the Gospels, Jesus was convicted by the Sanhedrin of blasphemy and turned over to Pontius Pilate, the appointed governor of Judea, for execution.

Cohen presents his arguments just as if he were writing a legal brief, complete with notes, in his book *The Trial and Death of Jesus.* He notes that of the approximately sixty thousand books written in the last century alone about the life of Jesus, very few relate to the trial itself. That makes sense, as there are no surviving records of the trial anywhere, and no eyewitness account of what occurred at the trial or crucifixion. With no record, the Gospel writers had a lot of leeway to invent or embellish what happened.[31]

Even without primary-source corroboration, most Christians take it for granted that the Gospel accounts are true, if not the actual revealed word of God. But just as other stories from the New Testament can be refuted (e.g., the prophecies, the date and place of Jesus's birth, the massacre of the innocents, etc.), so can the trial itself.

So, who did sentence and crucify Jesus, and under what laws and authority did they accomplish it?

Under Roman law, Jesus was clearly guilty of a capital crime, because only the emperor could appoint a king; therefore, when Jesus indirectly claimed to be King of the Jews, he was essentially admitting to insurrection and high treason. (*Lex Julia maiestatis, the law of treason,* was enacted by Caesar in 46 BCE and re-enacted by Augustus in 8 BCE.)

Further, the crime, *crimen laesae maiestatis*, causing injury to the majesty of the emperor, included not only treason proper, but all insurrections and uprisings against Roman rule, desertion from Roman forces, usurpation of powers reserved for the emperor or his agents, and all acts calculated to prejudice the security of Rome or the emperor or the Roman governments in the provinces. The definition of the offense is so broad as to include anything the emperor or provincial governor might consider harmful to the interests of Rome or himself. Senators and consuls were occasionally beheaded for showing the slightest contempt for the emperor or making jokes about him.[32]

Pilate had no option under this law but to find Jesus guilty and sentence him to death. Had he done otherwise he would have been violating his duty as governor. Nor did he have any qualms about crucifying Jews. Philo, a Jewish historian of the time, refers to Pilate as being "inflexible and stubbornly relentless, [committing] acts of corruption, insults rapine, outrages on the people, arrogance, repeated murders of innocent victims, and constant and most galling savagery."

Given the seriousness of the crime that Jesus admitted to in referring to himself as King of the Jews, all the associated stories, such as trading Jesus for Barabbas (a common criminal condemned at the same trial) would not have been viable options. But, according to the Gospels, pardoning a condemned person was common practice for the Roman judiciary during the time of a festival (e.g., Passover). However, research indicates that "there is little evidence for any such custom in Roman-dominated lands."[33]

Unfortunately for the Jews, the Barabbas story provided the authors of the Gospels with yet another opportunity to demonize us. It's in this story that Pilate asks the Jewish mob to choose between this good person Jesus and a common criminal. The Jews reject the offer and begin shouting, "Let him be crucified, let him be crucified!"

Somehow in the Gospel retelling, Pilate is transformed into a compassionate judge, who assures the assembled mob, "I am innocent of the blood of this just person."

But the Jews, not ready to let this thing go, again begin yelling, "His blood be on us and on our children" (Matthew, King James Version).

The Gospel writers differ to some extent about what occurred and what was said at the trial. Where Matthew has Pilate finding Jesus guilty, Luke has Pilate finding him innocent, even though Pilate asks the same question of Jesus: "Are you the King of the Jews?" Both versions report Jesus answering in the same way: "You have said it."

But all of them have the Jews shouting, "Crucify Him!"

These are the words that remain firmly embedded in my mind. It seemed to me that the ministers standing at the pulpit loved to raise their voices, like actors at the climax of a play, and call out, "Crucify him, crucify him," again and again, as if the congregation was at a baseball game with the crowds yelling, "Let's go, let's go Red Sox!"

The Gospels paint Pilate as a swell guy who was forced by the Jews to do something he didn't want to do. But Pilate's record as governor is actually one of brutal tyranny, in stark contrast to previous governors, whose tenures had been relatively calm for the inhabitants of Judea. There is no mention of civil bloodshed between Jews and Romans before Pilate, according to the historian Philo, who was living at the time.

Philo's assessment of Pilate had nothing to do with the trial, and it is believed the historian knew nothing of the existence of Jesus. His opinion of Pilate is confirmed by other writers, and we do know that not long after the trial there was such popular outrage against Pilate for his cruel behavior that Rome finally removed him as governor in 36 CE. Pilate had inflamed the population by desecrating the temple with graven images, stealing the temple treasures to build an aqueduct, and stationing troops in Jerusalem—all of which resulted in outright rebellion.

People in the Galilee were especially outraged, and the name "Galilean" became synonymous with "troublemaker." Jesus became a target of Rome, which referred to him as a Nazarene and a Galilean, according to the Gospels. The historian Josephus recorded how the Jews demonstrated against construction of the aqueduct, whereupon Pilate ordered his troops to dress as Jews and mingle among the demonstrators in order to surround them and club them to death. Roman soldiers stationed in the Galilee crucified thousands of Jewish rebels after scourging them as Jesus was said to have been scourged.

As public disorder grew, Roman soldiers became more aggressive, killing at the slightest provocation. The zealots rioted, and fanatics prophesied the end of the world and the coming of the Messiah, setting the stage for people to follow anyone who claimed to be the Messiah. There was widespread desperation and it was this climate and environment into which Jesus emerged and was himself finally tried and crucified.

Although the Jews were the victims of Pilate's brutality, the Gospels turn the tables, making the Jews into the victimizers, and pardoning Pilate:

> He [Pilate] took water and washed his hands in front of the crowd, saying, "I am innocent of this man's blood; see to that yourselves." And all the people said, "His blood shall be on us and on our children!" (Matthew 27:24, 25)

The early Christian leaders, Paul and others, transformed Pilate from Roman executioner to an actual believer in Christ. In the sixth century, Pilate was even made a saint by the Greek Orthodox and Coptic churches. This was a popular subject for artists, and there are many great paintings of Pilate washing his hands, including one by Calabrese (1633) hanging in the New York Metropolitan Museum.

This may be the first time in history when someone thought of "blaming the victim," making victim into oppressor, then recording it in a holy book to be read century after century until everyone believes it. There's no getting around the fact that, as the Gospels told it, Jesus committed a capital crime. Roman law is clear on that, and Jesus admitted to the crime by suggesting, or at least not denying, that he was King of the Jews. The Roman soldiers mocked him by hanging a sign reading "INRI" (*Iesus Nazarenus Rex Ivdaeorum*—Jesus of Nazarus King of the Jews) above his head on the cross. They also made a crown of thorns and placed it on his head and put a purple robe on him, "and say, Hail, King of the Jews" (Gospels of Mark, Matthew, Luke, John). But the important thing to understand is that, under Jewish law, no crime had been committed. Nevertheless, the writers of the Gospels concocted a detailed role for the Sanhedrin, the Jewish court, to give the impression of authenticity.

According to Matthew, 26, the priests and scribes and the elders, all being Jewish, met in the palace of the high priest Caiaphas. There they plotted to grab Jesus and kill him. However, they were concerned that since this was a festival period (the week of Passover), "There will be an uproar among the people."

The writers of the Gospels obviously had to spend a great deal of time thinking about how to write a credible story to illustrate how the Jews plotted to cover up the crime that they were about to commit. The Jewish priests needed to consider their options. They needed to consider how their actions would be seen by others, how they could set up the phony witnesses required under the law, and all the details they would carefully lay out as a group of men plotting an assassination. They needed to figure out how to get Jesus in a place where they could capture him, as is reported in the Gospels, "subtly." They needed to invent a Judas, a betrayer, to conveniently show up and offer his services to the priests for money.

And so, the authors of the Gospels gave us all that. They tell us that after the first seder ended, Jesus went with his disciples to the Mount of Olives to a place called Gethsemane. Judas followed with some soldiers and priests, and there he planted the fateful kiss. The soldiers captured Jesus and took him to the palace of the high priest.

At the palace that night, the Sanhedrin convened. It consisted of seventy-one jurists and was the highest court in Judea. The charge against Jesus was blasphemy. He was found guilty, sentenced to death, then handed over to Pilate for execution.

At the trial, according to the Gospels, the high priest asked Jesus to "tell us whether thou be the Christ, the son of God."

And Jesus answers, "Thou hast said: Nevertheless, I say unto you, hereafter shall ye see the Son of man sitting on the right hand of power, and coming in the clouds of heaven."

That was enough for the court to find Him guilty of blasphemy, a capital crime. "He hath spoken blasphemy; what further need have we of witnesses? Behold, now ye have heard his blasphemy," the high priest declared.

> *"Then did they spit in his face, and buffeted him; and others smote him with the palms of their hands."*

The trouble with the story is that what Jesus said was not blasphemy under Jewish law, for the Hebrew Bible says we are *all* children of God, the sons of God, which is understood to mean that we are all equal. Further, under Jewish law, blasphemy consisted of saying something derogatory about God, which Jesus did not do. Instead, he praised God, according to the Gospels. It is practically impossible to commit blasphemy under Jewish law, as two witnesses were required to warn and protect the person *before* he could utter anything blasphemous. The Gospel writers knew that two witnesses were needed, but they neglected the rest of the requirements of Jewish law. These two witnesses must first warn the person who is about to utter something blasphemous. The two witnesses must also be present at the trial, which they were not, because they did not exist.

Once again, I found myself obsessing about this idea on the day of my therapy appointment. "How did they think they could get away with this?" I asked my shrink, as if he was going to have an answer.

Beyond the fact that Jesus did not commit a crime under Jewish law, the entire trial could not possibly have been conducted by the Sanhedrin at the time or the place described in the Gospels. It was not allowed to sit as a criminal court, or to try criminal cases in any private house or anywhere outside the Temple precincts. Only by sitting in that chosen place, the Temple, was the Sanhedrin authorized to exercise their jurisdiction.

Nor was the Sanhedrin allowed to try criminal cases at night, since it was decreed that criminal trials must be commenced and completed during the daytime. They certainly could not convene a criminal trial on the night of the first seder because a trial for a capital crime could not be held prior to a holiday. This rule comes from the Mishnah:

> Civil cases are tried during the day and may be completed at night; criminal cases are tried during the day and must be completed during the daytime. If the accused is acquitted, the criminal trial may be completed on one and the same day; but if not, it is adjourned to the next following day, on which judgment will then be pronounced. Therefore, no criminal trials are held either on the eve of the Sabbath day or on the eve of a festival day. (M Sanhedrin IV)

"Furthermore, no person may be convicted on his own testimony or on the strength of his own confession, but only upon the testimony of two lawfully qualified eyewitnesses." But according to both Mark and Matthew, all witnesses were dismissed as untrustworthy, and the confession was based on Jesus's confession alone. "At the mouth of two witnesses, or three witnesses, shall he that is worthy of death be put to death; but at the mouth of one witness he shall not be put to death" (Deuteronomy 7:6).

Therefore, under Jewish law Jesus did not commit the crime of blasphemy, nor were there witnesses to warn him if he did.

Then I spent the rest of my therapy session telling my shrink how Christian writers have tried to explain the inconsistencies between what is written in the Gospels and Jewish law, by suggesting that this trial was held unjustly and was a travesty. They also tried to explain away the fact that Jewish law does not permit a trial to be held at night or prior to a feast day by saying that it all occurred two days *before* Passover. But that explanation conflicts with the timing of the seder Jesus had just attended. In the Gospel according to John, the

Jewish officials, upon being empowered by Pilate to execute Jesus, say with no basis, "We have a law, and by that law he ought to die, because he made himself Son of God" (John 119:7).

"It's very frustrating to me," I told my shrink as the session was about to end. "There is a belief, even among many Jews I know, that Jesus was a threat to the Jews and they needed to get rid of him. But it is obvious that he posed no threat and the fact that he said he was the son of God, sitting at the right hand of the father, wasn't particularly scandalous and wouldn't have raised an eyebrow at the time.

"We didn't find Jesus guilty because he wasn't guilty under our laws, and, besides, there could not have been a trial held before the Sanhedrin to begin with. But the Church, through the Gospels, found us guilty of a crime we didn't commit."

And with that I stood up and stormed out of his office.

Chapter 11

WHAT? WE KILLED LITTLE CHRISTIAN BOYS?

I was sitting at my dorm room desk trying to slog through my homework—a Middle English edition of Chaucer's "The Prioress's Tale"—when I came across these lines:

> *This cursed Jew did seize and hold him fast,*
> *And cut his throat, and in a pit him cast.*
> *I say, that in a cesspool him they threw,*
> *Wherein these Jews did empty their entrails.*

"Oh my God, that's disgusting," I blurted out before burying my mouth in my sweater for fear that I would attract attention (still thinking no one knew I was Jewish). The whole thought made me nauseous.

We killed the kid?

And this was Chaucer, not some ignoramus who's going to make something up. He's practically the father of English literature, the first author to be buried in Westminster Abbey's Poets' Corner. How could he be wrong?

And what are they going to say about this in class?

The Canterbury Tales is a collection of stories told in the first person by the fictional participants of a pilgrimage to Canterbury Cathedral, the shrine of Thomas Becket. The pilgrimage takes place around the time of the Third Crusade (1190), led by the English king Richard the Lionheart. We know this from the tale told by the knight who had just returned from that crusade. En route to the Holy Land, he and his fellow knights killed Jews to avenge the death of Christ, murdering the majority of English Jews living in Norwich, Stamford, Lynn, and York before murdering Muslims in Jerusalem. (Chaucer lived in the late 1300s.)

Our teacher left that Jew-murdering part out of the Chaucer discussion, and never mentioned that Robin Hood, the folk hero in tights from Sherwood Forest, who stole from the rich and gave to the poor, was also part of that crusade. When Robin returned, he found that his house had been taken by the authorities. The poor at that time were probably made poorer because Richard impoverished the country to pay for this crusade.

How was I going to concentrate after that cesspool business, or participate in yet another class discussion where I would turn out to be the villain once again? How could I hang out with my friends after class, knowing that every one of them had read the words "cursed Jew?" What would they think about me when my ancestors were the murderers of Christian kids just like them?

No wonder their grandmothers didn't think it was appropriate to invite me to their homes. Not only would I steal their money, I might pose an actual danger to their grandchildren, especially around Passover.

Of course, they didn't think anything like that, and if I'd had the guts to share my thoughts at that moment, I would have realized that the story hadn't fazed them at all. They were far more interested in "The Miller's Tale," an erotic story about how the miller's wife wanted to screw every man on the pilgrimage, and the miller didn't care a bit. Chaucer describes her as a buxom eighteen-year-old (not much older than we were), and we were obviously a bunch of horny teenagers. The only pictures we could get hold of then were of sexy models in bras and panties displayed in the *New York Times Sunday Magazine* ads. There was no *Playboy* available to us in the 1950s, and the most erotic thing we had was a recording that one of our classmates had of a couple screwing. We all huddled around the phonograph listening to heavy breathing and creaking bed springs, while laughing, making snide comments, and generally trying to avoid any details for fear of exposing our lack of firsthand knowledge.

So, while my classmates were happily flipping through the poem trying to find out how you say "tits" in Middle English, I was trying to make sense of the fact that my people had taken a crap on some child they threw into a cesspool after slitting his throat.

Fortunately for me, the class discussion focused on the beauty of the poetry, and when read aloud in Medieval English, it really was quite melodic. Our masters (teachers) occasionally played recordings of poets reading their own work. I remember that Robert Frost reciting his own poetry was ten times better than hearing it from someone else.

So, our discussion of Chaucer focused mainly on technique and use of language, and not too much on content. But sitting around that seminar table, I was once again distracted by the content. The knight had just returned from a crusade, where he had just participated in terrorizing and slaughtering Jews with his own hands, retribution for what he believed we had done to his lord, Jesus Christ.

How, exactly, was I supposed to participate in the discussion around that table? I must have appeared dull, uninterested, or just guilty of not reading the assignment. But I knew the story of the prioress all too well. Through her character, Chaucer accused the Jews of child kidnap and murder, and under torture, they admitted their crimes. So, the Christians burned some of them alive, expelled the rest from the town, destroyed their synagogue, and built a church where they buried the martyred child. It wasn't long after that (1290) that they finally expelled every Jew from England.

Where could the expelled Jews go? How were they supposed to cross the Channel, and if they did get across, where would they settle? Most of the Jews of England didn't survive the expulsion.

The prioress—the female head of a religious order—told this tale. It's about an incident that supposedly occurred in Asia and had to do with a child who was so devoted to the Virgin Mary that he memo-rized a song, which he sang over and over, praising the blessed Virgin as he walked from his home through the Jewish section to his Christian school. The Jews become inflamed at hearing the song, and Chaucer describes their anger:

> *Our primal foe, the serpent Sathanas,*
> *Who has in Jewish heart his hornets' nest,*
> *Swelled arrogantly: "O Jewish folk, alas!*
> *Is it to you a good thing, and the best,*
> *That such a boy walks here, without protest?"*

So, now I was learning that I'm the devil, with hornets in my heart and horns on my head. No wonder everyone hates us. The Satan thing comes right from the New Testament, as, according to John (writing one hundred years later), Jesus says to a group of Jews:

> *Ye are of your father the devil, and the lusts of your father ye*
> *will do. He was a murderer from the beginning, and abode*
> *not in the truth, because there is no truth in him. When he*
> *speaketh a lie, he speaketh of his own: for he is a liar, and*
> *the father of it. (John 8:44–45)*

Chaucer took this story from an incident that supposedly occurred in the city of Lincoln, England, one hundred years earlier. Around the time of Passover, a boy named Hugh was found dead in a well by his mother. The cesspool was near the house of a Jew named Copen. Under torture, Copen confessed that he had killed the child and used his blood to make matzoh, which he explained to his captors is a requirement under the laws of Passover. Although Chaucer places the prioress's tale in Asia, he tells us at the end of the poem that it was like the well-known story of Hugh of Lincoln, who was murdered by Jews for his blood in 1255. Thirty-five years later, all the Jews were expelled from England, not to return until Oliver Cromwell allowed it 350 years later.

Chaucer wrote *The Canterbury Tales* at a time when there were no Jews in England. He probably never met a Jew, but even in their absence there was plenty of antisemitic feeling to tap into. Wild myths about Jewish atrocities were reinforced by shrines to martyred children supposedly murdered by Jews. The myths, added to the story of the Passion, which was retold every Easter from the pulpit, made it practically impossible for Christians *not* to end up hating and fearing Jews.

The first of these blood libel accusations occurred in Norwich in 1144. Thomas Monmouth, a monk from Norwich Cathedral, wrote a seven-volume treatise claiming that through careful investigation, he had unearthed the source of these ritual murders. He found out that it was a sacred obligation for Jews to sacrifice a Christian boy every year to "the most high God in scorn and contempt of Christ." If Jews do not shed the blood of a Christian child, they will never be able to return to their homeland."

One of the popes responded to a similar incident in which Jews were accused of killing a Christian child to use his blood to make matzoh by asserting that this was untrue, since Jews under their own laws are forbidden to eat or drink blood. That's why we still use kosher salt to absorb all the blood in the meat we eat, and the reason why a kosher steak tastes like cardboard.

Back on the couch, years later, I found myself thinking about these child-torture and murder accusations. "The logic is that we are literally the devil and therefore capable of doing the most monstrous acts," I said to my shrink, pulling out of my pocket a paper I had brought with me.

"Let me read this to you. I know it's not usual in your office, but I want you to get the full flavor of how viciously this monk describes the torture we inflicted on these little boys."

The Rabbis of the Jews who dwell in Spain assembled together at Narbonne . . . cast lots for all the countries which the Jews inhabit; and whatever country the lot falls upon, its metropolis has to carry out the same method with the other towns and cities. . . .

"Then he goes on to say that the lot fell on the Jews of Norwich, and all the Jews in England agreed that the Jews of Norwich should carry out this wickedness. So, they kidnap this kid and bring him to the house of one of the leaders in the community. Now get this," I said, reading from the paper:

> *[The boy] was treated kindly by the Jews at first, and, ignorant of what was being prepared for him, he was kept till the morrow. But on the next day [Tuesday, March 21] . . . the chiefs of the Jews . . . suddenly seized hold of William as he was having his dinner and in no fear of any treachery and ill-treated him in various horrible ways. For while some of them held him behind, others opened his mouth and introduced an instrument of torture called a teazle [wooden gag] and, fixing it by straps through both jaws to the back of his neck, they fastened it with a knot as tightly as it could be drawn. After that, taking a short piece of rope . . . and tying three knots in it, they bound round that innocent head with it from the forehead to the back, forcing the middle knot into his forehead and the two others into his temples, the two ends of the rope being most tightly stretched at the back of his head and fastened in a very tight knot. The ends of the rope were then passed round his neck and carried round his throat under his chin, and there they finished off this dreadful engine of torture in a fifth knot. They then puncture his head with little stab wounds like the thorns the Romans put around the head of Jesus so that blood came running out of his head. Then they crucified him.*

I put the paper back into my pocket and got up as the hour was just about over. Then I turned to him as I left, and said, "It sounds just like the Nazi propaganda machine that put us into the gas chambers not so many years ago."

By this time, I had become a fanatic, so obsessed with this history that whenever anyone mentioned a place they had visited or some painting they had seen that had even the slightest relationship to anything affecting Jews, I was compelled to educate them about it. If someone casually mentioned they were going to go to Strasbourg to ski in the Alps, I would interrupt to say, "You know what happened there on Valentine's Day in 1349?" To which they would naturally say no, and then I was off and running:

"Well, that was the date when the Bishop of Strasbourg, the lords of the cities and the entire Christian population agreed to do away with the Jews for poisoning their wells. The Jews of that town, where you are about to go skiing, were marched into their cemetery, where a large wooden platform was constructed over a massive hole they had dug. The Jews were ordered onto the platform, about two thousand of them, along with their children. The platform was set on fire, with all of them screaming in pain, unable to escape, until the platform gave way and all were hurtled down into the burning pit of a mass grave. You'll be there in February, around Valentine's Day, right?"

Naturally, after my friends became familiar with my habit of steering the conversation to Jewish catastrophes, some would politely move away or change the topic, leaving some unsuspecting new victim alone to hear my rant. I guess that's why I needed to pay a shrink—to hear me out.

One thing I had to tell him about was the convening of the fourth Lateran Council in Rome in 1215, where the cardinals and bishops declared that the body and blood of Jesus is contained in a small wafer called the host, which is eaten at the communion service during the mass. It has to do with remembering the sacrifice Jesus made for mankind by taking his body and blood into one's self. There has been a controversy between Catholics and Protestants for hundreds

Profanation of the Host, for which a Jewish family is being burned at the stake, Uccello (ca. 1467-1469).

of years about whether the wafer is actually the body and blood of Christ or whether it is a symbol of the body and blood.

That part is okay, but listen to this. They put the story out that, to mock and denigrate the crucifixion, Jews would steal the wafers from nearby churches, take them to their synagogues, and crucify the biscuits. The myth adds that the wafers would begin to bleed when the Jews stabbed them.

In Bavaria, in the late fifteenth century, in a town where Hitler once lived, the Jews were accused of doing just that; it's all depicted on a woodcut that tells the story. According to the woodcut, a Christian in need of money made a deal with some Jews to steal a basket of wafers for them, and for each one he steals, the Jews would give him thirty pfennigs, not coincidentally the same amount given to Judas to betray Christ.

As I told my therapist, "The Christian steals the wafers and sells them to the Jews. When the Jews stab the biscuits and throw them into the oven, two doves fly out. Their theft is reported to the authorities, the Jews are arrested, and they confess under torture. Four of the Jews convert to Christianity and are 'mercifully' beheaded; four are burnt alive, two are torn to pieces with hot pincers, *then* burnt alive; and the rest are expelled. Their synagogue is torn down and replaced by the Church of Our Savior, where the wooden plaque depicting this history is displayed together with the knife used by the

Woodcut depicting
tale of host desecra-
tion, Passau, Bavaria
(late 15th century)

Jews to torture the host. There is no question in my mind that Hitler saw this woodcut. There is no way he could have avoided seeing it." (Near this church, the Mauthausen-Gusen concentration camp was built, where thousands of Jews were gassed and cremated.)

Myths like this flourished and spread throughout Europe and were later repeated by musicians, architects, and authors throughout the following centuries and well into our own time. Rudyard Kipling, a well-traveled, well-educated, popular writer, and winner of the Nobel Prize in Literature, is a good example. His writings include *The Jungle Book*, *Captains Courageous*, *The Man Who Would be King*, and numerous poetry and children's books, including one he wrote to teach history to his own children.

This book, *Puck of Pook's Hill,* was published in 1906 about a brother and sister, Una and Dan, who by chance call up Puck, an English spirit from the past. Puck appears and tells them little stories about significant events in English history. One such event was the signing of the Magna Carta in 1215 by King John of England. The Magna Carta sets out legal principles for fair dealings between the king and his barons in the feudal society of the time. It provided a framework for the various parties to obtain justice for disputes between parties.

In one of the Puck stories, "The Treasure and the Law," Una and Dan are playing in the woods, when suddenly, a tall, menacing old man appears from behind a bush, frightening not only the children but their dogs too. Dressed in a long dark coat with yellow fur, and "running his hands through his splendid grey beard," he approaches them and is confronted by Puck, who appears and speaks to this person in a foreign language. The man is Kadmiel, a Jewish moneylender with sneering eyes, a long nose, and bushy eyebrows. He relates how Jews control the world with their money. "You Christians," Kadmiel says, "always forget that gold does more than the sword." [34]

It amazes me that Kipling would assert that Jews owned the world's gold when they didn't even own themselves. Jews lived under the protection of the king or the lord of a given area, in exchange for paying the lord a tax on his earnings. Jews were also subject to strict one-sided contracts that gave them no rights of inheritance, no ownership of their assets, and no control of the terms of the contract, which could be canceled at any time and the Jews expelled. Furthermore, the Magna Carta, the very subject of this history lesson for Kipling's children, was signed not that many years after King Richard led the Third Crusade and massacred most of the Jews of England on his way to the Holy Land.

Why didn't Kipling include the Third Crusade in his children's story and explain that, far from manipulating kings and controlling the countries of the world, most of the English Jews were massacred?

I would love to have said this in class, but I didn't know any of it yet.

Chapter 12

HEADING OFF TO COLLEGE

Senior year at prep school meant focusing on getting into college, but my grades had suffered as I felt increasingly smothered by the constant feeling of not belonging. I had tried to remake myself to mirror the lives and attitudes of my classmates, the effort of which sometimes left me too distracted to pay attention in class. From this school in the 1950s, most students got admitted to pretty much whatever colleges they wanted to attend. What I learned later was that many of my classmates were considered "legacies," a term I had never heard back then. That tag magically handed you the key to an Ivy League school, and of course many of my schoolmates already had their names chiseled into the front of college buildings before they applied—names like Weld, Peabody, Wadsworth, Gray, Emerson, and Lowell . . . and that's just at Harvard.

Later, I learned that even classmates who were failing, or had been asked to leave, or were thrown out for some rules infractions somehow ended up being admitted to a prestigious college, maybe one year after doing some postgraduate work.

Now, that's what I call a legacy! I thought.

I did manage to leave a legacy of sorts at my school. I formed the Chamber Music Society and serve as its first president in 1956. It's a group that is still going strong today. I had forgotten about all this, but at my sixtieth reunion, an administrator from the development office handed me a large envelope, saying, "You'll like this." When I got home, I opened it and found copies of the school newspaper from

1956–57, with articles about how I had formed the society, including the word "brilliant"—the first time anyone had described me that way. The package included several of our early concert programs, a CD, and a group picture of our founding members.

One of our first concerts included Mozart's "The Musical Joke," a piece consistent with the protective persona I projected at the time and one Ms. Freeman, my violin teacher and faculty advisor to the society, knew would be right up my alley. The joke was subtle, understood only by musicians, as Mozart was poking fun at inferior composers. Because of its subtlety, I thought I would embellish the joke a bit.

In many pieces with a soloist (as first violin, I was considered the soloist), it is customary for the soloist to compose and play his own cadenza. A cadenza is used to show off the musician's talent, and when he is nearly finished, he signals to the rest of the orchestra by playing a long trill (rapid fingering between two adjacent notes), slowing it down and playing softer ("piano"), then signaling with a nod that he is finished. Well, in my cadenza, the final trilling went on and on. The rest of the orchestra members raised their instruments in anticipation of starting, but then I increased the volume of my trilling, getting faster again, bringing it to a crescendo, then once again signaling I was nearly finished. I repeated this several times until everyone got the joke. I also thought I would do what Victor Borge, the well-known Danish Jewish comedian, used to do at the piano: run his fingers rapidly up and down the keyboard as he seriously played a nocturne until he fell off the end of the piano bench onto the floor.

What I was planning was to let my bow go flying out of my hand at the end, but then I reconsidered, thinking that would work with a Borscht Belt crowd (those who frequented Jewish resort hotels in the New York Catskills), but not in Straus Library, an old family's gift to the school in 1927 that featured a grand vaulted room with rich wooden floors covered by three Oriental rugs, reading tables, and comfortable leather chairs.

Without a legacy, my mission during senior year was to get into some college. My parents asked a friend who taught at Harvard where he thought I should apply. He thought Lawrence College in Wisconsin would fit me well and help me become more serious about my studies.

Wisconsin? It's in the middle of nowhere.

The reason he suggested Lawrence was that Nathan Pusey had recently been named the new president of Harvard. He had come to Harvard from Lawrence, where he made a name for himself by speaking out strongly against Joseph McCarthy, whose hometown was Appleton, where Lawrence was located. In fact, Pusey's son was still a student there, a few grades ahead of me. With the McCarthy stance, and with Pusey's selection as president of Harvard, Lawrence was getting a lot of press at the time as an outstanding small college. I applied and was accepted.

All those years of desperately trying to belong clearly had had an effect on my self-confidence, but that started to change in this new environment. Going to Lawrence College was one of the better decisions of my life to that point. In Wisconsin, I was unique in that I came from Boston, although in the Midwest, social status was not nearly as ingrained a value as it was (and is) in New England. No *Social Register* in Appleton. My being Jewish wasn't an issue at all, and, in fact, there were plenty of other Jews there, both in my class and among the faculty.

So, I thought I was through with being excluded from certain clubs, but sure enough, it happened again. About a month after school started came the period of "rushing." The college had fraternities, and after freshman year, everyone lived in the frat houses, so most people rushed. Fraternity houses were all located in the quad, with each house having its own governance, officers, dining room, living room with a piano, card room, and dorm rooms that you would share with a roommate. The houses were comfortable and gave you the feeling of independence.

As it does everywhere, rushing consisted of freshmen visiting each fraternity so you could choose the best fit and give the upper classmen the opportunity to choose whom they wanted. Two or three of these fraternities were restricted—no Jews allowed! But the big difference at Lawrence was that a brother from each of the restricted fraternities came to me to apologize for their national body's discriminatory policy. It turned out that the fraternity I wanted to join, Beta Theta Pi, was not restricted and had the reputation of having the smartest, most serious students. They wanted me as well. Unfortunately, Beta did have a restriction against blacks, but when a black student from Chicago arrived in our senior year, our fraternity members wanted to admit him and agreed to fight it. Predictably, the national chapter was upset and sent an officer to talk with us. We threatened to dismantle our chapter, and with that they gave in. One small victory for social justice.

Soon after we had all gone through the fraternity rush process, it was time to elect the president of the freshman class. Someone nominated me as a candidate, and it turned out that three of the nominees were Betas. Naturally, the fraternity hoped the president of the class would be a brother, so the senior leadership thought it would be advantageous if only one of us ran, and a guy named Dick was chosen, an all-American boy with a lot of appeal. It was decided that it would be too obvious if the other candidate and I just dropped out, so we were asked to not campaign seriously in order to make Dick the obvious frontrunner. That was the plan.

The culminating event of the campaign was a speech all candidates had to give to the entire freshman class. The two of us hadn't done any campaigning, and of course our speeches were to be intentionally nonpresidential. My talk centered around how, being from Boston, I came from a long line of corrupt elected officials holding high office, and that, in fact, our previous mayor, James Michael Curley, had served an entire term as mayor from jail. I didn't promise to add washing machines and dryers in the dorms, or improve the food, as other candidates were doing.

I promised rampant corruption!

Well, that turned out to be the winning platform. I won in a landslide and was instantly transformed into a BMOC—Big Man on Campus. That new status proved to be a significant improvement over prep school, where I had actively tried my best not to call attention to myself, in class or in the dorms. Seeing myself as an accepted leader was a huge confidence-booster that lasted all four years of college and into my adult life.

My major was economics, and my professor, M. M. Bober (yes, Jewish), was my honors thesis advisor. He had written *Karl Marx's Interpretation of History*, which at the time was considered the premier text on Marx and his theories. Bober predicted that Marxist communism would ultimately fail, but he didn't live to see it happen.

I made good friends at Lawrence. They were serious, hard-working guys, but with a sense of humor and decidedly un-Yankee-like. One of my good friends there was Jewish, an entirely new experience for me, as he was my first close Jewish friend. We had a lot more in common than I would have imagined. It's a small thing, but when they served pork chops for dinner in the fraternity house, we would look at each other and leave, driving to a small diner up the street for something else. Neither of us was exactly kosher, but a pork chop was a bridge too far for both of us.

During the summer before senior year, I toured around Europe with Larry, another college friend, in the cheapest red English sports car we could find. When we neared Lake Geneva, we decided to take a detour to see the Château de Chillon, having both read "The Prisoner of Chillon" by Lord Byron. The poem tells of a monk who had been imprisoned for life in the dungeon of the castle, along with his entire family, for some offense against the Church. He was shackled to one of seven columns in the dungeon, along with his brothers, who were shackled to the others. His father had been burnt at the stake and all the brothers had died, leaving this monk to be the last. He mournfully relates his story to Byron, describing what he and his brothers had endured over the years, never seeing the sun and watching each other die without being able to help or comfort them. A plaque marked the spot where the monk was shackled.

We read this sad poem out loud to each other while sitting next to the column the monk was chained to, imagining that we could hear him plead with the guards to let him see the sun one last time and beg the gravedigger to bury his brother outside so even in death he might feel the sun. The gravedigger refused this simple request and went about burying his brother in a shallow grave near where the monk was shackled. Reading the poem in the damp darkness of the dungeon was unsettling; we felt we were right there with the suffering monk.

But a far more sinister activity occurred in this castle, one the tour guide never mentioned. Nor was it described in the Michelin guide or any of our other guide books. There was certainly no plaque on the wall to mark it.

The Jews had been accused of poisoning the wells in Europe, thus causing the Black Plague, and this phony indictment, based on fear and superstition, ended up wiping out most of the Jews in Europe. I didn't know this when Larry and I were touring Switzerland, but read about it much later, and realized I had stood on the very spot where the rumor began.

In 1348, the infamous Black Plague swept across the continent, ultimately killing twenty-five million people, one-third of the population of Europe. Knowing nothing about rats and fleas as disease vectors, ignorant, terrified people believed the rapidly spreading rumors that these deaths were "caused by an international conspiracy of Jewry to poison Christendom."

As a result, a number of Jews who lived on the shores of Lake Geneva were arrested, including the local rabbi, and brought to the very dungeon we were visiting. They were tortured until they confessed to the alleged plot to poison wells throughout Europe. They confessed that there was a Jewish trader by the name of Agimet from this area, who was about to send an envoy to Venice to buy silk and other items and who had also been tortured in this dungeon. When the rabbi heard of this, he gave Agimet a package containing poison and "venom in a leather bag [which he was to] distribute among the wells, cisterns, and springs about Venice and the other places to which you go, in order to poison the people who use the water. . . ."

> *Asked by the investigators if at the time that he scattered the venom and poisoned the wells above mentioned, any people had died, he said that he did not know inasmuch as he had left every one of the above-mentioned places in a hurry. Asked if any of the Jews of those places were guilty, he answered that he did not know. And by all that is contained in the five books of Moses and the scroll of the Jews, he declared that this was true. . . . ("The Confession of Agimet of Geneva, Châtel, October 20, 1348")* [35]

This Jew does not seem to know that the Five Books of Moses and the "scroll of the Jews" are the same thing. Every Jew knows, but the Christians who concocted this phony confession apparently did not.

The confession was relayed from town to town, down the Rhine River into Germany, resulting in thousands of Jews in more than two hundred towns being butchered or burnt alive. Those who survived fled east to the borders of Russia in what is now Poland, Lithuania, Moldova, and Ukraine.[36] Jews did not return or play any major part of German life again until the seventeenth century, some three hundred years later. This was the migration to the area that was later termed the "Pale of Settlement," the one region of Tsarist Russia in which Jews were permitted to live, but outside of which they could not go.

After Lawrence, I went on to graduate school at the London School of Economics (LSE), arriving early before the term began in order to find an apartment. At a party, I met Hugh, a teacher who had graduated from Oxford, and told him I was looking for a place to live.

He asked me if I wanted to go in with him and another fellow on a large place in Black Heath, a thirty-minute drive from the city. Black Heath happens to be where Caesar and his army camped during the invasion and conquest of Britain in 55 BCE. There were Jews in ranks of the Roman army, as we know from inscriptions in the catacombs, and who knows if one or more of my ancient Roman cousins didn't spread their DNA around while encamped on the Heath in England. Perhaps I really am of British stock.

On the day of enrollment, I walked into LSE and found a long queue in front of the bursar's office to register, pay the first-term tuition, and pick up the course materials they were handing out at nearby tables.

Queuing in London, as in "please form a queue," is poles apart from "line up over here." In England, everyone expects to stand quietly for half an hour or however long it takes to for the bus to arrive. No one barges in, no one lets a friend cut the line, no one bangs you with their umbrella or hits you on the head with a purse, as I have experienced in New York.

In this queue I saw quite a few students from the British Colonies, coming to London for their education as they have been doing since the grand Victorian period when the "sun never set on British soil." Many were from India and Pakistan, some dressed in traditional garb, even turbans. These students were all extremely bright. I remember being at a conference where one was presenting a paper on "econometrics." This was a new field of economics using physics and mathematical models to show that inputs into the economy are not static but dynamic, with one area affecting many others. The subject was so new and so complicated that, at the end of his talk, when he asked if there were any questions, a student replied, "Could you please go back to the part when you said 'Good morning, ladies and gentlemen'?"

I became friendly with one particularly brilliant individual, who used to tell us that the Foreign Student House, where he lived, was on the regular London bus route, and tourists were pointed to the building to indicate where students from the Colonies lived. If he happened to be sitting on the front lawn as the bus went by, my friend would get down on his hands and knees, with his colorful turban on, and pretend to chew the grass for the entertainment of the gawkers.

LSE was located on the Aldwych, across the street from the BBC, one block from the Royal Shakespeare Theatre, where we would often go to take a break from the library. Down the street was the Royal Court of Justice with the barristers in their powdered wigs and robes walking in and out of the building. On the Strand, which the Aldwych intersected, was the famous 1882 restaurant Simpson's in the Strand, and nearby, the Savoy Hotel. A pretty posh neighborhood, all in all.

I was in London when John F. Kennedy ran for president, and because he had also attended LSE as a student, there were crowds of reporters interviewing American students to see if we, and by extension Kennedy, had contracted the dreaded "Socialist virus." (LSE had been founded in 1895 by Sidney and Beatrice Webb, vocal socialists of the time.)

In the bursar's office queue that first day I was introduced to Shelley, along with several of his classmates from Harvard Law School, all of whom had come on scholarship. Unless I was missing something, it couldn't have been much of a scholarship, because the tuition for the first term was $500. Shelley also came to live with us at the house Hugh had located in Black Heath and became my lifelong friend.

That house we shared had no central heating; each room had a fireplace where you would burn coal or use an electric heater, which, when turned up to high, caused smoke to pour out of the basement. There was no central hot-water tank, either. In order to keep the electricity on, you had to feed the meter with coins; for hot water there was a little tank next to the sink called a "geezer"; its long arm could swing over the sink or over the bathtub. You had to feed it, too, with pennies to turn the gas on, and I remember Hugh often saying, "It's Saturday, I think I'll take a two-penny bath." Hugh couldn't get over the fact that the Americans took showers or bathed every day. That was unheard of in England.

Being a student in London and living in a house with a bunch of guys was terrific. Attending classes with people from such a wide variety of ethnicities, religions, and world views was fascinating. The knowledge that I was far away from my mother's portable Olivetti typewriter, which spewed out her poison letters, was the best of all.

After Shelley and I returned to Boston from London, he went to work for a real estate developer, Max K., building low and moderate-income housing. I was working at the hotel my father owned, doing pretty much whatever was needed. Max had purchased a large compound, perhaps twenty acres or more, near Nantasket Beach, and Shelley asked him if we could use it over the summer. Max agreed, so we rented a truck, pulled it up to the hotel, and took beds, dressers, chairs, tables, and lamps and transported everything we needed to the beach house.

Five or six of us moved in and we soon decided to throw a huge party, inviting everyone we knew. Three or four hundred people showed up. We hired a band, which one of our roommates told me some years later might have been the Grateful Dead before they were famous. (According to a June 2015 *Boston Globe* article, the Grateful Dead loved Boston and played there often in the mid to late '60s, so it's possible we did hire them.) The band and the crowd were so loud, and the party got so wild, that Paragon Park called the police to quiet us down. For years, every neighbor around this landmark amusement park had complained about the park's noise, which now must have seen an opportunity to blame someone else. With all the noise and the crowd, we were afraid of crashers, so when I saw this guy with a huge black beard walking up the driveway, I went out and told him this was a private party.

"My father owns this place" he said. And that's how I met Bob K., my future business partner. We eventually created a successful real estate development company together, building and operating federally subsidized elderly and market-rate housing.

Chapter 13

NOW I AM A DEVELOPER

Whether it's buying, building, or managing, real estate is a business that has attracted immigrants for years. The same, I suppose, applies to retailing and groceries. You don't have to apply for a job where you will likely be turned down anyway; you just start a little business of your own, and, if you're lucky, it grows. In the nineteenth and early twentieth centuries, there were notices published in the newspapers saying, "No Jews, Irish, or Poles need apply." By the 1960s, you never saw those ads any more, but even though they weren't printed in black and white, it was understood that the established (Yankee) law firms and real estate companies, with their Brahmin names arrayed on the letterhead, were not going to hire people named Bluestein or Feinberg.

I never actually tried that route, never wrote a resume or applied for a job. I never even thought of it. I liked the idea of construction—building buildings—probably a throwback to my love of playing in the sand with my little dump truck and steam shovel. My father was in real estate, and although he never built or developed anything, he did buy and manage a few buildings, so growing up I heard plenty of talk about mortgages, contracts, and leases.

In fact, all my father's contemporaries, including his brothers and cousins, started their own businesses. My uncle owned an upscale women's clothing store that he hoped to expand into a chain at the time when Jews were beginning to do that. I had two uncles who owned automobile dealerships and a cousin who started his own civil engineering company and eventually built the Mystic River Bridge—a huge structure that joins Boston to Chelsea and the North Shore.

After I returned from London to fill in for my father, who had suffered a heart attack, I managed one of his buildings while he recuperated. But I quickly saw that the management end was fairly boring, since this was a sleepy residential hotel catering mostly to elderly people. We provided our tenants with a small suite, daily maid service, and telephone switchboard service. Our full-time operator, Miss Kelly, who had been there since before the war, kept herself awake by listening in on the phone calls. Surprisingly, this habit once proved helpful when she informed me that a tenant and his wife had just walked out without paying, and she knew they weren't coming back, because she had overheard them booking an Eastern Airlines flight to New York leaving at 3:15 that afternoon.

I knew a couple of detectives from Station 16 around the corner, guys I would use from time to time to frighten off the occasional hooker who thought she could set up shop in the hotel. I called the station and told them I had a problem, and in a few minutes two detectives were at the front door. I described the situation and they said, "Let's go!" We all jumped into their unmarked Dick Tracy car and sped off to the airport, where the detectives and I ran down to the gate, they flashed their badges, boarded the plane, and took the couple right off. They brought the pair into a little side room, where they told the man that he was pimping the woman and they were in big trouble now. The detectives asked them where they had just been, and they named our hotel.

"Did you pay the bill?" the cops asked.

"Um, no. . . ."

"Well, here it is: pay up and you can leave." With that the guy reached into his pocket and paid the whole thing in cash.

Back in the car, the detective told me he had violated at least two laws—one state and one federal—as the airport was not in his jurisdiction and he had no right to board a plane and remove passengers.

Unfortunately, this kind of excitement didn't happen every day, and the rest was as boring as ordering toilet paper and counting towels.

My father knew everybody from Station 16, as all the officers were constantly coming in and out of the hotel to use the men's room in the basement. On Thanksgiving, when he would give all his employees a turkey, he included the men at Station 16. This practice turned his office on the Tuesday before Thanksgiving into a butcher shop, with dozens of turkeys wrapped in cellophane, lying on the floor and being bagged by the secretary for distribution later that day. I guess I had inherited everyone from Station 16.

But serving the elderly at the hotel did show me that there was a great need for clean, safe housing among this population, and that led me to try to replicate the Life Care Centers model in Massachusetts. These centers—attractive, new apartment buildings with the kind of amenities you would find in a resort hotel (community room, dining room with linen tablecloths, game rooms, library)—offered independent residential living, assisted living, and long-term nursing care, all available under one roof. The resident would pay a one-time fee of several hundred thousand dollars and that would last their lifetime and give them the security they needed. The dollar amount was based on actuarial studies of normal life expectancy, but the problem for nonprofit housing organizations run by churches, such as Presbyterian Homes, was that the care they provided was so good the residents lived well beyond their actuarial life expectancy, eventually bankrupting the nonprofits.

Nevertheless, I found a suitable piece of land in Newton and partnered with the owner of the land to build such a facility. We hired an architect, an engineer, and an attorney, got the land zoned, and did everything except get the project financed. It turned out that, by then, the banks thought it was too risky and wanted a large nonprofit behind it, so we never got it built. This actually turned out to be a good thing, as we too would have gone broke the way the churches did. However, this experience led the Masons of Massachusetts to hire me to build a facility for their own elderly members on land they owned in the western part of the state. A special program had just been announced from the Department of Housing and Urban Development (HUD) for nonprofits to build federally subsidized elderly housing, and they wanted my assistance.

I asked Bob K. if he wanted to do it with me. This was the guy with the big beard who had crashed the party Shelley and I had thrown the year before. Shelley had been working for Bob's father, and Bob had been living for a time in Jerusalem with his wife (hence the beard). When Shelley mentioned to Bob's mother that I was traveling to Israel, she asked me if I would bring him a pair of pants, and that's how I finally met him formally.

I knocked on his apartment door with the pants from his mother, and that started a long friendship. When he returned to Boston, he and his wife moved into the apartment building where my wife and I lived—a building his father owned. As the son of the owner, he had a beautiful corner two-bedroom unit overlooking the Boston Common. It had large windows and plenty of sunlight, whereas in our apartment, on the sixth floor in the back of the building, the only light we got was around sunset, when a beautiful red glow streamed in through our sheer curtains. We convinced ourselves this was the sunset, when it was actually the neon sign on the rooftop of an old hotel next door lighting up the other side of the alley.

Bob and I had talked about doing a project together, so when the Masons' opportunity came along, I asked him to join me. He was a lawyer by then, and had just passed the bar, so he would get the legal fee that was a line item on the HUD form and I would get the consulting fee—both allowable items. The application we prepared for HUD was so strong, due to the Masonic financial statements that go back to the time of King George III, that we were among the winners. Most of the nonprofits we were competing against did not have a lot of money behind them, and when asked by HUD officials reviewing their plans, "How are you going to deal with overruns from construction?" their answer was generally, "We'll have a bake sale."

This project was never completed because the Masons finally realized (after we had it zoned, priced out, drawings done, etc.) that anybody could legally apply for their housing and with the federal funding they couldn't restrict it to members of the Masonic Temple. They pulled out, but they did pay all the fees we would have received if it had been built, plus all the fees for the architect, engineer, and outside attorney.

Completing all that work trained us to write a strong HUD application, so when the next opportunity came from HUD, we weren't starting from ground zero. In 1976, the country was in a recession and nothing was being built, leaving construction workers out of work. President Gerald Ford worked with the building trade unions (carpenters, painters, electricians, laborers, etc.) to design the Demonstration Rehabilitation Program, whereby if they agreed to reduce their hourly wages and loosen their restrictive practices, HUD would award millions of dollars to developers to rehabilitate old mills and vacant buildings into housing for the elderly. This provided subsidies for elderly tenants so their rent wouldn't exceed 30 percent of their income. I imagine that was done to get votes from union members, but Ford did not roll it out in time for the election.

There was a short window of time to convince a city or town to designate an area for rehabilitation and then convince municipal officials that the designated area needed to include the building optioned—and that no other building would qualify. A developer also had to obtain signed agreements from the union business agents, complete an application, and deliver it to HUD in Washington, DC, by five o'clock on the designated day. We made applications in three cities and, surprisingly, won them all.

With that initial success we needed an office and a secretary, so we rented a one-bedroom/one-bath apartment with a kitchen in Bob's father's building. Bob took the bedroom, I took the living room, and the secretary took the kitchen, which worked out just fine, as she liked to snack and was only an arm's length away from the refrigerator. We figured that, if we grew, we could move to a two-bedroom, two-bath.

Almost immediately, a big problem came up. Two of the business agents, the Painters and the Electrical Workers who had signed the applications for the projects, one in Lawrence and the other in Lowell, Massachusetts, turned out not to be the real agents. They were located in Boston, and these guys were tough. They'd rather tear your arm off than reduce their wages by one cent. We would meet with them, Bob and I and a guy named Murray Movitz, who worked for another developer—three skinny Jewish guys trying to negotiate with Jimmy D., the painters' union agent, in his office located at the end of a narrow road, tucked under a bridge at the edge of the Mystic River. The whole thing looked like something right out of *On the Waterfront*.

Jimmy D. himself was a pretty scary guy, and so was the head of the Brotherhood of Electrical Workers. They weren't going to give us the required wage reduction or budge an inch on the "restrictive practices," the rules delineating, for example, that a union painter could not carry two one-gallon paint cans in each hand, and could not remove an electrical switch cover, but had to call an electrician to do that. Restrictive practices increased costs.

We needed both guys to sign, and they absolutely weren't going to, so we were faced with the prospect of losing all three projects and going out of business before we even moved into my dream two-bedroom/two-bathroom office.

As it happened, I knew the congressman from Lowell, Paul Tsongas, who wanted local construction workers to get jobs on these two projects. I called him and explained the problem. It turned out there was a bill going through Congress called the Common Situs Picketing Bill, which the unions supported. The bill gave unions a lot more power by stipulating that if one union with even a tiny percentage of the project wanted to strike, the whole job would have to shut down. Apparently, Speaker of the House Tip O'Neill also wanted this bill and knew that without Paul's vote it would fail. The heads of the building trade unions had pushed for this special demonstration project and wanted the jobs for their workers too. Paul told me to call them and say that he would vote against the bill if he didn't get those two projects.

The unions were all at their annual meeting of the AFL-CIO in Bal Harbor, Florida. I tracked down the vice presidents of those two unions and explained that their signatures had to be on the documents when we delivered the applications to HUD in two days.

"If they don't sign, we will. You'll just fly down to Bal Harbor and fly back, but hold on, I'll call you back in a few minutes." (No FedEx back then.)

In a few minutes they called back and said, "They'll sign."

Fearing the worst, including personal body mayhem, Murray and I went back to the union offices, and thank God, with no hassle, they signed our papers.

I zoomed back to Bob's father's office, where the secretary was typing out the HUD forms. She was like a machine, the fastest typist I'd ever seen, banging away on a new IBM Selectric. Barry F., our partner in Lawrence and Lowell, the funniest and most well-connected guy I ever knew, was struggling with the Xerox collating machine, its trays violently sliding back and forth. Every few minutes, the whole machine would jam up and papers would start flying all over the room, with Barry rushing around trying to catch them. We were pulling an all-nighter so everything would be ready and I could fly down to Washington, cab over to HUD with the carton of applications, run up the stairs, and slam the whole thing onto the reception desk to get it time stamped. (One of those developments was the Francis Cabot Lowell mill in Waltham, Massachusetts, which we rehabilitated into 250 units of subsidized elderly housing. These early entrepreneurs were the great-great-great-grandfathers of many of my classmates.)

Done! We were real developers, with the first hurdle completed.

Developing, owning, and managing HUD-subsidized elderly housing eliminates the market risk. The only risk is getting it built in the first place. I liked the process; it suited my personality, which is kind of risk-averse. The fear of losing money undoubtedly comes from my father, who went through the Great Depression and saw a lot of his friends and acquaintances go broke. Although none of them actually threw themselves out of a window, he told me plenty of stories that made the point. "You'll be okay in real estate, as long as your mortgage isn't so big that you can't survive a downturn in the economy . . . and you don't ever sign personally. In the long run, real estate will appreciate."

A friend I knew, who had been in the business for years, told me that he taught a course in development at Northeastern University. When one of the students asked him, "What's the secret in real estate?" He replied, "Living a long time."

Inflation "makes us real estate dopes look smart," as another friend in the business often joked. If you hold it long enough and you have enough cash in the property that you don't get foreclosed in a downturn, eventually you will make money.

Starting these three large developments was a dramatic change for me and required engaging a law firm familiar with construction contracts, a national accounting firm that could manage the complex financing, securing the required equity, as well as architectural firms, contractors, engineers, environmental specialists—the whole shebang. I went out and bought two white hardhats, one for me and one for Bob. I put mine on the ledge behind the back seat of my car, together with some rolled-up architectural plans, conspicuous enough so everyone could see I was a big-shot developer. I had never been a big-shot anything before, but with funding for three large developments in hand and high-priced consultants taking my calls, I was in the big time now.

Bob and I went into these projects with no experience and no track record as developers, which turned out to be a HUD requirement. I kept asking people in the Boston HUD office, "How do you ever get to develop HUD projects if you have to have been a developer before you are one?"

This must have been the problem the author(s) of Genesis ran into as they set out to write the first line of the Torah (the Five Books of Moses in the Hebrew Bible), so they simply wrote: "In the beginning, God created the heavens and the earth." I asked myself, "Does that go for a developer too?" We eventually figured it out.

What we really needed was to find a partner who had done HUD work in the past, but wouldn't try to take the whole project away from us. I had been introduced to a lawyer by the name of Gerry Doherty, who had done a lot of zoning work and was already a partner in many projects. I asked if he would represent us in our projects so we could use his previous experience to satisfy HUD requirements. He agreed and threw out a very fair percentage that he wanted in return for us using his financial statements to make us appear financially secure.

I used to joke that it seemed like we had more experience before we started than we had after years in the business.

Gerry was influential and politically connected, and very close to the Kennedys, having run Bobby Kennedy's campaign in Indiana, Jimmy Carter's campaign in New York, and Ted Kennedy's campaign for senator and president.

From then on, when we were negotiating to option a building, rather than do it in our modest little office, we would go over to Gerry's impressive suite on Beacon Hill, replete with Kennedy memorabilia, an original portrait of Rose, oriental rugs, and on Gerry's tie, a PT-109 clip. But the *pièce de résistance* was that when we were negotiating with the CEO of some major company who owned a vacant building we wanted to option, Gerry's secretary would come in and announce that he had a phone call from Washington. Gerry would say, "I'll call back."

"It's the president," Eleanor would quietly answer.

And it was!

Gerry often acted as a liaison between Jimmy Carter and Speaker of the House Tip O'Neill. So that whole little interaction, combined with the Kennedy aura, always sealed the deal.

Partnered with Gerry, we got what we needed every time. He was so generous with his time and expertise that I am indebted to him forever. We met for breakfast every Monday morning at the Parker House, with him advising us on next steps, recommending professionals we should hire, and sharing little pointers, such as, you never, ever discuss business in an elevator or a men's room.

Sometimes, when I had a meeting scheduled with Gerry, I would cut across the Boston Common to get from my office on Tremont Street to his office on Beacon Hill. Boston Common is our much smaller version of New York's Central Park—several square blocks of beautiful green space, shaded by trees two centuries old and criss-crossed with walkways, at the junction of which stands a hundred-year-old stone gazebo known as the Parkman Bandstand. The walks across the Common made nice little breaks in the work day, particularly in warm weather when I would often take a circuitous route to his office.

On one of those walks, as I passed by the corner of Beacon and Charles Streets, a really anxious and unsettled feeling came over me, which I couldn't understand until I started to piece together the memory of an incident that I had not thought about for more than twenty years. It was a day when I had accidentally come across a large anti-Jewish rally that took place at this very spot around 1957, led by the infamous antisemitic priest Father Leonard Feeney.

I was a boarding student then, and a group of us would often take the trolley from school to Boston on Sundays, getting off at Scollay Square. The area was really seedy back then, and our group was on our way to a notorious strip joint known as the Old Howard, a Vaudeville theater. In the late 1960s, the whole area was finally torn down to make way for the New Boston City Hall plaza.

We were too young to get into the Old Howard legally, but we all had fake IDs. A few men were scattered around the musty smelling theater, half of them wearing raincoats even though it wasn't raining outside. A bored-looking comedian would come out first to warm up the audience, along with a little band consisting of a drum, bass, and piano, but nobody cared about that—we were all there to see the girls.

Once the show started, they paraded around, throwing off their furs and other props to prolong the excitement, the drummer punctuating the removal of each piece of clothing with a drum roll, while the men in raincoats yelled, "Take it off, take it all off!" And soon, right there in front of us, were real live women's breasts, partially covered by miniature cymbals, which would jingle as their breasts bounced around. In hindsight, the whole show was as cheesy as the neighborhood.

From the Old Howard, we walked up Tremont Street and headed into the Boston Common. Near the corner of Charles and Beacon Streets, a crowd had formed around a priest who was standing on a riser in front of a huge cross with a life-size image of Jesus hanging up there in the most grotesque way, leaving no doubt about how much he was suffering. Behind the cross was a painted mural of the Virgin Mary. If that was not enough to stop me in my tracks, the words coming out of this priest's mouth nearly frightened me to death. He was spouting every vicious accusation about the Jews you could imagine. Everything wrong with the world was caused by us: Jews are the perpetual enemies of God, the ones who murdered Jesus, he screamed into his microphone, pointing up to the cross, and then he began quoting from Saint Paul: "The Jews who both killed the Lord Jesus and the prophets, have persecuted us, and pleased not God" (Thessalonians 2:15—16).

All I could think was, *Are you kidding? WE persecuted THEM?*

He railed against the Jewish merchants, who he claimed were taking over all the businesses and banks in Boston, referring to specific individuals by name: Rabinowitz, changed to Rabb, who owned a chain of supermarkets; Garfinkel, whose chain of department stores even included Brooks Brothers, that most Yankee of all New England men's stores. He threw out vividly descriptive buzzwords and catchphrases, such as "stuffing their bulging purses" and "squeezing" defenseless Christian merchants out of business, and brought up all the same old stereotypes used since medieval times.

Out of those loudspeakers I heard the words of Hitler, Himmler, and Goebbels, only they were being spoken right there in Boston, the so-called Athens of America. I found myself in the middle of a mob of angry Christians cheering along Father Feeney's speech, phrase by phrase.

What if they knew I was a Jew? What would they do to me? Would my friends stand up for me, or run for their lives? It was terrifying to be there, and easy to imagine myself at a Nazi rally in Nuremberg, Munich, or Berlin before the war. As the terror was about to start, few Jews believed it could happen to them in Germany in the twentieth century.

I later discovered that this Father Feeney wasn't exactly on the lunatic fringe; he had been a professor at Boston College, then a Respected Professor of Sacred Eloquence at the Weston Seminary, the local Jesuit theological school, and then, in 1943, became the leader of St. Benedict's Center, serving the Catholic students at Harvard and Radcliffe. When Feeney took over the center in 1949 it became the home base of a radical group of his followers called the Slaves of the Immaculate Heart of Mary, a virulently antisemitic religious community whose members always dressed in black and white uniforms. (To his everlasting credit, Bobby Kennedy, then an undergraduate at Harvard, wrote to Cardinal Cushing and asked that Father Feeney be removed.)

In 1949, Feeney set off a national theological controversy by contending it is heresy to believe that salvation is possible for anyone outside the Roman Catholic Church—an extreme medieval position the Church had modified over the centuries. The debate reached its

Father Feeney "preaching" on Boston Common, 1957

climax in February of 1953, when Pope Pius XII excommunicated Feeney and his followers for advocating that position in the name of the Church. But Feeney never recanted and his core belief—*Extra Ecclesium Nulla Salum* ("Outside the Church there is no salvation")—was etched on his tombstone when he died in 1978.

I would have thought his excommunication would have been based on his rants against the Jews, that the Church would have seen by now how such rhetoric aimed at angry crowds can end up in mass murder, especially with the horror of the Holocaust fresh in everyone's mind. But given the abysmal records of Popes Pius XI and XII before, during, and after World War II, I guess not. Pius XII gave sanctuary to members of the SS after the war, helping them avoid arrest for crimes against humanity, providing fake passports, and creating safe routes to Argentina and other countries using monastery "Underground Railroad" systems. In the aftermath of the war, it's no wonder that priests like Feeney felt they had free rein to spew hatred and incite violence. To add insult to injury, in 1972 Cardinal Medeiros of Boston revoked Father Feeney's excommunication and welcomed him back into the Church.

What is there to say?

After a few moments of being lost in thought about the Feeney rally, I turned away from the memory of what had taken place there twenty years before and turned my attention back to my upcoming meeting with Gerry. I shook off the uncomfortable feelings as I shifted gears and thought about how rare it was to have someone like Gerry come into my life and give so generously of his time to teach and mentor me. It's a relationship I still treasure.

But the memory of that scene in the Common got me thinking about the development community in Boston. In the business world I was now part of, there was a mix of Irish and Italian, Catholics, Protestants, Blacks, and Jews. We formed a remarkably close-knit family, sharing information, not competing in a city or town where a fellow developer was trying to get zoning for his project, and meeting every month at the law firm of Mintz, Levin with Howard Cohen, who was legal counsel to many of us. Together, we talked strategy about how to resolve a problem with the state finance agency or discussed pending legislation that affected all of us.

We all belonged to the Massachusetts Homebuilders Association, which lobbied for legislation and monitored what was going on at the state and federal levels. It included developers for multifamily and single-family housing along with contractors. We would get together from time to time for dinners, usually with a speaker from HUD or the state legislature. These dinners were casual and friendly, hosted by Walter Winchester, a fellow developer who loved to act as master of ceremonies, telling all kinds of funny stories. These guys were open and frank; there was never any fear that I'd hear those dreaded phrases, "He Jewed me down" or "that greedy Jew." It just wasn't part of their vocabulary, and the Homebuilders Association wasn't restricted in any way, but welcomed everyone equally.

Within this group of colleagues and friends there was great mutual respect and even an unspoken love for one another, with each of us ready to come to one another's aid when necessary. One contractor, whom we were especially fond of, ran into financial problems on one of his projects through no fault of his own. We closed ranks and helped him out, so no one came after him, including the banks, and he was able to work things out without going bankrupt. The warmth and encouragement I received from these business friends was like nothing I had experienced before. Their sincerity was genuine and right up front. They were not embarrassed to show their feelings; it was all quite wonderful. This was a cotillion I could dance at!

The association was made all the better by the fact that all of these guys were extremely charitable, each sitting on the boards of multiple community organizations like the hospitals, the Boys and Girls clubs, scholarship programs, St. Mary's Center for Women and Children, and a program that involved safe, clean housing for people in need called Caritas Communities. Its mission was to build apartment buildings around Metro Boston, all with single-room units for the homeless who had formerly been living on the street. Each building had a case manager who assisted these people to maintain sobriety and get back on their feet. All of us were willing contributors and would gladly come together with a pledge or to buy a table at a fundraising dinner for whatever casue anyone of us was interested in. It remains a great source of pride that I belonged to a group of people who were so committed to sharing their success with their community. Talk about repairing the world: that's what they did every day.

Jews have a long tradition of giving. *Tzedakah*, or charity, has been one of the pillars of Judaism for five thousand years, and I think we also invented the custom of putting up plaques on everything to acknowledge our donations—kind of like naming a street after yourself. There is a first-century synagogue in Ostia, an ancient city a few hours from Rome on the Mediterranean. With a little imagination, you can picture yourself praying and socializing with friends and family, and if you look up, guess what you see on the wall? A plaque for the nice gift from Mindis Foustos:

FOR THE EMPEROR'S HEALTH MINDIS FOUSTOS
CONSTRUCTED AND MADE AT HIS OWN EXPENSE
AND PLACED THE ARK FOR THE SACRED LAW

Today, you can walk down any corridor at the Beth Israel Deaconess Medical Center or the Brigham and Women's Hospital and see dozens of signs like this, acknowledging the donors. Even the elevators and broom closets have plaques!

Pillar from the Synagogue Ostia
Antica in the Port of Ostia on the
Mediterranean Sea (1st century)

Chapter 14

DORA: THE ROAD TO MARRIAGE

Shortly after Shelley and I returned from school in London, we met Mort Zuckerman, who later became a political commentator on *The McLaughlin Group* on PBS. He purchased *The Atlantic Monthly* and *The New York Daily News*, moved to New York, and became a big developer. But when we met him, he was still in Boston, about our age (mid to late 20s), and already quite a mover and shaker, working for the large real estate company Cabot, Cabot, and Forbes (sounds like a conglomerate of my prep-school classmates).

At that time, the company was building industrial parks along Route 128, the highway that formed a loop around Metro Boston. CC&F had offices in Boston and California, and Mort would fly back and forth—pretty impressive in those days. Having graduated from Wharton in business and Harvard Law School, he was smart enough to figure out that he could get mortgages on the industrial properties they were building for more than they cost to build, using the appraised value of the property based on the tenants' rents rather than the building cost, which allowed the company to walk away with immediate cash profits. The partners were naturally thrilled to put that extra cash into their pockets.

Those Jews, I could almost hear his Yankee partners saying while lunching in some private club Mort couldn't get into, *they sure have a way with money.*

Mort was making far more money than Shelley or I, and he lived in a really nice apartment, where, when you looked out the window, you didn't have a view of a brick wall twenty feet away. He had a spiffy new Jaguar convertible too, which he hated. "The problem is the damn thing won't start. I'm just going to leave it running on the street one day and hope somebody will steal it," he would joke.

He was not only very smart, but very competitive and a great athlete to boot. We were friends, but I never had the feeling I could be close to Mort, as he always had so many irons in the fire. He and I once went to Florida and stayed at the Fontainebleau for a week, but he would go up to the room for a few hours in the afternoon and trade stocks, even shorting the market, which at the time I thought was pretty sophisticated.

Shelley and I somehow found ourselves serving as Mort's "beta testers" of eligible girls. The process went something like this: Mort would mention a girl's name and suggest one of us should call her. After one of us went out with her, Mort would casually ask for a review. If it was positive, we would later find out he had called her for a date. That's what happened with Dora.

Dora and Mort were both from Montreal, and Dora's sister knew him from McGill University, which is how Mort got her name and phone number in the first place. He mentioned her to me and I called her. She sounded okay on the phone, so I went to pick her up at the appointed time at her apartment in Cambridge. A girl answered the door and introduced herself as Dora. She had just come out of the shower and still had an old striped towel wrapped around her with pink curlers in her hair. Quite a sight for a blind date. She smiled brightly and said, "You must be Arthur."

Yes, I replied, a little stunned. But just then, down the stairs came a truly stunning girl, and all four roommates started to laugh at how well the joke they had concocted turned out—and how startled I looked.

Dora was as much fun as she was pretty, and she suggested that we go to a jazz bar for a drink. I didn't particularly like jazz, but I agreed. Once we were seated at one of those bistro-style tables, she told me she had a friend who was playing trumpet there that night, and she wanted to see him play. Not a great start. Why would she take me to listen to a guy I assumed was probably a former boyfriend or, worse, a prospective boyfriend? Besides that, the bar was so loud it was impossible to talk–hardly the place to get to know somebody. She looked good, yes, but I wasn't sure I really liked her.

When Mort called the next day, I gave him my mixed review. A week or so later, while he and I were out together, he told me he had taken Dora to the Boston Symphony and thought she was great.

Maybe it's worth another shot, I thought.

That was a fortuitous decision, but since Mort was as competitive in the dating arena as he was on the squash court, he proceeded to invite her to a series of elegant events, just to outpace me. With Valentine's Day around the corner, I began to rack my brain for something creative to do. Then it came to me.

I went to a delicatessen and bought eight pounds of chopped liver, then to a candy store for a large, empty heart-shaped box. I formed a huge chopped liver heart, placed it in the box, tied it up with a pretty ribbon, and attached a card on the top that read:

You set my heart a-quiver,
You are my Gehackte Liver.

(Translation: *Chopped Liver—i.e., Jewish paté.*)

I sent it to her apartment by courier. She must have thought, *Wow, what a clever guy,* or maybe she just liked chopped liver. I don't know, but after that we dated frequently, and even went on a trip to the Chesapeake Bay to charter a sailboat with an old college friend and his wife. Dora, who was afraid to even step into a canoe, agreed to go on the sailing trip after a lot of persuasion and a guarantee that this trip did not mean we were going steady. But even though she insisted on separate rooms, I'm certain it was she who snuck into my room the first night, and not the other way around.

We did the normal kinds of things people did in the '60s: going out, then back to her apartment or mine, rolling around on the floor for a while, and then going home at an appropriate hour. But she had this habit, which she still does today, of always leaving behind at least one article of clothing, so after a while, most of her clothes ended up in my apartment, making it a necessity for her to move in. My mother had a cleaning man named Jesse, whose wife, Athaliah, came once a week to clean my apartment. They had separated, so everything was fine until they got back together and Athaliah told Jesse, "I think Arthur may be a transvestite. There's an awful lot of women's shoes and dresses in his closet."

With that morsel of gossip, Jesse must've mentioned to my mother that there was a girl living in my apartment, so she knew what was going on.

In the early 1960s, cohabitation was unheard of, and my mother took an immediate dislike toward this loose woman who was obviously corrupting me with her radical ideas. But Dora and I soon became engaged, and my parents threw a big party at their house for our families and their friends. Then, without our consent, my mother sent pictures of us that we had taken by the famous Boston photographer Fabian Bachrach to the *Boston Globe* engagement section. No one does that anymore, and I still feel embarrassed thinking about it.

Our engagement stretched on and on, way beyond the random wedding date we had set. Dora just couldn't commit, and even though her sisters were urging her to marry me, she was scared, and I was getting frustrated by her indecision.

Around this time Dora went to Montreal to babysit for her sister's two young daughters while their parents were on vacation. While she was away, I went with friends of ours, Bill and Judy, to see *The Graduate,* the iconic movie in which Dustin Hoffman realizes he is in love with a girl who is marrying someone else in a church. He drives to the church, climbs up to the rear balcony, and bangs on the stained-glass window yelling her name, "Elaine! Elaine!" She runs back down the aisle into his arms, and off they drive in his convertible sports car.

"That's what I have to do," I whispered to Judy, who knew my whole story.

After the movie, the three of us hatched a plot. I told them Dora was flying back to Boston from Montreal in two days.

"What do you think of this idea?" I said. "Judy, you pack up ten days' worth of Dora's clothes, I'll buy tickets to Rome, and when she lands, I'll meet her and give her an ultimatum: Either you fly to Rome with me right now and we get married, or it's over."

The next morning, I called Alitalia. It turned out there were plenty of seats on a nonstop flight to Rome leaving two hours after Dora was scheduled to land. I bought some travelers checks, collected my passport, and asked Bill if he would call my father to tell him we were going to Rome to elope.

I got to the airport early, walked up to the ticket agent at Alitalia, reserved two tickets, and told him my whole story.

"So romantic, so Italian, I love it. Just what Marcello Mastroianni would do," he said. Then he repeated the whole story to the other agents at the desk.

"Bravo! Bravo!" It was a scene right out of the movies; how could she resist?

"Come, sit down over here," I told her in a serious voice, after I collected her luggage from the Montreal flight. "I want to talk to you about something." This lent the moment an air of mystery, and then I laid out the plan and presented the ultimatum.

"Are you serious?"

"Absolutely. I have your luggage. Judy packed everything you need. I have two tickets waiting, but we have to confirm within half an hour to get our luggage on the plane."

The short timetable worked to my advantage, as she couldn't take too much time to contemplate, plus the romance of it all must have had some effect. Finally, she agreed. She took her passport out of her purse, looked at it, and announced, "Oh my God, it's expired!"

"*Oh, mi dispiace, mi dispiace tanto!* [so sorry, so sorry!]. *Ah, niente passaporto, tragico, tragico, una grande tragedia!*" the Alitalia agent passionately exclaimed.

Now we were in a scene from *Tosca.*

We went upstairs to one of the airport lounges to have a much-needed drink and talked about our life in a warm and loving way. Dora said she would see how quickly she could renew her passport.

But getting married in Italy, I discovered, wasn't so easy. You needed a two-week residency for a start, and there were a lot of other legal requirements. So, we thought, okay, let's get married in New York. Dora's sister, my sister, and their husbands lived there, and my sister's husband was the assistant rabbi at Temple Emanuel, the grand Jewish "cathedral" that included Senator Jacob Javits and other luminaries among its congregants.

With the inevitable delay, Dora's doubts began to resurface, and Mort marshaled a battalion of her old friends from Montreal to persuade her to reverse direction. Such a competitive guy he was. But somehow, with our friends persuading her to go ahead with it and the additional push of her roommate getting married the next weekend, our wedding plans were on again.

We reserved the main room at the Four Seasons restaurant and invited our friends. Unfortunately, my mother's ongoing resentment of Dora made inviting her impossible. I definitely wanted my father there, and we both wanted her parents, but the business with my mother cast a shadow on the arrangements. In the end, our sisters and their husbands came, so we had family and friends on both sides with us.

But before the ceremony came the legalities. We checked in to the Essex Hotel overlooking Central Park. The temperature was 90 degrees and the humidity close to 100 percent. Just up the street from the hotel was a clinic where we could go for our blood tests.

(It was required to test for syphilis back then.) We sat in the waiting room for quite some time, but when we got into the doctor's office, the needles were sitting in a glass container with cotton, soaked in alcohol to make them sterile, but the cotton was black with some disgusting-looking *schmutz*. This was a deal-breaker for both of us. But Dora's sister was a doctor who lived close by in New Jersey; she agreed to sign the certificate without the tests.

The next day we went to New York City Hall to get the license, and from there jumped in a cab. When the cabbie said, "Where to?" we said, "Tiffany's," feeling like we were still in the movies. Given the long period of time it took us to decide to get married, and now with the looming reality that we were finally going through with it, both of us became very nervous. Each step in the process brought us closer to that reality, so much so that as we sat on the stools talking to the jeweler, and as he showed us wedding rings displayed on a black felt square board, Dora began to feel lightheaded.

"I gotta get outta here," she struggled to say, as we both jumped off the stools, making for the door. With the salesperson wondering what was going on, and without the rings, we headed back to the hotel.

The following day was the wedding and much of it is still hazy, but somehow, we arrived at Temple Emanuel and met my brother-in-law, Rabbi Chuck, in his study. We signed the *Ketubah*, an ancient Hebrew marriage contract that guarantees support if the husband drops dead, which, the way I was feeling, might happen any second now. Having fought so desperately to convince Dora to marry me, the idea that it was really to happen hit me like a huge wave. I had been so busy convincing her, I had neglected to convince myself.

Our friends and family were already seated in the small chapel outside the rabbi's office. Dora and I came out, followed by Chuck, and we turned around to face him as he made the appropriate Hebrew blessings. Then he began to opine about marriage, using a sailing analogy that went on and on, describing our boat sailing peacefully over the water and coming up against storms and wind and rain, and

First sailing date with Dora, 1969

this and that—all this in the 90-degree heat and humidity. The longer he went on, the dizzier I felt. I motioned to him with my hand to hurry up, as I knew I wasn't going to last. But he was so caught up in his allegory that he kept going, until my knees buckled, saved only by one of our friends, who thankfully slid a chair under me as I passed out. Somebody ran to the bathroom for some wet paper towels to revive me. Once I felt a bit more stable, I made my own way to the bathroom, threw some cold water on my face, straightened my hair as best I could, and returned to the chapel.

As I think about it now, just a bit shy of our fiftieth anniversary, I'm pretty sure I never said, "I do," and never had the necessary blood tests. It's entirely possible that our whole marriage is illegal.

But despite our shaky start, I must say that our marriage has been filled with lots of laughter, great memories, and sometimes pain. Like many marriages, ours has been marked by occasional disagreements, issues, and rough patches. But with so many years together, we know we can depend on each other for support and unconditional love—surely the crucial elements of any relationship.

Even though I dated some non-Jewish women in my twenties and thirties, I always knew that I would marry someone who was Jewish. It was important to me to be able to share the values, the humor, the holidays, and all the verbal *shtick* that comes with Jewishness—it's not really something you can learn. Although Dora isn't any more observant than I am, we certainly have what you would call a "Jewish home," complete with the smell of brisket in the oven, gefilte fish (from a jar) with horseradish on top, *matzoh-brei* (fried matzoh and eggs) for breakfast on Sunday mornings, and Jewish holidays spent with friends and family, either in our home or theirs. It seems to me that marriage is difficult enough, and that when you share a culture, traditions, and family history, it gives you a slight step up. Of course, attitudes have changed a lot since we were married, and many of our friends' children have mixed marriages now. I expect they will find a way to make it work.

But Dora, for the Jewish home life you have given me, for the love and support you have shown to me, even when it was not easy, and for so much more, I can't thank you enough.

"Do I love you?" (as Goldie and Tevye ask one another in their well-known duet from *Fiddler on the Roof*).

Yes, very much.

Chapter 15

THE CRUSADES: KILLING TWO INFIDELS WITH ONE STONE

Dora and I mostly agree on the things we like to do, although maybe not so much on the boating thing (although I have many pictures of Dora smiling as we cruised around on our sailboat). We both loved traveling to Europe, staying at nice hotels, sitting in cafés, eating at the great restaurants, and naturally, visiting museums. Shopping for nice things was always fun too, until you realized that pretty much anything you wanted to buy was also available at Filene's, Jordan Marsh, or any department store at home.

We took lots of trips during the 1980s after I became interested in reading about Jewish history. It was on one of those trips that we visited Avignon in France, where the papacy had relocated in the fourteenth century. I discovered in my Michelin guide that the pope at that time agreed to protect his local Jews behind the walls, away from the Christian mobs who wanted to slaughter them. But the pope was unable to keep the mob away, and although he tried to convince the Jews to convert, they chose to commit suicide rather than face being hacked to death. This happened multiple times; each time they asked the local bishop to protect them, but unwilling or unable to, the he offered conversion instead. That was the single reference I found in any European guidebook about the Jews in medieval times—or later, for that matter. The discovery of that omission actually led me to write a guidebook about Jewish history in Europe. That effort morphed into a general history of the Jews, and finally into the memoir you are now reading.

There are no tangible remains of Jewish life, no Jewish sites from medieval Europe for tourists to see, largely because we were routinely slaughtered by the crusaders on their way to Jerusalem to fight the Muslims. There are no crusader castles in Europe as there are in the Middle-East; they did not need fortifications since the Jews were unarmed and it was simply a turkey shoot to hack and burn Jews in the name of Christ before they reached an armed enemy in the Holy Land.

There are no tours one can take through France and Germany to trace the crusaders' routes as they destroyed hundreds of Jewish communities and murdered millions of Jews.

At the start of the second millennium, as Rome began to emerge from the Dark Ages, the power hierarchy in Europe was reshuffled by the Church in what has been described as "one of the great tragedies of human history—and the central tragedy of Christianity." [37] It

Crusaders hanging and torturing Jews, who are portrayed as devils as they were called in the New Testament (ca. 1550-1580)

was accomplished with a single decree from Pope Gregory VII: the authority of the pope would now be understood as vested in Christ himself, and thus considered superior to that of any secular ruler, to be judged or defied by no one.

The popes' self-proclaimed infallibility spread across Europe, immortalized by the famous rupture in the mid-twelfth century between King Henry II of England and Thomas à Becket, his chief ecclesiastical officer. Henry had Becket murdered in Canterbury Cathedral for asserting his authority over the king's, based on many incidents of refusing to comply with Henry's prescribed punishments for capital crimes committed by members of the clergy. Becket had merely reprimanded a clergyman who had been convicted and sentenced to death by a civil court for the rape of a girl and the murder of her father, making it clear to Henry that Becket placed the power of the pope and the Church above that of the king.

The rise of papal authority inevitably led to the Crusades. Johnson attributes the Crusades to several interconnected causes. First, there had been a number of minor skirmishes between the Church and the Spanish Muslims. Second, Gregory VII wanted to expand papal territory to accommodate the rapidly growing European population. And third, the blessing by St. Augustine of the notion of a "just war" provided legitimacy for the campaigns. It was clear to the popes that the expansion of Muslim rule was threatening the power and wealth of the Church and needed to end.

From 632 CE to the beginning of the First Crusade, the known world was thrust into enormous turmoil as Islam took hold and Muslims conquered large swaths of territory. This meant that more than 90 percent of Jews were living under Muslim rule.

Although Muslims considered Jews second-class citizens, they did not persecute them as Christians did, but instead opened territories that had been closed to Jews under Christian rule, including Jerusalem. In Muslim-held countries, Jews who had been forcibly converted by the Church were allowed to return to their religious practices, and many Jews ended up emigrating to Moorish Spain, where Jewish culture thrived for several centuries.

But the Crusades against Muslims opened a terrifying new chapter in Christian behavior. Encouraged by the clergy, mobs inflamed against Muslims also turned to killing Jews indiscriminately—the result of demeaning rhetoric, degrading myths, and anti-Jewish laws promulgated by papal decree. Until the First Crusade, Jews had lived in *relative* peace in France and Germany. Although we were not allowed to own land, we were able to make a reasonable living as merchants. Intellectual life was permitted to develop during these peaceful times, including the study of holy texts. During this period Rashi (1040–1105), a rabbi living in France, emerged as a noted scholar and commentator of the Bible and the Talmud. However, as the Church gained more power toward the end of the century, persecution of the Jews became more common and this period of peace ended.

Increasingly, Church and local law decreed that Jews could be denigrated in any way. "In Toulouse the count in the city [would] have the right to slap the face of the Jewish leader on Good Friday." [38] In Rome, one pope dreamed up the idea that kissing the foot of the pope was too good for a Jew, so Jews would be forced to kiss the ground where the pope's foot had been resting the moment before.

But the insults were to become far worse. In 1095, Pope Urban II made an impassioned appeal to the Second Council of Clermont in France for all of Christendom to unite in a march to liberate Jerusalem from the Muslims. The men who answered the call attached to their outer garments crosses called "croises" or "crusades," from which the whole endeavor took its name. [39]

The crusading army was made up of nobles and "poppers (paupers)." The nobles saw an opportunity to confiscate the liberated territories for their own benefit; the poppers were driven by "pure religious fanaticism." [40] Although the stated intention of the pope was to liberate Jerusalem, the anti-Jewish accusations coming from the Church for centuries almost guaranteed that the Crusades would include the killing of Jews. In the New Testament, in myths and in local folklore, Jews were described as horned devils, Christ-killers, worse than vermin. So why wait to slaughter the infidels in Jerusalem when the hated Jewish infidels were living throughout France and Germany along the route to the east?

Godfrey Bouillon, one of the crusade leaders who later became the Christian ruler of Jerusalem, "vowed that he would not set out for the crusade until he had avenged the Crucifixion by spilling the blood of the Jews" and declared that "he would not tolerate that even one man calling himself a Jew should continue to live." [41] Encouraged by their leaders, crusaders enthusiastically took the pledge that Jews should be slaughtered first as they passed though cities and towns on their march to Jerusalem.

> *The first group which attacked the Jews assembled in Normandy, and fell upon the Jews of Rouen. . . . Meanwhile a number of other bands collected in Germany. A priest, Volkmar, collected an army in Saxony and marched through Bohemia, massacring the Jews of Prague. Another priest Gottschalk, descended from the Rhineland to the Danube and massacred the communities of Ratisbon, and possibly other Danubian cities. Yet another band was led by a Rhineland count, Emicho or Emmerich, and was responsible for the worst massacres in the Rhineland itself. His forces attacked Jews of Speier, Worms and Mainz. A band from Flanders, coming up the Rhine to join him, attacked those of Cologne.* [42]

These Jews were unarmed and unable to protect themselves, I thought as I read the detailed plans of the crusaders. Somehow, we still have images of these crusaders today as valiant warriors, wearing armor and carrying shields.

It was chilling to read how these crusaders developed such elaborate plans of attack, and that the Jews in the targeted towns had no idea that they were facing a massacre that would be their last day on earth. It must have been similar to Germany in 1940, when Jews were rounded up and told to pack some clothing because they were being "relocated." Then, still unsuspecting, and perhaps soothed by the orchestra music that greeted them at the railroad station, they were marched to the gas chambers.

A Christian chronicler of the time states: "We have set out to march on a long road against the enemies of God to the east, and behold, before our eyes are the Jews, His worst foes. To ignore them is preposterous."

Another writes, "Jesus Himself said 'that day will come when my disciples will avenge my blood.' We are those disciples and will fulfill the duty. God hates the Jews for their evil doings, and has made the Christians His portion."

And a third: "Whoever kills a Jew has all his sins forgiven." [43]

None of this makes sense to me. The Messiah was supposed to bring peace to the world. I heard this in the words of one of the Christmas carols I liked as a boy, singing along with the others on Beacon Hill: "Peace on earth, goodwill to men." That lovely winter scene, with snowflakes falling on cobblestone streets, lit by gas lamps, stood in sharp contrast to the images of crusaders wading knee-deep in blood, murdering Jews in the name of Christ.

The events unfolded much the same way in every town they attacked. The crusaders would assemble outside the city gates and plot to attack while the Jews were at prayer in their synagogue. If by some chance they heard of the plan beforehand, the Jews would leave the synagogue to hide in the homes of Christian neighbors or anywhere they thought safe. They would try to persuade the local bishop to help them by giving him silver to provide sanctuary in his castle or in church. The crusaders would eventually break through the gates, or the gates would be opened by Christian town folk, and they would rush through the streets, tearing Jews from their hiding places, breaking into their homes, offering them a choice of baptism or death.

In most cases, the bishops would be unable to protect the Jews from the rioting horde, and realizing their fate would attempt to persuade them to accept baptism. But rather than face the crusaders, who would slice their children in half with axes, force husbands to witness their wives being raped and then hacked to death, the Jews would often choose to kill their families and themselves. There are several written accounts of these mass suicides.

In May of 1099, the first crusaders reached Jerusalem.

> *The slaughter was fearful. The conquerors waded through streets which are ankle-deep with the blood of the vanquished. At night-fall they knelt in prayer before the [Church of the] Holy Sepulcher, sobbing with joy at their victory over the nonbelievers, [then] they drove all the Jews of the city into a synagogue and burnt them alive within it.*[44]

Except for their financial interests, local Christians didn't seem to care if we were slaughtered, I thought as I read. The princes who made up the secular authority and the wealthy feudal landowners made money from the Jews by taking a large percentage of the interest we were charging in order to make a living in their territories. Prior to the First Crusade, Jews were generally merchants who traveled the roads selling their goods, but with the advent of the Crusades, the roads were no longer safe for Jews. Since we were not permitted to own land, a new form of making a living needed to be found. A few Jews were able to find some duke or prince who would take a certain percentage of the interest the Jew would charge for making loans in exchange for a contract that would protect the Jew. The language was very broad in these contracts, resulting in the duke actually owning the Jew.

But it wasn't only the nobles and knights: the peasants among the Crusaders also found they could enrich themselves when they realized the Jews they were murdering had money and valuables for the taking.

And yet *we* are considered the greedy, money-obsessed people by

164

The Children's Crusade . . . Just like summer camp! (1212)

many Christians, both in the eleventh century and still today.

There were some "righteous gentiles" in medieval times, just as there were during the Holocaust of the twentieth century, people who saved and protected Jews, and we are grateful to them, no matter what century they lived in. The righteous ones were mostly working-class Christians who had become friendly with their working-class Jewish neighbors in the course of doing business together and living in close proximity.

The Fourth and final Crusade (1320) was called the Pastoureaux or "Shepherds Crusade" and was comprised mainly of young boys and groups of vagabonds who were incited to riot by a priest in France. These boys, whose average age was sixteen, together with the vagabonds, were every bit as vicious as the older Crusaders, and stormed through communities in France slaughtering or converting Jews. These Crusades were so barbaric and grew so out of control that Pope Innocent III (1198–1216) and later Pope Gregory IX (1227–1241) ordered the bishops to stop the massacres. But it was too late for the Jews. Before the Fourth Crusade was ended, these children destroyed 110 Jewish communities in the south of France.[45]

Many of the children wanted to go back home even before reaching Jerusalem. The trip was very difficult and many died from exposure to the elements and lack of food. When they reached Marseilles, a ship captain agreed to take them home, but actually took them to Africa to be sold as slaves. Two of the ships sunk and the bodies of the children eventually washed ashore on a little island called San Pietro, near Sardinia. Here a chapel was built to honor these "martyrs," which they named "Chapel of the New Innocents." This was a direct reference to the Gospel story of the children Herod slaughtered, called the "Massacre of the Innocents." The chapel, dedicated to these crusaders, whose swords still showed "the blood of babies and their parents" as they floated ashore, became a destination for pilgrims to pray for them.[46]

I told this story to my shrink one morning, and asked him "How can the Church be so blind to their sin of murdering other people to think of calling them 'martyrs?'"

Chapter 16

FROM THE RENAISSANCE TO THE GHETTO

Having immersed myself in Jewish history, I now wanted to return to Italy, but this time with a mission different from the one I'd had as a college student touring around on five dollars a day, looking at churches and historical sites, but mainly trying (mostly unsuccessfully) to pick up girls.

I needed to see for myself the Lateran church where vicious laws were enacted to tighten restrictions on Jewish life. I wanted to stand in the ghettos of Rome, Venice, and Siena to experience what it must have felt like to be locked up behind gates in the cramped, dank quarters to which the popes had relegated us for three hundred years. (Often associated with inner city slums today, the Italian word *ghetto* originally meant "ironworks," because an ironworks factory in Venice was the site of the first mandated Jewish enclave.)

Most of all, I wanted to understand the contrast between the way Jews had lived under the Roman emperors with full citizenship and without discrimination, and the way things had deteriorated for us in later centuries.

Off we went, Dora, our five-year-old son Ben, our au pair, a graduate student in Italian Jewish history we had hired who was also fluent in Italian, and me, carrying books and notes from the research I had done over the past several years.

We rented an apartment in Rome's Parioli section, on a hill just north of the city, and from our windows we had wonderful views of flowers spilling over the balconies of the buildings around us.

European apartments have a particular charm, and this one had it all: high plastered interior walls, tiled floors, and ceilings so high you could hear the echo of your steps as you walked. This was a beautiful section of Rome, where many of the embassies were located. At the corner of our street was a gorgeous flower market under a tent, next to a grocer and a charming little café. The whole market area was small enough that, after a few days, the grocers got to know us and always handed our little boy a sweet treat as we passed by.

Coincidentally, Primo Levi, the noted Holocaust survivor and author, had lived in this very same apartment, as our landlady informed us. I thought I might absorb a fraction of the great author's voice from those walls.

But years later I read Levi's first book, *If This Is a Man*, which he wrote just after being freed from Auschwitz. It is so poignant and so graphic that I realized I couldn't be inspired by his writings, but rather horrified and haunted by the savagery of supposedly normal human beings who considered themselves Christians. (The 1933 German census showed the country to be almost equally divided between Lutherans and Roman Catholics, with fewer than 0.75 percent Jews.)

Levi was from Turin in northern Italy and had studied chemistry at the university there. He joined the resistance movement and was captured in 1944, telling his captors that he was both Jewish and a citizen of Italy. With that, he was immediately shipped to Auschwitz.

Levi specifically told them that he was a citizen because, while the Germans expected all Jews in Italy to be sent to concentration camps, Italian bureaucrats insisted that only noncitizens could be deported. The Italians deserve thanks and gratitude for purposely fumbling around and confusing the records of who was a citizen and who was not. As a result of their actions, only 25 percent of the Jewish population in Italy was sent to the death camps. (How sad to feel grateful that only one-quarter of the Jews were sent to their deaths, because in most other European countries it was closer to 100 percent.) Pope Pius himself, who might have shown spiritual leadership during the war, did nothing to save Jewish lives. It is said that, at one point, he watched from the Vatican windows as trucks rumbled by, packed with Italian Jews being deported to concentration camps. I wonder if it occurred to him as he watched that he was witnessing a true "massacre of the innocents?" He could have played the same game as the bureaucrats, but remained silent and let so many go to their deaths. Later, he went out of his way to hide members of the SS and help them escape from Europe to South America.

In his book, Levi speaks directly to his captors. "Now that I am free, I make my voice heard to the German people and talk back to the SS and their heirs. I am alive, and I would like to understand you so that I can judge you." [47] It became his lifelong effort to understand the kind of immorality he had witnessed and experienced firsthand, carried out by human beings against other human beings. "Oppression corrupts the oppressed." The Nazis, he tells us, had a knack for making their victims feel shame for surviving, and just as they brutalized us physically, they also brutalized our minds and spirits and turned us into the vermin they thought we were.

They would assign prisoners to perform low-level functions, like cleaning out the latrines, carrying full buckets of urine out to the snow to be dumped, where victims would feel grateful just to get out and breathe some fresh air, to be out of the vermin-infested beds they shared with other men, head to toe. Victims assigned to the position of *kapos*—bunk/group leaders—were even grateful to be selected to cooperate with evil, just to be able to survive for one more day. It is incredibly callous to suggest that some Jews collaborated with the Germans, and to shift some of the blame from these church-going Germans, if you yourself did not witness or experience firsthand the starvation, torture, and slow death.

Levi's purpose in writing was to try to make sense of "a phenomenon that is devoid of sense by civilized standards." He says, "I want to understand in order to judge, not to punish because that is someone else's job. Not to forgive, as I do not know of any human action that can undo all the wrong. Germans cannot escape guilt, as ordinary citizens who must have known, should have known, looked the other way, or willfully forgot . . . those who worked in, lived near, built, supplied, or purchased from the vast network of slave labor camps that were integral to the German economy, a mass of invalids huddled around the core of savages." [48]

Primo Levi was tormented by these questions, none of which seemed to have any answers, and suffered long periods of depression during which he could not be comforted. Desperate, he took his own life in 1987, just a few years before we stayed in his apartment.

After reading his book, I couldn't help but think that there is no other creature on earth as cruel to its own species as man. We have an extra layer of brain tissue and a large skull to contain it. Our large brains give us language with which to understand the past and speculate about the future, to compose beautiful music, write books, create all manner of beautiful objects, and to enjoy and reflect upon the meaning of our lives. Why has it also given us the need to denigrate and destroy anyone we believe to be different or inferior? No other creature on earth does that. Can you imagine a herd of horses getting together and deciding that "the zebras kind of look like us—except for those ugly stripes. We're bigger than they are; why don't we just kill them all?"

All I can say is: Are we human beings living at the bottom of the moral ladder?

Primo Levi's son, Renzo, knew that his father would commit suicide. He said, "Just read the conclusion of his book, *The Truce.*"

In it, Levi described a recurring nightmare, which always began in a beautiful, sun-filled spot, where he was surrounded by friends and family. Then, slowly, the scene would degenerate into a turbulent, black eddy of fear and madness, and he would hear once again the dawn command of Auschwitz—"a foreign word, feared and expected: Get up, 'Wstawach!'" And he would understand that the warmth and beauty were an illusion; the cruelty and madness were the true reality of human life.

Reading this, I felt his fear at a visceral level, and it was made even more relevant by the knowledge that I had stayed for several weeks in the very rooms where he had lived and worked. The desperate, numbing thought Levi and all those in the camps must have experienced—that this might be their last day on earth—has been our historical reality for much of our seventeen hundred years under Christian rule.

After we settled in at the apartment, the first thing we did was to go to the Vatican, where I had arranged to visit the archives with the help of a priest I had met at the Hebrew College library in Newton. These archives had just been opened to scholars doing research, and although I wasn't exactly a scholar, he said he could get us in. Once the archives were opened, it was discovered that they contained many old Talmuds the Church had confiscated from the Jews of Rome in 1553. They searched every house over a nine-day period. The books they found were taken by wagon loads to the Campo de Fiori, where they were burned on September 9, Rosh Hashanah. (This was a place of public executions, and a statue still stands there of Giordano Bruno, a philosopher accused of heresy and burned alive in 1600.) Members of the clergy understood that without the Talmuds, Judaism would disappear, as it was our holy texts that bound us together and saved us from extinction. A plaque also hangs in that piazza commemorating the burnings of the Talmuds. (I understand that some American Jew received permission to put up the plaque. It didn't seem too complicated a process; perhaps I should start doing that.)

As is every visitor to Rome, Dora and I were struck by the grand architecture, the majestic columned buildings, domed churches, piazzas with their magnificent statuary and fountains throughout the city. The similarity of contemporary Rome to the architecture of the ancient city is not an accident, but the result of a desire during the Renaissance to rebuild pagan Rome into the most beautiful of Christian cities. The builders were aided in their efforts by the discovery around the year 1400 of a book by Marcus Vitruvius Pollio—

the only surviving text on classical architecture and design, written a century before the birth of Christ and recopied seven hundred years later.

The Renaissance (1400–1600) was a unique period of creativity that also ushered in a welcome interlude of peace and prosperity for the Jews of Italy. It was an era that saw an explosion of human talent, long suppressed during medieval times, but now enthusiastically embraced and supported by wealthy merchants, land holders, and the papacy itself. St. Peter's Cathedral, the Sistine Chapel, the statues and sculptured fountains dominating the piazzas of Rome all date from this period, which also produced the great masters, including Michelangelo, Bernini, da Vinci, Titian, Tintoretto, Botticelli, Caravaggio, Raphael, and others.

The popes had abandoned Rome for most of the fourteenth century, as the elected pope, a Frenchman, insisted on remaining in Avignon. The papal seat remained there for almost seventy years, a period referred to as the "Great Schism," during which there were two competing popes, one in Rome and the other in France. Rome suffered terribly during those seventy years, as many of its inhabitants left the city, returning in 1418 to find it in utter disrepair—hardly the great "City on the Hill."

The seventy-year hiatus is also referred to by the Church as the "Babylonian Captivity," another instance of the Church appropriating Jewish history by plagiarizing our exact terminology without even a footnote.

Such chutzpah, I thought to myself as I read about this. *Yes, it took seventy years to rebuild the temple in 516 BCE after the Persians defeated Judea and destroyed it in 586 BCE. But that doesn't give the Church the right to steal a meaningful phrase related to the seventy-year period from our history of two thousand years earlier.*

The Babylonian Captivity is remembered each year at the celebration of Purim (a holiday honoring the Biblical story of Haman and Queen Esther). When Cyrus the Great defeated the Persians, he permitted the Jews to return to Judea in 538 BCE, and he issued a declaration that forms the very last words of the Hebrew Bible:

> *All the Kingdoms of the earth the Lord, God of Heaven, hath given me; and He hath charged me to build Him a house in Jerusalem, which is in Judea. Whosoever there is among you of all His people—the Lord his God be with him—let him go up.*

As it is today, the commitment to return to Jerusalem was powerful, even though it was daunting because of the country's destruction, and forty-two thousand Jews made the choice to return. They knew the Jews who had remained were living in severe poverty, but arrived (as we know from Psalm 126) with singing and celebration:

> *Then was our mouth filled with laughter,*
> *And our tongues filled with singing.*

When the popes returned to Rome, their desire was to rebuild it into the great city it had been under the Roman emperors. When the emerging intellectualism and scientific curiosity of the fifteenth century was coupled with the architectural and engineering achievements of the Roman period (visible all around them in the ancient ruins), the resulting humanism stood in stark contrast to the rigid Church-dominated spiritual life of the medieval past. This new vision dominated all areas of life and quickly spread north throughout Europe.

The contrast between the old and the new visions of man and his relationship to the Church was dramatic. In medieval times, it was the afterlife that faithful Christians had focused on, since this life was, as Thomas Hobbes said, "nasty, brutish and short." The Renaissance, on the other hand, emphasized a more pleasant and a somewhat more secular life, in which material comforts were meant to be enjoyed. The idea of a rebirth is often attributed to Francisco Petrarch, an Italian intellectual whose vision gained wide popularity in his own time (1304–1374). Not surprisingly, it was also a period of widespread economic growth, fueled by international trade and banking in the cities of Venice, Florence, Genoa, and Milan. The accumulation of great wealth by ambitious merchant banking families made it possible to finance this rebirth in Italy.

Venice is an island, and the necessity of building oceangoing ships led it to become the center of trade on the Italian peninsula. But as trade grew, it was Florence that became the international banking center as well as the major producer and exporter of fine cloth and silks. These activities made the House of Medici and other prominent families extremely wealthy. It also guaranteed employment and a living wage to many, resulting in an increase in the standard of living for much of the population around Florence. This newfound wealth and ability to purchase luxury foods, wines, spices, and exotic goods from all over the world fueled the economic boom.

For many, especially in the upper classes, the pleasure of indulging in these luxuries was far more appealing than waiting for the promises of an afterlife. This transformation from the constrained view of life in medieval times to the opportunities of the Renaissance spread steadily as more of the population had access to a comfortable life, formerly available only to dukes, princes, and the clergy. Opportunities to make money were found everywhere, from ship building to importing and exporting, to manufacturing and sales, and to the borrowing and lending of money to finance these ventures.

The pursuit of material comfort became so widespread that the Church had to relax the strictures against money-lending. The popes and the members of the papal court almost all had relatives whose wealth had helped grease their way into the clergy and higher office. Lorenzo Medici's son was even elected pope, becoming Leo X. You can see Lorenzo himself looking out coyly from the right of Botticelli's painting, *Adoration of the Magi*, as if to say, *Hey, take a look at who's kneeling in front of the baby Jesus. Sure looks like cousin Cosimo.*

The invention of the moveable-type printing press by Gutenberg, Fust, and Schoffer in the mid-1400s helped advance the social and

Adoration of the Magi Botticelli. (ca. 1475-1476)

intellectual progress of the Renaissance by making written texts, formerly hand-copied by scribes, widely available. The technique of making paper from water and cloth (originally developed by the Chinese) replaced the use of parchment and further expanded the reach and impact of the printing press.

For Italian Jews, all this progress and relative secularism was a welcome change. They now enjoyed equal rights with Christians and were permitted to engage in commerce for the first time since the reign of Constantine, nearly a thousand years before. Jews quickly took advantage of this new period of openness, during which they were able to educate their children, hire tutors in philosophy, mathematics, and medicine, and study their own holy books. Even restrictions on socializing with their Christian neighbors were relaxed. It all created something of a renaissance in Jewish life in Rome.

Soon after the papal return from Avignon, the Tiber River overflowed its banks, flooding parts of the city and causing a serious plague from the foul water. Jewish physicians freely offered their services for anyone who fell ill, which prompted Roman officials to reduce Jewish taxes and bestow citizenship on a number of Jews—a rare expression of thanks rather than blame for causing the flood.

This welcome humanitarian tone continued with succeeding popes. Pope Boniface IX (1389–1404) extended Jews' privileges and legislated that all Roman Jews enjoy the liberties of citizenship. Pope Gregory XII (1406–1415) accepted a Torah scroll given to him by the Jewish community, as was required as a formal welcoming of new popes. But this time, to the surprise of the rabbis, the new pope didn't respond with customary indictment of the rabbis and all Jews for murdering Christ—a traditional crowd-pleaser everyone looked forward to—but accepted the Torah scroll as a gift. Pope Martin V (1417–1431) issued edicts that protected the rights of the Jews and publicly encouraged Christians to develop friendly relationships with their Jewish neighbors. In these good times, Jews became productive members of society, engaging in many professions, including banking. Pope Martin was interested in theology and philosophy and invited Aaron Abulrabi, a famous Jewish scholar from northern Italy, to discuss Biblical and Talmudic topics with several cardinals who had become increasingly eager to expand their understanding of humanity and the sciences. The cardinals developed close relationships with Jewish scholars, some even learning Hebrew.

Unfortunately, the good relations between the Church and the Jewish community under the tolerant popes proved fragile. With the election in 1442 of Pope Eugene IV, who was influenced by the anti-Jewish persecutions in Spain, came the reinstatement of restrictive laws against Jews. Eugene once again forbade contact between Christians and Jews, halted the construction of new synagogues, denied residency to Jews in certain areas of the empire, forbade the reading of Jewish religious texts and eliminated the right of Jews to hold public office. But threatened by the prospect of a mass exodus of all Jews from Rome to the lands of the Duke of Mantua (who invited them to come), the apostolic court reversed its decree and accepted the offer of a large sum of money to the Church from the Jews.

The next pope, Nicholas V (1447–1455), was interested in maintaining the cosmopolitan culture of Rome and returned to the earlier policy of protecting the Jews, but he too came up against the deeply ingrained anti-Jewish attitudes held by the Church. A powerful anti-Jewish friar by the name of John Capistrano traveled around Italy inciting Christians to riot against Jews. (He was later made patron saint of judges and honored in the United States by having a couple of monasteries named after him.)

There were a number of these reversals, but outside events derailed popes from fully rescinding Jewish rights. The threat of invasion from Turkey distracted Pope Calixtus III (1455) from reinstituting the restrictive laws. But when the threat subsided, before he could follow through, he dropped dead—one small miracle for the Jews!

This safe and serene period continued as the next pope, Paul II (1464–1471), revived the ancient Roman carnivals, games, and races for Jews and Christians alike. In 1471, Sixtus IV was elected pope, and it was during his reign that the Renaissance reached its architectural and intellectual peak, for it was Pope Sixtus who hired Michelangelo to paint the ceiling and walls of the Vatican's Sistine Chapel, which he named after himself. Sixtus would not tolerate the persecution of the Jews and would not support fanatical friars who hoped to stir up the masses with their fictitious tales of ritual murders and well poisoning. The anti-Jewish laws that had been enacted earlier and promulgated by the Lateran councils were no longer enforced anywhere; everyone could now enjoy the fresh air of freedom emanating from a more humanistic, even secularized, papacy.

To the west, in Spain, things were quite different. Queen Isabella, outraged that the Marranos (Jewish converts to Catholicism) were secretly practicing Judaism and committing heresy, directed the Spanish ambassador to the Vatican to insist that Pope Sixtus act to stop this desecration. Sixtus resisted, but pressure from King Ferdinand and Queen Isabella was too great, and in November 1478 he issued the infamous bull (papal edict) that authorized the Inquisition and ultimately led to the expulsion of all Jews from Spain in 1492. Although Italy was one of the few places allowing Jews to immigrate, only about nine thousand were able to do so. With no place to go, most died of hunger, were murdered by robbers, or died of exposure to the elements as they looked for refuge.

But in Italy, Jews continued to enjoy a life fairly free of torment as another pope, Paul III, emerged in the mid-1500s. Paul employed a Jew as his personal physician, admitted Jewish refugees from Naples into his territories, authorized the free emigration of Jews to Palestine, permitted the establishment of a Hebrew printing press in Rome, and discontinued the annual presentation of the Passion Play in the Coliseum, an event that depicted Christ's crucifixion at the hands of the Jews.

The pope's extraordinary decision to ban the Passion Play was a reaction to the violence perpetrated against the Jews following the performances. Professor Nerida Newbigin of the Italian Language and Literature Department at the University of Sydney found records in the Vatican Secret Archives that described the activities of a religious fraternity in Rome known as the Confraternity Gonfalone. In the years between 1490 and 1539, during the Holy Week of Easter, the Confraternity performed plays in the Coliseum, re-enacting the last week of Christ, including the betrayal by Judas, the crucifixion, and the resurrection. An estimated seventy thousand spectators filled the Coliseum. Newbigin writes:

> *The Gonfalone assembled on Good Friday and walked in a devout procession from the Santa Lucia church through the Jewish quarter to the Coliseum. [At the end of] the play, they carried an actor representing the dead Christ back from the Coliseum to their church, singing hymns and flagellating*

as they walked. In a dramatic text printed in 1501, we find that a series of choruses added to the basic text of the play are against the Jews and arouse hatred of the Jews. We have evidence that in other cities the Jews were advised to stay indoors during Lent, six weeks before Easter, when preachers whipped up the populace to a fever pitch. Although we can't find a document that states exactly the nature of what happened in 1539, we do know that the Gonfalone used such preachers. As the Confraternity passed through the Jewish quarter, a riot erupted. The violent incident prompted Pope Paul III to put an end to the play, despite the Confraternity trying several times to start them again. In subsequent years, their procession went to St. Peter's, there were no plays and they no longer passed through the ghetto.[49]

Five hundred years later, I find myself asking why Pope John Paul II in our own time didn't take the opportunity to speak out publicly against Mel Gibson's 2004 film, *The Passion of the Christ.*

"Did you see it? I didn't," I said to my shrink. "John Paul II is a modern pope, not one from the Middle Ages. But he actually endorsed it, saying, "It is as it was.""

The Passion is performed every ten years in the Bavarian town of Oberammergau, Germany, as it has been since 1634. It was the fulfillment of a vow the villagers made to Christ if he would answer their prayers and spare them from the bubonic plague of 1632. The plague finally ran its course after taking many lives, but believing their prayers had brought it to an end, they fulfilled their vow and mounted the first performance in 1634. Today, the play still attracts more than half a million people. It is five to six hours long and employs a huge cast of local townsfolk as actors, orchestra members, and choir. Hitler attended the three-hundredth anniversary performance in 1934 and endorsed the play for its antisemitic agenda.

"Wouldn't you think that after the Holocaust, they would close it down for good? The Second Vatican Council in 1965 added a seder with a *kiddush* (prayer over the wine) and *hamotzi* (prayer over the matzoh), which Jesus recites in Hebrew. They even have one of the Apostles, the youngest one undoubtedly, ask the four questions. Only the matzoh ball soup is missing.

"They dropped the part about the Jews shouting that the blood of Christ is on us and on our children, and Pilate no longer washes his hands of the whole business. But the Jewish high priest is still the major villain.

"Check it out for yourself; you'll be shocked," I said as I walked out of his office.

In the end, the new freedoms Jews enjoyed during the Renaissance were suddenly halted, and the heavy foot of the Church was again planted on the necks of the Jews, slowly strangling them. On July 12, 1555, Pope Paul IV issued his infamous bull, *Cum Nimis Absurdum*. I saw a copy of the original at the Jewish Museum in the synagogue located where the Jewish ghetto once stood, and I saw the machine used to create the official stamp on the various bulls in the Vatican.

> **Cum Nimis Absurdum.** *Forasmuch as it is highly absurd and improper that the Jews, condemned by God to eternal slavery because of their guilt, should, on the pretext that they are cherished by Christian love and permitted to dwell in our midst, show such ingratitude to Christians as to insult them for their mercy and presume to mastery instead of the subjection that beseems them. . . .*

Jews were given ten days to make yellow hats and veils and wear them when in public, and only two weeks to vacate their homes and squeeze into a low-lying area on the banks of the Tiber that is often flooded. Here, in crowded apartments, with disease rampant due to four, five, or six people sharing a room, the Jews of Rome were imprisoned for the next three hundred years. Today, it's easy to see that the ghetto buildings are much taller than those in surrounding areas, because with nowhere to spread out, Jews were forced to build high-er and higher. (In the 1930s, Germans ordered Jews to sew a yellow star on their clothing, as the pope had required on 1555. The color was chosen to signify urine.)

This period of isolation was interrupted only by a short period of respite when Napoleon was in power. Napoleon actually tore down the walls of all the ghettos across Europe and granted the Jews cit-izenship and freedom, which they lost again after he was defeated. It wasn't until 1870 that the Jews were finally given citizenship after Victor Emmanuel defeated the pope's army and entered Rome. The large white monument in Rome, Altare della Patria, commemorates the unification of the country and, in some way, the freedom of the Jews. (Puccini's opera, *Tosca,* takes place during this time of unifica-tion, and we hear Tosca's lover Cavaradossi crying "Victoria!" when he hears that Victor Emmanuel has won a decisive battle.)

Only seventy years after this moment of freedom, the Third Reich would begin to rise in Germany.

Chapter 17

IF WE WERE THE USURERS, WHERE ARE OUR PALACES?

As we traveled from Rome to Florence, we saw all around us the rich legacy generated by the wealth, industry, and creativity of the Renaissance. Elaborate palazzos, where I presumed the wealthy merchants lived (then and now), were filled with the magnificent friezes, frescoed ceilings, statues, and portraits they commissioned. The most famous painting in the world, the *Mona Lisa*, is a portrait of the wife of a wealthy Florentine silk merchant, Francesco del Giocondo, who hired Leonardo da Vinci to paint her.

She never got the painting though, because Leonardo messed around with it for years, trying to make it perfect, then died before he was satisfied with it. Can you imagine how furious she must have been?

You tell him I want it, and I want it now! I sat there in his freezing studio for months and months, with him all the time staring at my breasts. Now go get it, you wimp, I can picture Mona Lisa yelling at Francesco.

When I read about this, my immediate train of thought was: Jews–silk–ghetto. I might be the only person in the world who would make such a connection with the *Mona Lisa*. Am I so absorbed with how everything relates to the Jews, intellectually curious, or just a nut job? I don't have a shrink any more to tell me which, but I'm going to follow that train of thought here.

It turns out that a Venetian Jew by the name of Magino di Gabriele discovered and was given a patent on a process that doubled the yield of the silkworm, which naturally doubled profits of the merchants and farmers. At this time, Magino and his family were confined in the Venetian ghetto, as the doge had established the first ghetto in 1516, long before the pope issued his infamous bull, *Cum Nimis Absurdum*, which relegated the Jews of Rome and all the Papal States to ghettos for the next three hundred years. However, the pope was so pleased with Magino's discovery that he magnanimously granted him and his family the right to live outside the ghetto for fifteen years. And, I guess, to repay himself for being so gracious to a Jew, the pope took 50 percent of the Jew's profits for his sister.

So, where were we Jews living back then? Everybody knows that Jews are clever with money, that we've constructed international financial empires for centuries. We have lent to kings and queens; we have lent to business enterprises large and small, and at exorbitant rates. We were so sophisticated.

If all that is true, where are our palaces? I was in Italy and I wanted to see them. But, what do you know? Just like I couldn't find a Star of David in our "nondenominational" chapel back at prep school, I couldn't find our Jewish palaces anywhere in Italy.

We took a train to Florence and stayed in a lovely hotel on the Arno, within walking distance to most everything. We strolled over to the Palazzo Medici and joined a small group.

"This is one huge house. What did this guy do for a living?" I asked the enthusiastic guide leading us through the Medici Riccardi Palace, a particularly enormous and impressive palazzo. The guide hesitated a moment, then replied, "He was one of our great Italian bankers."

Oh, so he must have been Jewish . . . right? I never realized we became so wealthy. I wanted to say this, but didn't.

After all, Jews were the ones who lent money; we were the usurers, weren't we? Everyone knows that. So, what were these Italian Catholics doing in the banking business? For them it was a sin, and the Medici family certainly wasn't Jewish. Four members of the family had even been elected pope, with a generous sprinkling of bishops and cardinals in the family tree as well.

I knew there had been plenty of corruption in the Church, but who knew that it supported usury as well? Luther railed against the sale of indulgences in the Ninety-five Theses that he nailed to the door of All Saints Church in Wittenberg, Germany, in 1517, launching the Protestant Reformation. But he never mentioned usury. Maybe there were more Christians guilty of that sin, so he didn't want to touch it for fear of infuriating some of the wealthy Christians whose patronage his movement might need.

When the guide said, "Medici was one of our banking families," I wanted to know more about it, including how these Christian bankers managed to get around Church doctrine on the subject of lending money. After much digging, I found a book by Raymond de Roover, a medieval economic historian who had the answer.

Under canon law, usury is defined as requiring a borrower to repay any amount of money that exceeds the loaned principal. In other words, it was illegal to charge interest. However, it was legal for the lender to extract "damages" for infractions by the borrower, such as a failure to repay the principal at the maturity of the loan, and it was also legal to consider the loan as an investment and tack on a percentage of the profits of the venture being invested in. Sounds like a pretty friendly loophole to me.[50]

The way the Catholic bankers managed it was quite complicated and required both sophistication *and* great financial worth, which made it difficult for most people (including Jews) to get into that business. They figured out that by using the normal fluctuating differences in the exchange rates between different currencies (arbitrage) and understanding how currencies fluctuated between countries and city states as a result of weather and seasonal changes, violence, and other variables, they could take advantage of the borrower's lack of understanding to make substantial profits. Over time the bankers were able to detect these patterns and predict swings in the exchange rates with a high degree of accuracy. Original banking records from various archives, collected and examined by economists and historians, indicate that it was rare that bankers suffered losses in the process of exchanging currencies; they generally ended up with profits averaging 17 percent. Now that's exorbitant!

It worked like this: If an individual, company, or government, say in England, wanted to borrow a sum of money from the Medici Bank in Florence, the bank would have its agent in England arrange to make the loan in English pounds, but tied to the Florentine ducat. When the loan was repaid, if the pound was now worth less than the ducat, the borrower would need to increase the amount of sterling needed to pay off the loan and make the lender whole. Thus, what the borrower repaid the lender was equal to the amount borrowed, satisfying the requirements of canon law. The additional sterling above the original amount was the profit.[51]

(To use an actual transaction from the Medici account books: Five hundred Venetian ducats are lent to a borrower in England at an exchange rate of £47 per ducat, calling for the payment of £97,18s.4d sterling to the borrower. The loan was for six months and when it became due, a "bill broker" in London testified that the Venetian ducat had increased in value against the pound sterling, the pound having dropped to £44 as quoted in the Lombard Street exchange in England. That meant that the borrower now needed to pay the Venetian lender 535 ducats plus a service charge, giving a profit to the Medici family of 35 ducats or 14 percent for the six-month period. This transaction was termed a "Bill of Exchange," which was not considered a loan, but just an act of changing money. Stated in the language of the law, it read: "*Cambium non est mutuum*," an exchange transaction was not a loan, versus "*Usuracolum in mutuo cadit*," usury occurs only in a loan.)

Very cute. Why couldn't we have thought of that? Well, for one thing, we were constantly being thrown out of one country after another, so how could we ever acquire the power, wealth, or influence to set up an international network of anything?

But we didn't have to set it up to take the blame anyway for hording all the gold and knowing all about the fluctuation of currencies. In his 1906 children's book, *Puck of Pook's Hill*, Rudyard Kipling has a Jewish character express the same understanding of markets that Christian bankers like the Medicis in Renaissance Italy had three centuries earlier. These bankers were familiar with the markets and knew when money was "either tight or easy. . . . These alternative periods of stringency (*strettezza*) and abundance (*larghezza*) even followed a seasonal pattern, which was described in merchant manuals, and is still in print." [52]

Kipling's Jew says: "There can be no war without gold, and we Jews know how the Earth's gold moves with the seasons, and the crops, and the winds; circling and looping and rising and sinking away like a river—a wonderful underground river." [53]

The banking families sent their sons and relatives to set up branches in all the major financial and trading cities, developing the earliest international banking conglomerates. Profits on the exchange rates ranged from 7.7 to 28.8 percent a year, the upper range being 14 percent higher than Jews charged for interest on their loans. Jews were generally serving the poor, whose needs were modest and of little interest to the large merchant bankers.

"And *we're* supposed to be the international bankers? It was them all along, and for all these years we've taken the rap. This is why I get so angry," I confessed to my shrink. "This is exactly what the Jews have been accused of, spelled out in that antisemitic book *Protocols of the Elders of Zion*" (a tract widely distributed in Germany during the early 1900s and in America for free by Henry Ford).

"What a damned lie. How can someone whose citizenship has been denied to him for centuries, who has been banned from participating in any profession, and only allowed to trade in pennies, become an 'international banker'?"

The papal bank was actually the major source of funds, as large amounts of money flowed into it from all over Europe through its network of churches. The Church would designate the papal bankers who would follow the Roman Curia, the term used for the governing offices of the Universal Church—clearly a great prize for the chosen banking family. The heads of these large banking families found that encouraging family members to enter the priesthood, then with their influence move up in the clerical hierarchy, helped cement banking relationships with the Church. Four members of the Medici family became popes. The popes functioned like emperors ruling over the Catholic countries, but with the advantage of having moral power as well as political, military, and financial power. The cardinals, prelates, and clerics residing at the Roman Curia also deposited in the bank funds received from various sources and received interest on the funds that were loaned out.

In addition to managing the money for the Church, the bank did exactly what Jesus thought was so terrible when he entered Jerusalem and supposedly threw the money-changers out of the temple. But the function was just as important at the time of Jesus as it was for the Church later on. As the Church Curia and its bank traveled around, pilgrims hoping to see the pope and emissaries who had business with the Curia would come with letters of credit rather than carrying money in belts or saddle bags, and exchange the letters of credit for cash. (Siena was the main banking center in Europe for seventy-five years, beginning in the early 1200s, its largest company being the Gran Tavola—great table or bank—which failed in 1298. Florence then became the center, its most powerful companies including the Bardi, the Peruzzi, and the Aciainoli. They called themselves "the pillars of Christian trade." They all collapsed just prior to the advent of the Black Death in 1348, due to loans to sovereigns who defaulted.)

Money lending was not relegated to just one family in Italy, as I found out later when we went to Padua, a short drive from Venice.

The graduate student traveling with us went with me to the Arena Chapel, knowing that its walls and ceiling were covered by Giotto frescoes painted at the beginning of the 1300s. Rivaling the Sistine Chapel in magnificence, the chapel is called the Arena since it was built on the ruins of an old Roman arena where its owner, Reginaldo degli Scrovegni, built his palace.

What surprised me was the chapel's size. Typically, faithful Catholics of the time built small, private chapels for family prayer. But this is huge, about sixty feet long by twenty-five feet wide by thirty-six feet high—bigger than the stone church at prep school.

"They must have been incredibly pious to build such a large chapel, and it must have cost a pretty penny. Why do you think they did that?" I asked our guide.

"Yes, they were very pious," he quickly answered, brushing me off, as everyone else was more interested in discussing Giotto's work. Well, what I found from reading about medieval Catholic bankers was it wasn't built out of piety and faith; it was a deal Reginaldo's son made with the pope to obtain forgiveness for his father's crime of being a money-grubbing usurer.

Lending money by Christians was no secret, nor was it practiced by just a few Christian bankers. Dante wrote about this in his epic poem *The Divine Comedy,* where he journeys into the Inferno (Hell), guided by Virgil. Here he describes the corruption within the Church and the guilt of the Christian moneylenders. We read the poem in school, but somehow, I missed the part about the Christian usurers, who had been sentenced to one of the harsher rings of hell to suffer forever for their sins.

Giotto painted Scrovegni into his painting on the back wall of the chapel, showing him hanging over a fiery pit, weighted down by the moneybag tied around his neck. The Blue Sow, his coat of arms, is clearly highlighted for all to see. Scrovegni must have made just a little too much of a fortune in the usury business for the pope to overlook. This caused a big problem for his son Enrico, who needed to work out a deal with the pope to ensure his father's afterlife, and keep the family fortune for himself so he could have a nice life in the here and now. The deal they struck called for Enrico to build a glorious chapel dedicated to the Virgin Mary adjacent to the family's palazzo, its walls covered with frescoes portraying the life of Mary and Jesus.

Enrico hired Giotto to design the Arena Chapel and paint the frescoes. The Medici family did exactly the same thing and worked out a similar deal with the pope, keeping their ill-gotten profits in return for building the Monastery of San Marco in Florence. In hindsight, I'm struck by the complete lack of information from the guide about the fact that the chapel was built as penance for a usurious father who was charging astronomical interest on the loans he was making. Nor did our guide mention that Dante, a contemporary of Giotto (both of whom most likely attended the university just up the street), had portrayed Christian moneylenders as being consigned to the fires of hell. I wondered if he even knew.

"Forget the guide. Why didn't my English teacher bring this up when we read the *Divine Comedy* in school?" I wondered out loud to

Giotto frescoes, Arena Chapel, Padua (ca. 1305)

my shrink. "Did they knowingly withhold relevant facts that would have questioned the stereotype of the Jews as moneylenders, or were they just ill-informed? Our teacher had obviously studied *The Inferno*; it's hard to ignore the fact that Dante depicted no Jews in hell, but only Christian usurers and the corrupt popes who sanctioned their work."

I have a vague recollection that one teacher mentioned the corrupt popes, as that would have been relevant when we studied Martin Luther in history class later on. The Protestant Reformation launched by Luther was to occur two hundred years after Dante; one of his major complaints against the Church was its widespread financial corruption. Luther expected that Jews would flock to the purer version of Catholicism that he envisioned, but turned against them once he realized they still weren't interested in converting. He spelled it all out in one of his lesser known tracts, "The Jews and Their Lies."

Quite predictably, *The Divine Comedy* was awarded a top spot on the Church's *Index of Forbidden Books,* along with the Talmud, and was not removed until 1908. In Italy, the book was available, but the parts the Church found offensive were redacted.

A friend once told me that she and her aunt had taken a tour of the grand mansions in Newport, Rhode Island—marble edifices built as "summer cottages" by the Astors, Vanderbilts, and other New York industrial tycoons. The tour leader was a frail and elderly lady from the Newport Historical Society, who obviously took great pride in these old families. She started off on the first floor of one of these great houses, pointing out the art, the Greek columns, and the ballroom with its extensive gilded molding, then proceeded to the second floor. The old lady took the elevator while the tourists took the stairs. On the way up the staircase, our friend's aunt, in a booming voice so all the tourists couldn't help but hear, added how the Astors had pushed the contractor to get the house finished in time for the summer social season, pushed them so hard that they skimped on safety measures. As a result, several workmen fell off the scaffolding on the roof, killing or badly injuring themselves.

By the time the tour group reached the second floor, their former enthusiasm turned a bit more skeptical, and by the time they reached the third floor, they were angry enough to throw the guide right out the window.

I would love to go back to that chapel in Padua and do the same thing with our Italian tour guide, but I guess the tourists who had made the pilgrimage to this chapel to atone for their sins would not take my actions lightly, and in all likelihood, I would start a pogrom.

Giotto's magnificent frescoes couldn't help but draw you in. He captured the expressions on the faces with such emotion that I could feel exactly what the characters were thinking; their pain, their sorrow, and their joy were all on full display. He had created the Renaissance equivalent of a slideshow on the walls, so as you walked around, Jesus's whole life unfolded before you. This is the role that art played in those days, intended for the illiterate Catholic population to follow the illustrations and understand the meaning of the biblical stories.

One of the first panels in the series shows the Massacre of the Innocents, and I couldn't help but stare at it for a very long time. I saw the pained looks on the faces of the screaming mothers, clinging desperately to their children as Jewish soldiers sent by Herod pulled their babies from their arms, stabbed the babies to death, and threw them into a heap on the ground. The severed head of one baby peered out at me near the bottom of the canvas, while King Herod the Great looked on from a balcony above the scene of mayhem.

Even though I had read that this massacre never occurred, it was hard not to be moved by the vividness of the horrific act shown in the painting and to understand the rage of the faithful Christians who had stood in front of it for seven centuries. What they were getting was a good dose of Church propaganda, intended to gin up their hatred of Jews. First infanticide, then deicide. You couldn't get much worse than that.

Massacre of the Innocents, a common theme in Gothic and Renaissance art, depicted in the frescos in the Arena Chapel

On the other hand, what *I* saw, as I stood in front of the painting, were the Jewish babies being torn away from their mothers by German guards in concentration camps—the guards who threw the infants up in the air and caught them on their bayonets just for fun. And all of this took place in front of their parents, who were then stripped and marched off to the gas chambers. These events *really* took place, documented and even photographed or filmed in the twentieth century.

As I moved around the chapel, examining the frescoes in order, it was evident that Giotto wanted to discredit the priestly Jews too, clearly identifying them by their distinctive *peot* (braided sideburns) and their full beards.

192

In one of the panels, the leaders of the Jewish community and members of the Sanhedrin, are seen bribing Judas to betray Jesus. The dark figure of the devil stands behind Judas, holding him by the shoulders while two priests discuss what Judas will do for them. Christian observers would easily be able to distinguish the bad guys from the good guys by their alien beards, and just to make it clearer, the good guys all sported golden halos. Everyone viewing the fresco was undoubtedly familiar with this "Jewish look." The old feelings of discomfort came over me, intensifying as the crowd of tourists pressed around me.

In the next panel you can see the fatal kiss by Judas and the arrest of Jesus. Then comes the fresco showing Jesus standing before Caiaphas, chief priest of the Sanhedrin, who sits on his throne. He has just found Jesus guilty of blasphemy. Jesus with his halo, his hands bound by a rope, is being held by a guard who looks eager to hit him before he is delivered to the Romans. After viewing that fresco, every Christian pilgrim now knew for certain that the Jews were evil and the Jews were guilty.

At the center of the back wall is a scene of the crucifixion, and to the bottom right is a depiction of hell, where we see Reginaldo Scrovengi, the Christian usurer, hanging by the money pouch tied around his neck—exactly as he is portrayed in Dante's *Inferno*. Dante and Giotto were contemporaries, and both spent time in Padua. Giotto obviously took what Dante had written and painted it on canvas. The guide never even mentioned that the man who built this palace and chapel was the same man seen hanging from his money purse, together with other Christian moneylenders from Padua.

Giotto's fresco showing Jesus throwing the money changers out of the temple portrays the Jews with no halos and no eyeballs, but again, the good Christians have both halos and eyeballs because, presumably, they have the ability to "see."

"What a hypocrite this Giotto was," I said to my shrink the next time we met. "He just painted the Christians hanging from their

One of the people Giotto depicts hanging from ropes attached to money purses—halfway up to the right—is Scrovegni, shown with his family coat of arms, a blue sow.

money pouches over fires of hell, and yet he used his art to rehash the false perception that Jews were the only moneylenders. The big-time bankers were all Christians."

After that outburst, I imagined my shrink reaching over to make a note in my chart: *Experiences frequent paranoia . . . a hopeless case?*

In Roman times, Jews were never involved in lending money, and in medieval Europe, we did what the Christians were already doing, only on a smaller scale. The irony was that the Church held most of the currency. There was a Christian class of moneylenders known as Lombards, who emerged around the tenth and eleventh centuries, most likely in northern Italy. They had a reputation of being especially unscrupulous.⁴²I actually went to school with a Lombard, and now I know why Jim and I were such good friends—we were both usurers. I think I'll tell him at the next reunion. The only difference was that the Lombards were Christians, so his ancestors were given privileges the Jews never had. Maybe those privileges extended all the way to the twentieth century, so that Jim was allowed to attend Miss Hall's dancing school, while I wasn't.

As usurers, the Lombards were occasionally expelled from cities and countries the way the Jews were, but they were granted the courtesy of advance notice. In addition, they could enter into the same kinds of charters and contracts with the dukes, lords, and kings as could Jews, but they were considered free individuals; you could not rent a Lombard or sell one, as you could a Jew.

Their other advantage was that they could leave a given territory at any time and had more freedom of movement and choice of where to settle than did Jews. Most importantly, they had very little liability: contracts were always drawn up in their favor and they weren't subject to the office of the Inquisition.

"You know, this stigma of usury is just never questioned. Everybody accepts that it was a sin for Christians to loan money, so Jews filled the vacuum. Even Jews believe this," I continued from the couch. "There's a lot of evidence that refutes this, and original sources prove Christians charged more interest, often double what their Jewish counterparts charged. Christian writers have acknowledged that one negative consequence of expelling the Jews from a territory was that people had to turn to Christians to borrow money, and at rates much higher than they would have gotten from Jews."

In 1253, the Bishop of Lincoln stated that terms offered by Jews were often better for the debtor than those offered by Christians.⁵⁴ In 1306 a Norman (French) writer, referring to the expulsion of the Jews from France, complained that "after the expulsion of the Jews, they could not find any money, except by borrowing it through agents from certain Christians, both clerics and laymen, who lent at such

Jews (with yellow badges on their clothing) being expelled from France by
King Philip August, 1306 (miniature from a French chronicle, 1321)

an enormous rate of interest that it was more than double what was
charged by the Jews, and who did it in such a way that the debtors
did not know the lenders who were in possession of their pledges." [55]

In Perugia in 1462, a Franciscan friar by the name of Fra Michele
da Milano was intent on getting rid of the Jews, but there was real
pushback from Christian borrowers seeking the small loans that
Jewish moneylenders provided. The loans were critical for the farmers, for example, who needed money to purchase seeds and supplies.
The friar went from town to town giving sermons about the need
to replace Jewish loans with Church-administered loans without interest from the Funds of Piety. However, the new practice of not
charging interest to cover losses and the expense of running these
Funds of Piety quickly created a problem. It was magically solved
by a pope of the early 1500s, who declared that in these cases it was
legal to charge interest and would not be considered a sin. Before the
end of the century there were about thirty of these funds set up in

Pescara, Genoa, Mantua, Verona, Pisa, Florence, and other towns.

"The more you read about Jewish history, the sadder it becomes. The Church was relentless, and if the popes weren't after us, launching a crusade or inquisition, there was always some group like these friars thinking up yet another way to tighten the noose around our necks. No wonder the Jewish population never expanded much after the first century."

My shrink, also Jewish, must have been feeling some of that sadness too. He was silent for a long moment before saying, "I'll see you next week."

"But at least this usury noose is off our necks now," I said as I left.

Chapter 18

THE INQUISITION AND THE END OF SPANISH JEWRY

As Dora and I headed down the Italian peninsula to Pompeii, I started to explain to her that early Christians saw the destruction of the Second Temple by the Roman army in 70 CE as divine retribution against the Jews for failing to accept Jesus as the Messiah.

But a few years after the destruction, Mount Vesuvius blew up and many Romans, who were very superstitious, believed the destruction of Pompeii was their divine punishment for having destroyed Jerusalem and the temple. Maybe the Romans' belief was closer to the truth, because the volcano exploded almost to the day of the ninth anniversary of the sacking of the temple. It would be easier for God to explode a volcano than start a war, wouldn't you think?

Whenever anything bad happens to the Jews, Christians see it as divine retribution, but not so for anything that happens to one of their sacred sites.

"The Basilica of St. John Lateran in Rome, the first Christian church ever, was built by Constantine to symbolize the triumph of Christianity over paganism around 312 CE," I told Dora as we drove.

"Less than 150 years later, the Vandals destroyed the church and stole all of its treasures, so they tried restoring the church in 460. But again, it was destroyed by a huge earthquake in 896. Not one to give up, Pope Clement V tried to rebuild it in the early 1300s, but it completely burned down a few years later in 1360.

"Again, they rebuilt it. I can just imagine God thinking they would never learn. He had to destroy it six times to get the message across."

Church leaders and thinkers, both ancient and modern, have long expressed their belief in divine punishment in their writing and preaching:

> But the Jews who rejected him, and slew him, . . . after that were miserably spoiled by the Romans . . . and dispersed over the face of the whole earth. (Saint Augustine, The City of God, XVIII: 46)

> The apostles had scarcely set foot on the land of exile when Judea fell to Titus; her people, driven forth, were scattered all over the earth. (Gregory the Great, Moralia, IX: 6, 7, 9; Homilies, XXXIX)

> The Jews refused to acknowledge their king; they mocked him, condemned him to death, crucified him . . . and God [punished] them. He took away the land he had given them. . . . They are scattered over the surface of the earth, without a land of their own. . . . (Jean Bosc, "Le mystere d'Israel," Reforme, November 23, 1946) [56]

When we arrived in Pompeii, we could see it was not only a pretty vivid example of divine retribution, but also a perfectly preserved example of some of the classical art and architecture of ancient Rome that the Church wanted to bring forward into the Renaissance. The shift toward secularism and intellectual open-mindedness in Italy during that period brought about a rebirth of freedom for the Jews that seemed to mirror exactly what had taken place in Spain. Spanish Jews had enjoyed their own renaissance of a sort, though it had been achieved through conversion. Nevertheless, their conversion, though forced, carried with it many of the social advantages Christians had always enjoyed.

These "conversos" (whom Christians referred to as "marranos") used their newfound social access to make themselves wealthier in many cases than their Christian counterparts—not unlike what the Jews in Italy had accomplished. This was certainly not what the Church or the nobility had intended, so both communities eventually got the axe. The papal bull known as *Cum Nimis Absurdum*, which brought an end to the good years, posed the question: "How absurd is it that these Jews among us are doing so well?" Italian Jews were consigned to ghettos for the next three hundred years; in Spain, they faced torture, mass execution, and expulsion.

In Spain, the lives of Jews had changed dramatically after they converted. It was immediately off with the old rags, on with smart clothing; off with the beard and the identifying badge. It became possible to ride a horse and conduct business of any kind, to enroll in a university, even to become professors or legislators. With their new freedoms, Jews grew wealthy and consequently became prime catches for impoverished widows of the nobility who hoped to save their titles and estates through marriage.

The result was that "within a couple of generations, there was barely a single aristocratic family in Aragon . . . from the Royal house downwards, which was free from some Jewish admixture or alliance. Half the important offices at court were occupied by conversos, or their children, or else their close relatives." [57]

For example, Noah Chinillo, a convert who had changed his name to Santangel became secretary to the royal household and was thought to be responsible for the patronage Christopher Columbus received from Ferdinand and Isabella.[58] Converted Jews also began to dominate the intellectual life of Spain, becoming confident enough to mock one another in their poetry and writing, suggesting that they did not come from as grand a background as they pretended.

Wandering with Dora through the ruins at Pompeii and thinking about the fates of Italian and Spanish Jews, I remembered the unique way in which my childhood rabbi, Dr. Roland Gittlesohn, would conduct the *Erev* (evening before) Yom Kippur service known as *Kol Nidre*—the holiest night of the Jewish calendar. He made it so theatrical that it vividly came to life for the congregation.

"If we had lived in Spain any time from the 1400s to the 1800s," he told the congregation, "coming together for worship like this would have meant curtains for all of us." He slowly set the stage: "Imagine yourself back in Spain five hundred years ago. We are secret Jews attending services, and because we have publicly converted, it is against the law for us to gather here. Catholics see us as false Christians and call us *marranos*—pigs. In private, we call ourselves 'the forced ones,' because we were given the choice of conversion or death, the sword or the cross. We have quietly assembled here in secret in the basement of our neighbor's house and darkened the windows before we begin our *Kol Nidre* service."

As the rabbi spoke, the sanctuary lights dimmed and our cantor began to softly chant the mournful words of the *Kol Nidre* (All Vows) prayer. When he was finished, Mrs. Webber, who happened to be our neighbor, would replay the melody on her viola from out of sight in the balcony. It was quite an emotional show.

After the music, the Rabbi continued: "The office of the Inquisition has issued 'Edicts of Faith,' and has posted them in all the cities of Spain. They spell out how faithful Christians must report anyone observed performing any of a long list of Sabbath rituals—lighting candles on a Friday night, placing a new tablecloth on the table, making a blessing over wine, a father placing his hands on his son's head without making the sign of the cross, and many more.

"It is the duty of Christians who spot such activity—exactly the things we are doing right here in our temple—to report it to the authorities." I remember that a shiver went through me as he spoke, imagining how terrified our Spanish ancestors must have felt at the thought of being turned over to the Inquisition police.

Once in the hands of the Inquisition, we would be tortured until the truth of our pretended conversion was discovered. We would be suspended by a rope tied to our wrists, arms behind us, raised by pullies up to the ceiling and then dropped. Because the rope stopped us just inches before our feet touched the ground, the abrupt shock would dislocate our bones.

If no confession came, this would be followed by a simulated drowning (similar to what is now called "waterboarding"), followed by the roasting of our feet after they were coated with fat. When a confession would finally be wrung out of us, we would be found guilty of slipping back to Judaism—the capital crime of heresy. Our sentence would be burning alive at the stake along with other "guilty" conversos—often on a date coinciding with a Christian holy day or a celebration of the king's birthday. On the way to the stake we would be accompanied by a religious friar who graciously offered that if we truly converted now, we would be spared the agony of death by fire, but in Christian love and mercy, would be strangled to death instead. Those who chose to convert were marked with an image of flames pointing down sewn to their clothing, as opposed to an image of flames pointing up for those of us not willing to renounce our faith.

As I remembered the *Kol Nidre* services of my youth, it flashed through my mind that the pastrami sandwiches my father occasionally brought me at school would have been more than enough to consign me to the Inquisitor's dungeon.

I was born in 1939, as were my fellow classmates. But this particular piece of European history seemed to be mine and not theirs. At home, as a child, I remember hearing constant talk of Hitler's activities, about the restrictive laws being imposed on Jews in the countries he had conquered, and the reinstatement of ghettos in Warsaw and other cities. I remember my parents' whispered rumors of labor camps and even death camps, where Jews were being systematically murdered. My classmates and I were seven years old at the end of the war when many of the German atrocities were revealed during the Nuremburg trials. Why didn't my friends know these things as well? It was right there in front of them, on the radio and in the newspapers.

Like the Germans of the twentieth century, Spanish Catholics of the fifteenth century became furious at how prosperous and powerful converted Jews had become. This resentment quickly came to the attention of Church authorities, who saw Jewish success as a blasphemy against the Catholic faith. From the pulpits, priests sermonized about how these false Christians were undeserving of the blessings of Christianity, especially because they were still secretly practicing Judaism.

Once the Catholics had taken Spain from the Moors, there was growing demand to rid the country of Jews as well. In the summer of 1391, the Archbishop of Seville's message of hate finally erupted into the gruesome massacre of 50,000 Jews in the kingdom of Castile. Historians report that Toledo was set on fire and the corpses of Jews were piled up in the streets of Segovia.[59] The king ordered that no one participating in the murder of Jews and the looting of their property could be harassed, punished, or fined.

The massacres spread to Aragon and to Barcelona, where the Jewish community was completely destroyed, and in the year 1400 it was ordered that no Jew could ever return there. The Church did nothing to bring a stop to the massacres, seeing them as "an act of God to bring the stubborn Hebrews into the fold of Christ," and in fact encouraged preaching that reminded the population that "kindness to the Jew was a sin against God."[60]

The fear of being slaughtered convinced many Jews to accept baptism. M. Llorente, citing original documents of the period, reported that one hundred thousand families converted, representing nearly half a million individual Jews.[61] Fray Vincent Ferrer, a Jew-hater who was later made a saint, traveled from town to town revving up Christian mobs. He would arrive at synagogues with a Torah scroll in one hand and a cross in the other, accompanied by angry followers, who threatened conversion or death. All this was happening in a country that was home to more Jews than all the others in Europe combined.

According to Llorente, the spark that ignited the Inquisition happened by chance. On the evening of March 18, 1478, a young Christian who had fallen in love with a converso went to visit her at her home on what happened to be the first night of Passover. To his amazement, he saw that, although it was also Easter week, the family was engaged in a celebration that did not appear to be at all Christian. The young Christian told a Dominican friar from San Pablo, who in turn informed Queen Isabella. Having no love for Jews herself, she contacted the Spanish ambassador to the Vatican to demand that Pope Sixtus do something about this heresy.

In November, the pope issued a bull that authorized the establishment of a court, which would be overseen by bishops learned in theology and common law and would have a free hand in dealing with heresy in the kingdom of Castile. And so was launched the Spanish Inquisition.

Two years later, on September 17, 1480, formal guidelines for dealing with conversos who had secretly returned to Judaism were written and installed. The Dominican friars were assigned the power to carry out the inquiries and execute the heretics. The two bishops chosen to head up the inquiries were Miguel de Morillo, Master of Theology, and Juan de San Martin, Bachelor of Theology. On Christmas Day (Merry Christmas!) they arrived in Seville, and the following Sunday held a solemn procession to announce their purpose.[62]

Llorente states that no sooner were the inquisitors installed than many conversos left their homes to travel to the lands of the dukes of Medina and Sidonia and other nobles—territories where they felt that they would be safe. However, the grand inquisitor, the infamous Thomas de Torquemanda, not wanting them to escape, issued a proclamation on January 2, 1481, declaring that these noblemen were to arrest the fleeing Jews, confiscate their goods, and send them back to Seville. If the noblemen refused, they would be excommunicated, their own lands confiscated, and their offices lost. Threatened in this way, they readily complied with the order.

Within six months, in Seville alone, 298 conversos were burned at the stake and twenty-nine others imprisoned for life. Across the whole province, more than two thousand people were burned and another eighteen thousand suffered various canonical punishments. Not surprisingly, many of the condemned were people of wealth, whose estates were confiscated by the treasury. Many of those who died in Seville were locked inside one of four hollow statues placed on top of a stone pyre called the quemadero, with the intention that they would die more slowly. That structure stood outside the city until 1820.[63]

The procedures for dealing with heretics were very elaborate, and handbooks were issued covering all aspects of the so-called "inquiries." Soon after a tribunal was established in a particular location, an Edict of Grace would be posted, inviting persons who had committed heretical acts to voluntarily come forward and confess their sins, with the promise that they would be treated mercifully. Once they confessed, their inquisitors would demand, under threat of torture or death, that they denounce anyone they knew who was guilty of observing Jewish traditions. Following a thirty-day "term of grace," the Holy Office would begin arresting the second wave of people whose names they had obtained under duress. Finally, they issued Edicts of Faith asking Christian neighbors to come forward, "under pain of excommunication," to denounce others suspected of being heretics. This series of edicts allowed the Holy Office to compile a long list of persons subject to arrest.

Another edict issued in Valencia in 1519 enumerated the activities that would prove someone was a secret Jew. These included: observing Friday evenings and Saturdays; changing into clean personal linen on Saturdays and wearing better clothes than on other days; preparing on Fridays the food for Saturdays; not working on Friday evenings and Saturdays as on other days; kindling lights in clean lamps with new wicks on Friday evenings; placing clean linen on the beds and clean napkins on the table; celebrating the festival of unleavened bread, eating unleavened bread and celery and bitter herbs; observing the fast day when they do not eat all day until after the evening star; observing the fast of Queen Esther; swaying back and forth; slaughtering poultry according to Judaic law; becoming circumcised; lighting candles when someone has died, etc.

The edict went on to demand that:

> *If you . . . see any of this behavior and do not tell the authorities, the Holy Office will go after you as "abettors of heretics, in various ways; but, wishing to act with benevolence, and in order that your souls may not be lost, since our Lord does not wish the death of the sinner but his reformation and life" . . . you will be excommunicated, publicly denounced, cursed, segregated, and separated as an associate of the devil, from the union with and inclusion in the Holy Mother Church, and the sacraments of the same.*[64]

The brutality of the Inquisition lasted for 330 years until 1809, when Napoleon abolished it following the defeat of the pope's army and the resulting loss of papal military power.

As I have pointed out, unfortunately, all these interludes of freedom didn't last long, for as soon as Napoleon was defeated in 1815 at the battle of Waterloo, it took the Church almost no time to rescind our freedoms again. But during the brief time when Napoleon was in power, he demanded that the Church archives be searched and the history of the Inquisition's ecclesiastical tribunal be written down and made public. He chose Dom J. Antonio Llorente, an eyewitness and insider, to write the cruel history, having first been installed as commissioner of the Inquisition of Logrogno and later appointed secretary-general of the Inquisition, offices which gave him access and possession of the archives. Llorente gave us the most graphic, detailed, and horrific description of the "the cord, the water, and the fire," as the forms of torture during the Inquisition were known. His descriptions were long, but clearly convey what victims endured.

> *[The prisoner was led to] a subterranean vault. . . . The profound silence which reigned in this chamber . . . and the*

terrible appearance of the instruments of punishment . . . seen by the vacillating light of two flambeaux, must have filled . . . the victim with a mortal terror. The inquisitors and executioners, clothed with long robes of sackcloth, and their heads covered with hoods of the same, pierced with holes for eyes, mouth and nose, seized and stripped [the prisoner] to his shirt.

In the first case, they tied his hands behind the back . . . by means of a cord passed through a pulley attached to the roof, and raised him up as high as possible. After having left him sometime thus suspended, they loosened the cord so the prisoner fell suddenly within a half a foot of the ground. This terrible jar dislocated all the joints; and the cord cut the wrists and entered into the flesh, even to the very sinews. It was not until after a physician declared that the sufferer could no longer support the torture without dying, that the inquisitors remanded him to prison. There they left him . . . till the moment they prepared for him a torture still more horrible.

The second trial was made by means of water. The executioners stretched their victims in a wooden instrument in such a position that the feet were higher than the head. Respiration became very painful, and the patient suffered the most dreadful agonies in all his limbs, in consequence of the pressure of the cords, the knots of which penetrated into the flesh. . . . In this cruel position the executioners introduced at the bottom of the throat . . . a piece of wet linen, part of which covered the nostrils. They afterwards turned the water into the mouth and nose, and left it to filter so slowly that one hour was exhausted before the sufferer had swallowed a drop, although it trickled without interruption. Thus, the patient found no interval for respiration. . . . When the torture was finished, they drew the linen from the throat, all

> *stained with blood of the vessels which had ruptured by the*
> *struggles of the unfortunate one. It ought to be added that*
> *every instant a fatal lever was turned [which caused] the*
> *cords which surrounded the arms and the legs to penetrate*
> *even to the bones.*
>
> *The inquisitors afterwards had recourse to fire. To make*
> *this trial, the executioners commenced by tying the hands*
> *and feet position this trial, and then rubbing the feet with oil*
> *and lard, and placed them before the fire until the flesh was*
> *so roasted that the bones and sinews appeared in all part.*[65]

The burning alive of those who confessed became grand public celebrations. There were a number of these spectacles each year and they took place all over Spain, but the grand *auto-da-fé* ("act of faith" as penance for heresy) was reserved as entertainment prior to a royal coronation, marriage, or birth of an infant.

Five hundred years later, on March 13, 2000, Pope John Paul II apologized, asking forgiveness for sins committed against Jews, heretics, women, the Roma people, and native peoples by the Church. "Never again," the Pope said. "We forgive and we ask forgiveness. We are asking pardon for the divisions among Christians, for the use of violence that some have committed in the service of truth, and for attitudes of mistrust and hostility assumed towards followers of other religions. We are deeply saddened by the behavior of those who in the course of history have caused these children of yours to suffer, and asking your forgiveness we wish to commit ourselves to genuine brotherhood."

After Catholics finally conquered the last remaining part of Spain, defeating the Moors, they had total control of the peninsula. The increasing frenzy to rid the entire country of the Jews was led by Torquemada, the first grand inquisitor of Spain, who had for years wanted to expel them all. The king, however, had resisted, recognizing the economic consequences of doing so, but was now made to see the value of confiscating Jewish wealth and possessions and adding it to his treasury. On March 31, 1492, an edict was issued that all Jews in Spain must leave within four months or be executed. Jews had lived in Spain for fifteen hundred years, and now had to sell everything and leave in a matter of months. The confessions they had wrung out of the Jews during the Inquisition could now be used as evidence that there were lots of other "secret Jews" infecting those Jews who had converted voluntarily. They received almost nothing for their possessions as the population understood that they had no choice and little time to liquidate. In return for a large house they would be lucky to get a donkey in payment.

On the second of August, 1492, some historians claim that as many as eight hundred thousand Jews left Spain. (Often population estimates refer to families, so the total could have been four or five times greater.) There were few places where they could go. England and France had already expelled their Jews, and Germany and Italy felt they already had too many. The Jews of Italy were barely able to support themselves and feared that more people would add to their problems. Some went to Italy anyway, and some to north Africa, where many were murdered or eaten by animals, or prevented from entering the cities and towns, leaving them to live in open fields where they starved to death or died of exposure to the elements. Others paid ships' captains to take them abroad, but once out to sea, many were thrown overboard or delivered into the hands of pirates. Rumors spread that the Jews had swallowed diamonds and other jewels, leading bandits to capture them and slit them open to search for their valuables. Others were sold into slavery, and many Jewish children were baptized and sent off as settlers to the newly discovered island of St. Thomas.[66]

The time of the expulsion is confirmed by the very first sentence in Christopher Columbus's diary, which reads: "In the same month in which their majesties [Ferdinand and Isabella] issued the edict that all Jews should be driven out of the kingdom and its territories, in the same month they gave me the order to undertake with sufficient men my expedition of discovery to the Indies." With no place to settle, many of the Spanish Jews wandered from place to place:

> *Friars wander[ed] among the famished groups, . . . a crucifix in one arm and loaves of bread in the other, offering food in return for conversion. You would have thought that they [the Jews] wore masks. They were bony, pallid, their eyes sunken in the sockets; and had they not made slight movements it would have been imagined that they were dead. They were given the choice of embracing Christianity or being sold into slavery.* [67]

Another account, written by an Italian Jew in 1495, provides a vivid description of the reality of the expulsion:

> *One hundred and twenty thousand of them went to Portugal, according to a compact which a prominent man . . . had made with the King of Portugal, and they paid one ducat for every soul, and the fourth part of all the merchandise they had carried thither; and he allowed them to stay in this country six months. This King acted much worse for them than the King of Spain, and after the six months had elapsed, he made slaves of all those that remained in his country, and banished seven hundred children to a remote island to settle it, and all of them died.* [68]

"Did no one weep for us?" I asked my shrink after I learned of these events.

Chapter 19

SHRINK #1 GIVES ME THE BOOT

There has been an extra bonus from writing this memoir: it has forced me to think about issues I never fully understood and, consequently pretty much ignored throughout my life. One occurrence that anyone might think would be serious enough not to ignore was my first therapist firing me. He made it clear that he'd had enough of me, that I wasn't going any further in analysis, and he had come to the point where he thought we were both wasting our time.

I started going to this doctor a few years after I was married, when I was thirty-seven or thirty-eight years old. I had never thought about seeing a psychiatrist until I met Dora, but I probably should've known something like that was about to enter my life as she had a doctorate in psychology, specializing in childhood development. All her friends from graduate school were into psychology and quite a number of those became our lifelong friends. Some were psychologists and some were psychiatrists, and they gravitated together, kind of like the way stockbrokers like hanging around with other stockbrokers to exchange tips.

All Dora's friends and colleagues believed everyone should be in some form of therapy, because we all had issues and if we didn't know it, it was because we had obviously repressed them. They all seemed to have become trained salespeople, pushing something you never knew you needed—kind of like a Veg-O-Matic infomercial.

Finally, with all that pressure, I was convinced to go. I knew I had issues. I knew I was conflict-averse. I knew my mother's toxic personality had clearly influenced me, although I did open up and tell her what I thought of her the night my father died. I knew being the only Jew at school had been a heavy emotional burden, but I never thought that talking about it was an option.

Once I decided, the next step was finding a therapist who would be the right fit. There was a shrink matchmaker who would meet with you and make a referral, or you could just go through the grapevine. Eventually, I picked Doctor G.

He looked like he came from central casting. He had kind, friendly features, dressed neatly in an old tweed jacket, and cupped a pipe in his hand to convey a sense of calm authority. His office was attached to his house (which I later learned was a standard arrangement, and something I immediately pegged as a tax deduction). The first thing I saw was a small waiting room with a chair or two and a white noise machine so patients couldn't hear what was being said in the office. On my first visit, I nervously sat down and tried to settle in. Soon, he opened his door and welcomed me.

His office came from central staging. There were bookshelves on one wall, framed certificates and university affiliations hanging in clear view on another, so you would know he was legit, and Kleenex boxes on every surface. He had the regulation shrink sofa for those in analysis, and a chair for patients in regular therapy. His was a comfortable leather chair, well-worn from sitting all day long listening to people *kvetch* (Yiddish for complain).

And this is a business? I thought to myself.

We started off in regular therapy, sitting facing each other. I went over the issues I thought I had, mother and school, blah blah blah, with Dr. G. asking probing questions like, "What was it about your mother's behavior that bothered you most? What was happening at school? Were you feeling insecure, did you feel depressed, did you feel anxious? Tell me about that." And off I would go. I will admit that once I started talking about things, I did feel better, and as I talked, more issues bubbled to the surface. At some point, perhaps a month or so later, he strongly suggested that I switch to analysis, which entailed coming three or four days per week. The idea of the analysis is that the shrink is supposed to become, in the patient's mind, the individual or environment that caused the trouble in your childhood—something called transference. The difficult part of analysis, for me anyway, is that I went so often that eventually I ran out of things to talk about, which is how ranting about Jewish history and unraveling the Christian myths and misperceptions about Jews became a topic for me to focus on. It took up analysis time, but it also brought back some of those early memories that bothered me more than I had realized.

This analysis went on for several years, more than I think I needed, but I had the best time slot, 8 to 8:50 in the morning, which I didn't want to give up, just in case. I spent a lot of that time complaining to him about being rebuffed (marginalized? side-lined? made invisible?) by the Yankee world I had grown up in, in terms of being excluded from their clubs, prevented from socializing with them, yet still going back and back again like an addict needing a fix.

So, when I said to him one morning that I needed to take the next week off from therapy to race in the Edgartown Regatta, he angrily came back at me: "Re-*gat*-ta, re-*gat*-ta. Listen, Arthur, I think we've gone as far as we can go in your analysis. I think it's time to say goodbye!"

I didn't get what he was saying at the time; I thought that he was being hostile and inappropriate, but I understand now. I had complained to him for years about being thrown into a community where I didn't belong, and here I was at the same time craving more and more of it.

I liked the Yankee lifestyle, and what's not to like? They have fabulous summer places on the water, spots they claimed as soon as they arrived in the 1600s or 1700s. Purely by accident, Dora and I happened to find one of those old Yankee houses on land a family had owned for two hundred years. The family had been into shipbuilding,

Me practicing for the fateful Edgartown Regatta in the Alden 44

whaling, and textiles and owned hundreds of acres, which they sold off lot by lot as they needed money. (The family money slowly dried up as each subsequent generation saw more and more descendants trying to live on it.) We were the first people outside the family to move in, so we now could accurately boast, "We've been here since the 1700s . . . along with the New Bedford Hathaway family."

Not only did I now own a house in one of those small seaside towns with a name that's not on the map, but I got the lineage to go with it.

214

We bought the house the day we saw it. It's right on the water and has four large chimneys painted white with a black ring at the top, supposedly to alert British ships that this is a Tory house, so don't blow us up. They called it a cottage, even though it has nine bedrooms (six of which were designed for servants). It came with all the proper amenities, including a large lawn that gradually sloped toward the water, large enough for a tennis court, pool, and a game of touch football. I added all the requisite equipment: kayaks, a small sailboat we could carry into the ocean, a swim raft, a vegetable garden—everything I could think of. It was nicely situated as well; it had a long private road with a double fence at the entrance (only half of it closed to indicate it was a private drive), old fieldstone walls bordering the driveway, the smell of dry grass outside . . . and that faint, authentic whiff of mildew inside.

The yacht club sailboat race starting line was right off our beach, so if we weren't racing ourselves, we could watch from the deck we built at the water's edge, sitting on Adirondack chairs and sipping summer cocktails.

Our renovations focused on the basic things: new heating system, updated electrical and plumbing, while keeping the old marble sinks with their separate hot and cold faucets (which I finally realized were totally impractical after guests complained they were getting scalded). I reluctantly installed modern faucets, but with a vintage look. It took me longer to cave in and replace the old claw-foot bathtubs with modern shower stalls.

We filled the house with my parents' furniture, which we had in storage—lots of antiques that fit in perfectly, old rugs and all my mother's old dishes. We went on a buying spree in Maine and picked up a whole roomful of vintage wicker chairs and tables for the porch. I screwed a Chelsea clock and a barometer onto a panel on the side of the fireplace in the living room, and a wind speed/direction indicator on another panel in the hall, where I could look out to see the condition of the waves in the bay. I found out about an auction in

Newport solely devoted to ship models and sea-themed paintings. The day turned out to be rainy and miserable, keeping most people away and resulting in sparse bidding competition. We walked away with seven old model ships and two or three beautiful paintings. And that completed the look.

I'd had the advantage of seeing some of my old classmates' houses when someone would volunteer his home for a class party. It was obvious that these houses had been passed down from one generation to the next and were furnished with the same pieces they had brought from England, last reupholstered half a century ago. I liked that well-worn, old-patina look, even the chipped paint here and there. It's a look of studied non-ostentation.

We use the house just like the previous owners probably did. It's large enough for our family, cousins, and friends to come down, even a lot of them at once—ten for breakfast, twenty for dinner. I love that. I think I've adopted the best part of my classmates' lives without taking a nickname like Bunny or Boopsie or naming the house something corny like "The Look Out," and certainly without the jokes about falling off the deck while drinking. Some of my old school friends live (or summer) in this harbor community, which I never even knew existed until I got here.

When our renovations were complete, and I was alone one day, I looked around and said to myself, *Oh my God, what have I done?*

I had turned myself into some kind of nouveau Yankee wanna-be

But what the hell, I thought, sitting in the living room looking out at the waves splashing on the rocks, *I haven't converted. So, what's the big deal?*

The big deal, which I still find hard to admit, is that I was jealous of my WASP friends. Yes, I was able to buy the big shingled house right on the water, but what I couldn't buy was the mental freedom they had. They could skip through life, completely comfortable in their skin, secure in their status, without the kinds of worries I carried. The worry that someone would look at me differently because they could tell I am Jewish. The worry that someone would tell an inappropriate joke or make an offhand comment because they couldn't tell I was Jewish. The worry about being at a restaurant with other Jews who might be too loud (even though people at the next table, drunk and screaming with laughter, were significantly louder).

Being loud, I was surprised to find, is a stereotype that goes back all the way to the sixth century and the reign of Pope Gregory, who unilaterally declared himself to be pope and decided, while he was at it, that all power resides in the pope, who is the only one who talks directly with God.

The restrictive laws that had been enacted by Justinian and Constantine against Jews did preserve a few of their civil rights. But there was a bishop in Terracina, a small town just north of Naples, who threatened to punish the Jews if they didn't convert. When they refused to comply, the bishop complained directly to the pope that the chanting of the Jews in their synagogue was so loud that it was disturbing the congregation in his church. Pope Gregory sent a couple of bishops to investigate and they confirmed their colleague's claim.

Gregory immediately ordered the synagogue closed and required the Jews to open a synagogue well away from the church. This move still didn't satisfy the bishop's underlying animosity, and he once again complained to Gregory that the praying of the Jews was too loud. Gregory replied with the following order to his overzealous bishop: "We forbid the aforesaid Hebrews to be oppressed and vexed unreasonably." [69] (But "reasonable" oppression and vexation was probably still okay.)

I offer this story as a humorous example, but it does demonstrate how the stranglehold on Jewish life, enforced by the Church, ranged from the tiniest infraction of praying too loudly to being slaughtered or forced to convert (the cross or the sword) through successive centuries. Although Jews are now living in one of the longest periods of relative peace and freedom (1945 to the present), if we are honest, we all carry the weight of the possibility that things could change at any time.

My son Ben was born three years after we purchased the house, and I loved running around with him, pushing him on the old wooden swing the previous owner had hung from the chestnut tree next to the garden shed. He and I built and shot rockets off on the lawn, running to pick them up as they parachuted down. We tied two kites together, letting them fly way up, pushed by the predictable southwest afternoon winds. I loved swimming with him out to the raft we had anchored off the beach, holding sandwiches packed in sealed plastic bags up out of the water. I joked with him that it was a Bar Mitzvah rehearsal party. We would drive down to the yacht club and take the launch out to our sailboat, which we had childproofed with netting all around so he wouldn't fall off. His little life vest was hooked to my belt with a dog leash as we sailed over to the Vineyard or Nantucket for a few nights. Ben picked it all up quickly and I would sit beside him as he maneuvered the dinghy from the boat to the shore, taking it all in, both of us enjoying our time together. His sleeping bunk doubled as a seat for the navigation area. He would stand up and start playing with the instruments, and soon figured out how the ship-to-shore radio worked and how to work the radar and the Loran (the navigation tool prior to GPS). It was all so much fun.

I'm digressing a bit, thinking about those days. Getting fired from shrink #1 was so sudden and unexpected and humiliating that I thought I should find a replacement. A Dr. M. was recommended. He was a good choice, a little less Germanic, and he immediately made me feel comfortable as I brought him up to speed. But it wasn't long after we started that everything changed.

Chapter 20

MY LIFE TAKES AN UNEXPECTED TURN

On the July Fourth weekend of 1991, I went out for my usual morning bicycle ride—just far enough to keep myself healthy, I used to say. It was a racing bike, complete with skinny tires and turned-down handlebars. I had purchased all the cool gear—spandex pants, neon racing shirt, and aero-dynamic helmet. As I cruised down a rather steep hill on my familiar route, gaining speed to make the next hill easier, my front wheel got jammed in a pavement crack at the side of the road. The bicycle stopped abruptly and I flew over the handlebars, landing on my chin. The impact pushed my head back, stretching and injuring my spinal cord between the sixth and seventh cervical vertebra, in what is called a hyperextension.

Although I could see that the bike had fallen on top of my legs, I realized I could not feel the bike, could not move my legs, and could not get up. A neighbor across the street, who happened to be a doctor, saw all of this and came running. Being a physician, he knew not to move me, and he immediately called an ambulance. I was conscious long enough to ask the police officer who had arrived on the scene to call my wife, and then I blacked out.

I have no memory of being moved, but I was flown to the Massachusetts General Hospital, where I woke up some time later alone in a strange hospital room. I found I could move my arms and had feeling in both hands, but my fingers didn't seem to work at all. I tried to poke around under the covers, touching my legs and chest, and realized I had no sensation below my rib cage. I knew I was in

219

serious trouble. Soon, my wife and a nurse came in and gave me the diagnosis. I remember that the nurse used the term "catastrophic injury," then added, "you'll probably never walk again." I was fifty-one years old and right then, I knew that nothing would ever be the same.

When the doctor arrived, he told me they needed to immobilize my head and upper spinal cord with a halo device. This is a medieval-looking contraption consisting of two round metal rings, the top one literally screwed into my skull, the bottom one resting on my shoulders. Between these two metal rings were five vertical bars. Oddly, the whole thing reminded me of a light fixture we had hanging in our hall, but instead of light bulbs hanging from the top, there was my head. It almost looked like I was in the stocks—those colonial-era devices used to punish people for adultery or some other moral infraction.

My wife began a search for a good spinal cord rehabilitation facility, and through some friends found what was widely considered to be the best, Craig Hospital in Denver, Colorado. A woman flew in from Craig to meet with me and assess my condition, then suggested that they arrange for a medi-flight to Colorado. The same woman and a nurse accompanied me on the plane, together with my cousin Fred Sherman and nephew Josh. I remember them taking turns feeding me grapes all the way until we landed.

I could see it was pitch dark as they carried me out of the plane and into an ambulance. Since my room was not ready when we arrived, I was wheeled on a gurney into a large room with a group of other recent arrivals, a lot of them young kids who were crying, some even screaming. It was like being in bedlam, or a battlefield hospital, unable to move, unable to sleep, alone without my wife and in the dark. It was a harsh introduction to quadriplegia. That's the technical term for paralysis involving all four limbs. To this day, I hate that description of myself; it sounds so much more severe than I feel.

Sometime the next morning they assigned me to a double room, with a roommate already installed, which I also hated. "I want a private room!" I guess was feeling pretty sorry for myself and thinking it was acceptable to be demanding.

My wife finally arrived, and she and Fred went to speak with the administrator to figure out the next steps. I was furious and frustrated that I wasn't expected to be in the room with them. I was the one who was paralyzed. I wasn't dead yet, I was fully cognizant and able to make my own decisions, and I was desperate to understand exactly what was in store for me. But I couldn't get out of the bed and walk down there myself.

I must've made such a fuss that they finally agreed to roll my bed, with me in it, halo and all, pushing and squeezing into the administrator's small office. I asked her for a single room, but she thought it would be more helpful and less lonely if I had another person to talk with. At my age, I didn't need a new friend; I wanted my own room. They didn't have many private rooms, but somehow, a day or so later, I got one.

That was better, and I was somewhat comforted by the fact that I had my family around me. I noticed that many of the other patients, mostly teenagers or young guys in their early twenties, seemed to be alone. I must've seemed so spoiled (I cringe to think about it now), even refusing to eat in the main dining room, but prevailing on Fred to go out to the nearest delicatessen and bring me chicken soup with matzoh balls, a brisket dinner with potatoes and carrots, and all the comfort foods I craved. Sleeping was the worst part, as the halo was incredibly awkward and uncomfortable and prevented me from resting my head on the pillow.

The three months at Craig were spent exercising, stretching, and learning how to balance my upper body while sitting up. Eventually, I was able to sit in a manual wheelchair and slowly propel myself along during walks with other patients, who all seemed to be much stronger than I was. They zipped around, up and down hills, while I struggled to hold up the rear with my physical therapist trotting along beside me holding a spray bottle filled with water, squirting me to keep me cool and lower my anxiety. It got me wondering how I would have fared in the army, and I was grateful I had never been drafted.

The staff at Craig introduced us to being semi-independent, taking a group of us to a local shopping center as an exercise to show us we could function and navigate in the world again. The assignment was to team up with somebody who was ambulatory. My nephew Joshua volunteered, and they sat him in a wheelchair and drove us all to the shopping center. Seeing him in a wheelchair was a strange and disturbing sight that made me realize how terrible it would have been had he or my own son Ben suffered the same injury.

The instructions for this "getting back to life" activity required that we go around together, but that Joshua should hold back from helping me so I would do as much as possible by myself. We went to a restaurant for lunch, where I used a special strap that wound around my hand and fastened with Velcro, with a fork or spoon bent at an angle and inserted into a little sleeve in the strap. During this first restaurant meal, I realized when we finished eating that I now needed to ask the server to wash my silverware, explaining that this was my own fork and spoon and not one of theirs I had destroyed. Then, another whole discussion was required to ask her to put it in the top compartment of my knapsack, which was hanging off the back of my wheelchair. In that moment, I understood how much more there was going to be to this paralysis business than I first imagined. The most difficult part is that, all day long, you have to ask other people to do the simplest tasks for you, like getting something out of the refrigerator, or picking up a pen that has fallen on the floor, or helping you get a sweater over your head. Not only does all this make you feel like a child, but each one of these requests requires your saying "please" and "thank you" dozens of times. Add it up and you're saying please or thank you thirty or forty times a day, seven days a week, fifty-two weeks a year, for the rest of your life. To tell the truth, it's a colossal pain just to get a drink of water. I can fully empathize with my dog as the two of us sit in front of the refrigerator, waiting for somebody to come and open the door to get us a snack.

After the eye-opening lunch at the mall, we proceeded to go shopping, with the goal of making a purchase. This required another whole series of instructions to the sales clerk, since my wallet is stowed in a pouch hanging *in front of* my chair seat. I always have to depend on the clerk's willingness to help me out.

On the upside, this whole complicated process occasionally works to my advantage. I recently ran through a traffic light, reluctant to jam on the brakes as the yellow light turned red. As soon as I went through the light, a policeman came up behind me with his blue lights flashing and approached the window to ask for my license and registration. I began my usual spiel: "Well, officer, you need to go around to the passenger side and in the glove compartment you'll find my registration." After he retrieved that, I continued, "Now come around to this side, and open my door, and then you need to reach under my wheelchair and take my license out of my wallet."

"You know what?" he said. "Let's forget the whole thing."

I thanked him and drove off (smiling).

The process of learning to drive a specially equipped van with a chairlift began at Craig and was particularly challenging, because your feet and your brain have been conditioned for years to work the accelerator and brakes, and not your hand, which is now needed to push the toggle forward or back to move and stop the car. The instructor and I practiced this in an empty parking lot over what seemed like a very long weekend, she with her foot at the ready near a brake on the passenger side in case I screwed up and was about to run into something. Eventually, this daredevil of an instructor led me onto the highway—which was a terrifying idea at first. But she knew I would get used to it, and eventually I did.

When my months in rehab were over and we returned home, we ordered a Ford van, the type used to deliver flowers or dry cleaning. When it arrived with a foot brake on the passenger side, I drove with my five-year-old son Ben to the parking lot at the yacht club five minutes away, knowing the lot would be empty and I could continue to practice. Ben sat on the floor near the brake pedal, since his legs couldn't reach the floor, and I instructed him that if I yelled "brake!" he was to push down on it as hard as he could. Once I learned to get in and out of the van without assistance, I began to feel quite comfortable driving myself around, which was incredibly liberating.

But the conversations I have to have with strangers are endless, *especially* when it involves the van. It has no seat on the driver's side, because that's where my wheelchair locks into place with a mechanism on the floor. So, whenever I drive up to a hotel or restaurant valet zone, the parking guy comes over and opens my door, expecting me to get out so he can drive it away. I have to tell him, "You can't drive this car. There is no chair for you to sit on." The guy looks at me blankly, not understanding what I'm talking about.

"I'm going to take care of you," I continue, waving a ten-dollar bill, "because you can't drive this car. So just give me a spot near the front of the restaurant and I'll put it there myself." The prospect of the tip does the trick every time. I keep a stack of tens and twenties on hand, and we pretty much stick to the same restaurants around the city, places where they already know me. It's easier that way.

It was pretty hard in the first years after the accident to avoid mourning the loss of the activities that meant the most to me, especially sailing, playing my violin, and traveling in Europe (where almost nothing is accessible). But as time has passed, I have found that it's really the little everyday things I miss most: getting myself a cup of coffee, getting in and out of bed without assistance, cutting my own steak. Being dependent on other people to do the simplest things occasionally requires some imagination when no one else is around. I was alone one afternoon and cut my finger on something or other, and it started to bleed like a son of a gun. I couldn't feel it (paralysis prevents sensation as well as mobility), and only noticed it when I saw the blood all over my pants. I knew it wasn't serious enough to call an ambulance, but there was no way I could bandage it myself, until it dawned on me that a pizza delivery guy might do the trick. I called and ordered a small mushroom, green pepper, and onion and a Coke. When the doorbell rang, I answered and said, "I'm so glad you're here. I need you to do a little something for me," as I directed him to the cabinet with the gauze and tape.

At Craig, I met with a psychologist several times a week. I would be lying on my bed and he would be sitting in a chair next to me, and both of us would be eating See's chocolates while we talked. I was filled with fear at this enormous life change, suddenly finding myself imprisoned in my own body with the realization that I could do very little on my own. I began to envy salamanders and starfish, who can grow back their injured or severed limbs. But eventually, the sessions with this therapist, plus meeting with people in the Denver area who had suffered similar spinal cord injuries but were now back to driving and working, showed me what was possible.

I carried on a continuous dialogue with myself during those weeks (and long afterward). "Roosevelt won a whole war from a wheelchair, so why can't I survive this?" I told myself I had two choices: be depressed all the time, stay home and feel sorry for myself, or just make up my mind to get going. Once I realized that I could learn to drive an adapted van, that I could dial and talk on the telephone, and that I could feed myself in a restaurant, I knew I would be okay, because that's pretty much what my workdays consisted of—phone calls and work lunches with colleagues and consultants.

I knew that, from a physical point of view, I was back in business, but that was also when a period of deeper reflection set in as I began to imagine what form my working life would take moving forward. I started to question whether I still wanted to be in the business of building and managing buildings. When you lose everything you consider essential in your life, your priorities can't help but change.

Chapter 21

MY SECOND CAREER AS A LOBBYIST

That same year, 1991, the real estate market suffered a huge downturn. Many local and national banks went under, making loans difficult to come by and bringing development to a near stand-still. I used to joke that the market and I crashed at the same time.

Fortunately, because we owned mainly federally assisted housing, the downturn had little effect on our properties. But with less business to focus on during this period, my attention turned to the possibility of work that might be more fulfilling—and that turned out to be the state of medical research. Someone said to me at the time, "Everything happens for a purpose," and although I didn't subscribe to that fatalistic view, it did strike me that I could begin to repair myself by working to "repair the world." I became convinced that I could turn my accident into something positive in terms of curing diseases and disorders, not just my own spinal cord injury (SCI), but possibly the whole range of illnesses and injuries that millions of Americans were suffering with.

Clearly, more money was needed for medical research. I was accustomed to lobbying local politicians who needed to be persuaded that what their community needed was a hundred units of elderly and low-income housing right in their neighborhood. Now, those had been real fights, and I thought it couldn't possibly be harder to lobby Washington politicians for more funding to cure paralysis and other conditions. I began to put those personal relationships to work to arrange meetings with members of

MY SECOND CAREER AS A LOBBYIST

Congress who came to Boston to raise funds for their campaigns.

I soon discovered that many senators and congressmen and women had a personal interest in a specific disease. Often this was because they had a family member struggling with that disease or disorder. For example, Connie Mack, then Republican senator from Florida, was concerned with melanoma, because so many members of his family had died from it. Tom Harkin of Iowa, chair of the Subcommittee on Appropriations for the National Institutes of Health, had a nephew with a spinal cord injury. Bill Cohen from Maine had a sister with Parkinson's. Arlen Specter was himself struggling with a brain tumor. They were all interested in increasing medical research funding.

With the help of the dean of Harvard Medical School, I would often arrange to bring a senior researcher to those meetings—someone who could serve as my wing man, and speak to the politicians firsthand about new discoveries they were working on and the prospect of finding treatments and cures.

I had an interesting meeting with Senate Majority Leader Bob Dole, who was running for president at the time. During World War II, he had suffered what would have been a fatal wound, had it not been for a physician who treated him using experimental antibiotics. Senator Dole and I sat for about fifteen minutes in the elegant formal office reserved for the Senate Majority Leader, right across the hall from the entrance to the Senate chamber. We commiserated about how difficult the simplest tasks were for us and he confided that he always carried a pencil in his useless right hand so people wouldn't try to shake it. We compared notes about the simple but aggravating tasks that were so frustrating to do when you were alone, and we agreed that one of the worst was trying to button your damn shirt. I told him I had a little tool that I would send him, which you poke through the buttonhole, then hook over the button, and then, with your teeth holding the shirt, you can pull the button through with your good hand.

Me with Bob Dole, 1993

"How did you figure this out?" he asked.

"Well, to be honest, I learned it by watching my dog eat a bone, using his paw to hold the bone down, then yanking the meat off with his teeth. It's amazing how many times in a day I use my teeth to do things. After so many years, it's just a natural reflex.

". . . And I go to the dentist a lot."

After we had finished *kvetching* to one another, we shook hands—left hand to left hand—and I left for my next appointment.

Out in the hall, as we made our way to another senator's office, I said to Dmitri, my personal care attendant from Kiev, "You know what I talked about with the majority leader, the second most powerful person in the country? How to button a shirt. Funny, isn't it?"

On another visit, Senator Ted Stevens of Alaska, who had a reputation for being a bit brusque, spent an hour with us describing the many members of his family who had suffered and died with Alzheimer's disease, and how dreadful those losses had been for him. In response, I told him about Dr. Dennis Selkoe, a Harvard research scientist we had recently brought to a Senate hearing, where he announced the groundbreaking discovery his laboratory had made regarding the cause of Alzheimer's (beta-amyloid plaques) and stated that he now envisioned that a vaccine could be developed to prevent the disease, or at least slow its progress.

From my housing advocacy days, I had a pretty good idea of how much I didn't know about getting things done in Washington, so I contacted former Congressman Chet Atkins and asked him to advise us on how to get legislation passed or attach riders to appropriations bills requesting special consideration for spinal cord injury research. This was relatively easy to do, since it didn't require a vote but had the effect of making the disease category a priority for the NIH institute overseeing it. Chet would coach us on what to say and advise us on what materials to prepare for the meeting. Most importantly, he warned us that the member might agree with us on the spot, but after he left, his staffer would explain how difficult it would be to single out spinal cord injury for extra funding when there were advocates waiting out in the hall to make the same request on behalf of cerebral palsy or ALS. There was a lot of competition for the same federal dollars.

The answer soon became clear: we needed to raise the *entire* NIH budget, not just fiddle with the percentages each institute would receive from the overall pot. So, we set about creating an umbrella organization that would advocate for all the disease groups. By including everybody, we effectively represented tens of millions of Americans who either suffered from chronic disease or had relatives who did.

Through these early efforts I was assisted by my niece Rachel Samuels and her roommate, Eleanor, two bright young women who had just graduated from Harvard. In a corner of our development company, we created an office for them the size of a closet right next to my own, with its large conference table. We tried everything we could think of to get our name out, including creating a speaking event on the Senate-side lawn of the Capitol building. In the front rows, we placed one hundred empty wheelchairs. We didn't gather a crowd, but sent around pictures that made it look as if we had. We created a network of people, including some celebrities, who had a child or close relative with a crippling disease, and this strategy provided the opening we needed. From zero, we built a real nonprofit organization and began to raise operating funds.

You'd think it would be easy to make a difference in Washington if you have talented help and your organization represents tens of millions of people. But I discovered that even though the senators were interested in curing disease, they were also listening to health-care economists who believed research led to expensive new drugs and devices that would ultimately push health-care costs higher. They were concerned that the increases to Medicare and Medicaid would further increase the federal deficit.

Around this time, Rachel and her friend left to pursue their careers, and I was fortunate to find an extremely talented writer who had been brought up in a public relations family, her father having founded Arnold Worldwide, one of the largest advertising agencies in the country. You learn a lot sitting around the dining room table talking shop, and Leslie Kenney had public relations in her DNA. We clicked during her interview, and eventually worked together on advocacy for ten very productive years.

In 1997, we read a *Boston Globe* article about a Duke University economist who was the lead investigator on the National Long-Term Care Survey, a longitudinal study that had begun in 1982, surveying thirty-five thousand persons over sixty-five years of age at regular intervals and measuring the decline over time in chronic disability that represents the costliest part of Medicare and Medicaid.

I contacted Dr. Ken Manton, and with his research results as ammunition, we began to take a different approach on Capitol Hill. The idea was that with cures and therapies developed through the pipeline of increased basic and translational research, chronic disability (defined as requiring help in three or more activities of daily life) would be converted into acute, short-term, treatable conditions. This shift would, in turn, result in enormous savings to Medicare and Medicaid.

Dr. Manton and his research team began to work with us on writing a series of articles for peer-reviewed medical and health-care journals. Our focus was on how medical research results in cures and treatments that shorten the number of sick days over a working lifetime, thus increasing what was termed "human capital productivity." These articles, and the press releases that accompanied their findings, began to make a convincing argument that, in the long run, research reduces the cost of health care. We met with the Medicare actuary to convince him that changes in behavior resulting from new medical knowledge available to the public would also lead to a decrease in chronic disability. For example, in the years following the 1964 surgeon general's announcement that smoking is hazardous to your health because it causes lung cancer and decreases life expectancy, the number of smokers in the country decreased from 50 percent of the population to 25 percent.

On the Hill, we found that members of the Senate, who were by and large older and therefore more concerned about health issues than their counterparts in the House, expressed a lot of interest in finding cures and treatments for chronic disease through research. The representatives were still young enough to think that a daily turn on the treadmill and a salad for lunch would take care of them.

When I first began to approach these members of Congress, I knew I needed a platform. I had heard about the National Council on Spinal Cord Injury, an organization that spoke for several paralysis groups and had originally been organized by the Veterans Administration. I became advocacy chair and eventually president of the organization known as NCSCI (the acronym is pronounced nick-see). At that point, I spoke for several hundred thousand individuals nationwide. Soon after, I was appointed by the Department of Health and Human Services to the Advisory Council of the National Institute of Neurological Disorders and Strokes, and later to the Advisory Committee to the Director of the entire NIH, Dr. Harold Varmus.

Publicity was going to be important if we were going to have any impact in Congress and with the public. Leslie, with her background in marketing and public relations, said, and I remember it so well, "A company like Volkswagen spends millions every year to continually reinforce their brand and message in people's minds. Obviously, we don't have that kind of money; what we need is free publicity from articles and stories on radio, TV, and in the press about what we are doing to cure disease." And that's what we set out to do—to make me the poster boy for our cause.

My being in a wheelchair made this easier. Through a friend, I met with the chief of the editorial page at the *Boston Globe*, who agreed to

On the cover of *The Boston Globe Magazine,* (April 9, 1995)

232

write an editorial about the value of medical research. That triggered a lengthy cover story in the *Globe*'s Sunday magazine, showing me sitting in my chair at the base of the Capitol steps, looking up. There is nothing better, if you want to call attention to yourself, than to wheel through an airport with photographers in front of you clicking away, with everybody wanting to know, "Who is this guy?" Then we'd head over to the Senate office buildings with the cameras still clicking and meet with senators (who are always more than willing to get into the picture). That early exposure led to more, and soon, whenever someone suffered a spinal cord injury, I would get a call from a local TV station asking for my comments. Now I had credentials.

The NIH Advisory Councils, on which I was fortunate to serve, are made up of super scientists, many of them Nobel laureates and presidents of universities, and two lay people like me. I remained connected to the NIH for twelve years, getting to know many major luminaries from all areas of medical research. Eventually, I became sufficiently well educated about the science to be able to talk with confidence in public about cutting-edge research.

My growing credentials and body of knowledge about the state of our national medical research portfolio allowed us to take the next step. We formed the Task Force on Science, Healthcare, and the Economy. This was a working group that included Duke University economist, Ken Manton; Charles Vest, president of MIT; Herb Pardes, dean of Medicine at Columbia University; and Eric Lander, director of the Broad Institute and head of the Human Genome project at MIT. As Herb Padres observed, "We have great convening power." He was right; everyone now took my calls.

With all that academic firepower behind us, we brought together multiple patient advocacy groups for a major forum on the Hill to discuss the impact of research on the U.S. economy. We were joined by a consortium of research universities, the Association of American Medical Colleges, chambers of commerce from cities where biotechnology was an important part of the economy, the Biotechnology

Industry Organization itself, some representatives of big pharma, Advamed (Advanced Medical Technology), and other key groups. This was a group with credibility.

In the spring of 1995, the actor Christopher Reeve, who had played Superman in the movies, fell off his horse and sustained a C-2 injury—the most severe type of spinal cord injury. Given his celebrity, the media covered his accident extensively.

When we heard about the accident, we had already scheduled a hearing before the Senate Appropriations Committee, chaired by Republican Mark Hatfield, a real friend and strong advocate for medical research. This is the largest of all U.S. Senate committees, whose duties are to set the budgets for the various government agencies, including the Department of Health and Human Services. We immediately realized how powerful it would be to bring Christopher's mother to Washington to testify. As it happens, Christopher's in-laws had a summer home in the same Massachusetts coastal community that Dora and I did, and he moored his boat in the same harbor as mine.

It wasn't easy to find out where he was hospitalized; no one in his family wanted the press to descend on them. But I knew from experience that someone at your boatyard always knows your whereabouts. So, I called Brody, the boatyard owner, and asked him about Christopher. Brody knew of my activities in Washington and told me where he was hospitalized in Virginia. We FedExed a letter to his mother, asking if she would be willing to speak at the hearing. In the end, Christopher's younger brother, Benjamin, the spitting image of Christopher, agreed to come. His presence made the hearing a big press event, drawing all the senators on the committee and a packed gallery. (A celebrity at a hearing brings the press and the TV cameras, which bring the senators—that's the trick.)

A month later, after Christopher was stabilized, I asked his family if I could visit him and bring along a prominent spinal cord injury neuroscientist, Dr. Wise Young from Rutgers University. They agreed, and we drove down to the Kessler Rehabilitation Institute in New Jersey. On the wall of Christopher's room was a large poster of all the NASA astronauts. They had all signed the poster, and above their signatures someone had written: "Everything is possible." Christopher was an imposing figure in his oversized motorized wheelchair. Due to the severity of his injury, he was equipped with a ventilator—a machine that forced his lungs to breathe in and out. It was difficult for him to speak with his tracheotomy and ventilator, but he was upbeat and eager to get to work on behalf of research funding. It was his goal to create his own organization and to work cooperatively with ours. His mental strength and positive attitude left me with the feeling that I really was in the presence of Superman.

At that first meeting, Christopher shared a wonderful story about his Julliard roommate, fellow actor Robin Williams. Robin had come to visit him unannounced the week before, barging into his hospital room dressed in surgical gear and mask, speaking with a heavy Russian accent and insisting that he needed to conduct an examination immediately. He was holding up a scary, invasive-looking medical instrument. It didn't take long for Christopher to realize who was behind the mask, and he went on to tell me how they both laughed and then cried together.

We grew close as time went on and we discovered how much we had in common: our love of boats and sailing and, now, a shared determination to achieve the same goal—a cure for spinal cord injury.

I had a friend from Newport, Rhode Island, an accomplished sailor who had multiple sclerosis. He was part of an organization called Shake-a-Leg, which helped people with disabilities to keep sailing. He also competitively sailed remote-controlled scale models of America's Cup yachts. I asked him to build one for Christopher. It was to be painted flag blue, the color of Christopher's boat, the *Sea Angel*, whose name I had reproduced on the model's stern in the same lettering. We were able to modify the remote controls to work like a motorized wheelchair using "sip and puff" mouth controls.

Dora and I had met Christopher's wife, Dana, when we first visited. When the model was ready, I asked Dana's mother to deliver it to their home in New York. I got all choked up just asking this, and she cried too, as her husband, Chuck, had frequently sailed with Christopher, and both of us were just stricken by the calamity of his accident. Dana's parents really became Christopher's parents at this point.

My phone calls with Christopher were fraught with emotion, as both of us had lost so much, above and beyond our beloved boats. We found we had both dreamed about pulling up to our boats in the yacht club launch, throwing our boat bags onto the deck, and then easily climbing aboard to go for a solo sail. We imagined setting just the jib, dropping the mooring line, and sailing off without having to start the engine. With the autopilot engaged, we could still see ourselves standing at the bow holding on to the stay, feeling the wind in our faces and gliding through the water as our boats cut through the waves.

I read somewhere that after he was confined to a wheelchair by polio, Franklin Delano Roosevelt used to dream of his boyhood, of pulling his sled up a hill, then lying on his belly to glide down the snow-covered slope. Christopher told me how he had loved to play the piano and missed it so much. I told him how incredibly sad I was when I first realized I might as well sell my violin because I would never be able to play it again. I put it off for a year or more, hoping that my fingers would suddenly, miraculously, start to work again. We spoke to each other about the many dreams we had at night in which we were still walking, only to wake up and find it wasn't true.

But we were both moving on in a new direction, motivated by the astronauts who had urged him to believe that "Everything Is Possible." Christopher was still very competitive; it was hard to keep up with him, even though he was much more seriously injured than I. Even speaking clearly was a problem for him because of the breathing tube placed in his throat and the fact that he had to speak with the rhythm

Me with Christopher Reeve, 1998

of the machine that was keeping him alive. But he had that Superman drive and determination, and would organize all kinds of events to further the cause. The most memorable was a grand black-tie gala at the Pierre Hotel on Fifth Avenue, where he invited me to sit at the head table with him, between Paul Newman and Barbara Walters.

Dana and my wife confided in one another as well. They spoke about the difficulty of being tied down and limited because of their husbands' disabilities, and how we now received most of the attention from friends and family members. They weren't just complaining; these are serious issues for couples after traumatic accidents have occurred. Both partners must be sensitive about making sure that the uninjured spouse doesn't feel trapped or left behind or just stuck in the role of caretaker.

Christopher soon created his own foundation, and we worked closely together for several years until his untimely death, followed closely by Dana's tragic and unexpected death from lung cancer. While he was alive, our common goal was to create convincing economic arguments to show that medical research not only saved lives and prevented suffering, but saved dollars and slowed the growth of healthcare expenditures as well. With Christopher's media connections and the press coverage of the articles Ken Manton was publishing, we were invited to be interviewed on some of the morning shows. Leslie and I flew back and forth from Boston to Washington quite often, working with staffers to organize Senate hearings and informational meetings with members of Congress in their offices. We invited scientists, economists, and celebrities to testify at these events, making sure the scientists were from universities in the senators' home states.

For one important hearing, which combined the Senate Special Committee on Aging, chaired by Bill Cohen, and the Senate Appropriations Committee, chaired by Mark Hatfield, we brought Travis Roy, a talented young Boston University hockey player, who, in the first few seconds of his first game, slammed into the boards with his head, resulting in a C-4 spinal cord injury. At the hearing, Travis sat next to his father, Lee Roy, who struggled to fight back tears as his handsome, blond, eighteen-year-old son asked that Congress create a Manhattan Project to cure diseases like spinal cord injury. As he said, "All I want to do is be able to hug my mother one more time." With that, his father did burst into tears, and the senators were visibly moved. After a long silence, each senator, directing comments to Lee Roy, talked about their personal fears for their own children.

"It was the most remarkable hearing I have ever attended," Mark Hatfield told me later. (I choke up myself every time I think of what Travis said that day.)

Not long after that, Ted Kennedy invited us to convene a forum in his name on the economic impact of medical research. (Only the majority party can schedule a hearing, but any senator can host a forum.) We had been working for some time with the senator and with Nick Littlefield, his staff director and chief counsel for the Health, Education, and Labor Committee, for which Kennedy then served as the ranking (minority) member.

The senator became passionately involved in our cause. I found that the great thing about Ted Kennedy was that once he got hold of an issue, he was a pit bull, never letting it go, and using all his considerable resources to move it forward. Eventually he even arranged a meeting for us with Alan Greenspan at the Federal Reserve. In the language of economics, for an innovation to be of significance, it must increase productivity, which in turn increases economic growth. We convinced Chairman Greenspan that extending the number of healthy days an individual could spend at work in his lifetime would increase "human capital productivity." He replied that he had never thought of it in exactly that way and agreed.

For our forum with Senator Kennedy, we needed witnesses who would attract the press, and Morton Kondracke (whose wife Millie had Parkinson's disease), then editor of *Roll Call*, an influential paper on Capitol Hill, suggested Dr. Judah Folkman of Harvard and Boston Children's Hospital. Dr. James Watson (of Watson and Crick) had commented in the press that Dr. Folkman's discoveries about the process of angiogenesis could lead to a cure for many cancers. The press had been after Dr. Folkman for comment, but not wanting to raise false hopes, Harvard Medical School had advised him against speaking publicly. Mort thought that if we got him to come, the press would follow. We also invited Boston financial guru Peter Lynch (the man behind Fidelity's Magellan Fund) to testify about the economic impact of medical research.

We created a large chart for Peter's presentation, tracking the percent of GDP that went to support all federally funded research from 1960 to 1995. It showed that in 1962, the U.S. had spent 2 percent of GDP in federally funded research (space program, internet, etc.), but by 1990 the figure had dropped to 1 percent and by 1995 it was only

.06 percent. Peter held up this chart and said: "If I had a company that looked like this, I would sell it short."

The senators all laughed, appreciating the short-sightedness of reducing basic research funding, which not only results in so much good in humanitarian terms, but could also drive U.S. economic growth.

"We are eating our seed corn," Lynch concluded.

Dr. Folkman had been working with worms for twenty years before discovering a biological process he called angiogenesis, which involves cutting off the blood supply of cancer tumors. He was clear with the senators that, without NIH funding, his work

[back row] Henri Termeer (Genzyme), Sen. Bill Frist,
Peter Lynch (Fidelity); *[front row]* Dr. Judah Folkman, me

Henri Termeer, Peter Lynch, Sen. Ted Kennedy,
Dr. Judah Folkman testifying on Capitol Hill

could not have been done, and he carefully explained the impact
this work could have in curing multiple diseases. I remember Dr.
Folkman as the most gentle, humble, and extraordinary man. He
told me that his father, grandfather, and great-grandfather had all
been rabbis, and that it had been assumed that he would follow in
their footsteps. But throughout high school and college, he found
himself fascinated by biology and chemistry and knew in his heart
that he wanted to go to medical school and pursue a career focused
on research. Finally, he gathered the courage to tell his father that
he would not be going to rabbinical school. His father was silent for
some time and then replied, "Well, if you have to be a doctor, then
be a doctor with the spirit of a rabbi." Anyone who knew Judah will
attest that he did exactly that, inspiring scores of colleagues and
younger researchers along the way.

From the forum, we went to see House Speaker Newt Gingrich
in his spectacular office, a meeting arranged by the CEO of Delta
Airlines (whose hub was in Newt's Atlanta district and who served

with me on the Harvard Medical School board). Again, we were followed down the hall by members of the press asking for comments. We gave Speaker Gingrich the same arguments we had made in the forum, and after a brief back-and-forth, he said, "I don't think I could double the budget of the NIH in five years, but I'll agree to do it in eight."

We knew we had it then, and were excited to hear that, at the next Republican caucus, Connie Mack proposed to double the NIH budget in five years. Remembering Gerry Doherty's advice from years ago, I told our little group not to go skipping down the hall just yet.

But in 1998, Congress did in fact vote to double the research budget of the NIH over five years, bringing the total from $13.7 billion to $28 billion annually. (When we started lobbying in 1993, the total NIH budget was slightly over $10 billion; it had slowly inched up to $13.7 billion by 1998.) [70]

All this new money flowing into medical research significantly raised the grant application success rate for scientists and resulted in many new therapies for a wide range of diseases and disorders. The sequencing of the human genome, which occurred at that time, in turn opened up the prospect of new stem cell–based therapies. Unfortunately, stem-cell research progress was slowed down by the Bush administration's faith-based ban on stem-cell research using federal dollars. In the years following this doubling, the NIH budget remained flat from year to year (an actual reduction when inflation-adjusted) and in some years declined in real dollars.

Buzzing around the Senate office corridors in a wheelchair made me stand out as an advocate, and for the first time, I found that being the only one in the room in a wheelchair—in other words, being different—was an advantage, which I used to maximum effect. I loved this work and was totally energized during those years. I never thought of myself as disabled or handicapped.

Leslie and I flew to Washington a lot, together with Dmitri, who often took pictures standing on tables or chairs to get a better shot.

I would tell the senators that Dmitri was from *Pravda*, the Moscow newspaper. Once, in Bill Cohen's office, the senator (who later became secretary of defense) handed Dmitri a large CIA plaque and told him to hold it up in front of himself. Then the senator snapped a picture, joking, "Now you'll never be able to go home again."

I once asked Dmitri what his profession had been in Russia, and he answered in his broken English: "I was airplane engineer." But when I would ask him to fix something, even the simplest little thing, he would just wrap it up with duct tape. I used to think we didn't need the CIA to tell us the Russians military wasn't as good as ours. I knew that their planes would fall out of the sky as soon as the duct tape loosened up.

All in all, the unexpected turn in my life, which I thought at first had *ended* my life, actually brought me many opportunities for new learning and fascinating work. It introduced me to a network of brilliant scientists and passionate advocates, who became not only colleagues but friends. It gave me the sense that I could make a real difference in the world, that I could actually help change people's lives. On top of that, it brought me all kinds of awards and recognition for my work in the form of engraved clocks, plaques, complimentary articles in my school magazines, and, most meaningful of all, an honorary degree from Rutgers University. As Leslie recently reminded me, "You never got an honorary degree for being the only Jew at school."

So, I count myself to be a very lucky man. A few years ago, my cousin Fred and his wife, Leslie, and Dora and I were sitting around the table after dinner. Fred proposed that each of us rank our life on a happiness scale of 1 to 10. As we went around the table, Fred, Leslie, and Dora all put themselves somewhere between a five and seven. But when it came to me, I said nine and a half.

"Are you nuts?" my cousin exclaimed. "You've spent the last twenty years in a wheelchair."

But my self-evaluation was true.

Chapter 22

"KVELLING" OVER BEN

Back when everything about the accident was new and the learning curve loomed large—the limitations, the loss of privacy, the need to relearn so many simple tasks—some of my biggest challenges came in my family relationships. Though my instinct was to focus on my own needs back then, Ben was only five the day I said goodbye to him, went off for a half-hour bike ride, and basically came home four months later a completely different father from the one he had known. The trips we had talked about taking as a family, the kinds of games and activities Ben saw his friends doing with their fathers, and even my ability to pick him up and hold him—they were all gone in a minute. The loss of the normal life we had enjoyed together had to have had a traumatic effect on a five-year-old, but it took quite a while for me to recognize his pain and confusion; I was too embroiled in my own fears and losses.

Ben flew with Dora to Colorado, where they stayed in a rental apartment and visited me at Craig Rehabilitation Hospital every day. The facility was filled with all kinds of weird-looking rehab machines, and there were lots of kids suffering from various crippling conditions—kids who had been injured diving into shallow water, surfing, or falling off a motorcycle or a ladder. Teenage boys and young men most often sustain spinal cord injuries, since they are the ones who are most active and heedless of danger. I was the exception there, together with Willie Shoemaker, the famous jockey, who lay in a hospital bed across the hall from me watching horse races on satellite TV.

Me with Ben and Dr. Kenneth Viste, then president of the American Academy of
Neurology, receiving our Leadership Award, 1998

At Craig, Ben would sit on my lap as I wheeled around a large activity room filled with equipment and a few computers on tables designed to accommodate wheelchairs. He liked playing games on these
early-generation computers—not the shoot-'em-up type, but games
you would see on TV like *Jeopardy* and word or puzzle-solving games.
He was good at them, and we played them together, as he had already
mastered reading. He could busy himself creating a whole new language using little symbols to signify letters and then writing something with his new code, which we later realized was his earliest foray
into computer programming and coding, which is now his passion as
an engineer. He could sit on my lap in front of those computers for
hours, until my legs hurt, but I was glad to have him right there, where
I could hold him close, and both of us could enjoy the same activity.

Before I was shipped off to Colorado, I'd met with a hypnotist at
the Massachusetts General Hospital, who taught me how to hyp-
notize myself, to shift my thoughts to something more pleasant
when I was feeling anxious and frustrated about being unable to

move, which was pretty much every minute I wasn't sleeping. His instruction was to pick some favorite activity I had enjoyed and focus on that, which always turned out to be something Ben and I had done together, like walking around the zoo with him riding on my shoulders, holding on to my head so he wouldn't fall off. I'd introduce him to the monkeys and zebras and the others, saying to them, "Mr. Zebra, this is my son Ben. Would you like to say hello to him?" I had a hat I would wear whenever we went to the zoo. It featured the head of a wolf with its large mouth wide open, and I would wear it backwards so the wolf faced Ben. My father was a funny man and would do those kinds of silly little things, which became wonderful memories for me. I thought about the impact it would have had on me if my father had broken his neck. How would I have dealt with such a calamity, with losing so much of the relationship I had with him?

The self-hypnosis worked surprisingly well, relaxing me, taking my mind off what I was going through and what I would continue to go through for the rest of my life—a heavy burden in those early days.

What I learned from the hypnotist was that the more I became involved in an activity, the more I would forget my own problems. For me, this turned out to mean immersing myself in the task of increasing federal funding for biomedical research. In that capacity, I was hearing about cutting-edge discoveries across multiple medical fields, and often shared these new discoveries with Ben, who was quite a budding scientist and mathematician as a boy. There were several exciting new fields emerging: genomics, stem cells, the breeding of what were called "knock-off" mice, omitting a specific gene that researchers thought might cause cancer, diabetes, etc. Dr. Larry Smarr, who served with me on the NIH Advisory Council to Director Harold Varmus, was, at that time, advocating for the creation of "centers of excellence" in universities around the country to grow a new field he called bioinformatics, which would make sense of all the mega-data arising from these new fields. I talked at length with Ben about all of this, because he loved computers more than anything.

To my surprise, Ben, who was about fourteen at the time, had heard of Smarr, and knew he was director of the National Center for Supercomputing Applications at the University of Illinois. But he didn't know that we had just voted to set up those centers of excellence around the country to develop the engineering needed to mine the data.

Around the time Ben was entering high school, I heard about an exciting program called City Lab at Boston University Medical School, which the dean, Carl Franzblau, had created to teach high school students biotechnology by doing hands-on DNA analysis in a modern lab. As he so aptly put it, "You don't learn how to play baseball by reading a book—you give the kid a glove."

I encouraged Ben to sign up, and he loved it. I shared with Carl Ben's enthusiasm for science and computers, and how he followed the development of every new device. Carl told me that he too had loved scientific gadgets as a young man, and even now would buy whatever was new, encouraging me to do the same, much to Ben's delight. This paid off educationally as you might expect, but surprisingly, it paid off financially as well. He used a $10,000 gift Dora's mother gave him (as she did all her grandchildren) to invest in the technology he knew best—Apple—buying the stock at $4. With that bet, he could eventually have bought every conceivable scientific gadget, and a Ferrari to boot.

The year before my accident, we had enrolled him in Solomon Schechter Hebrew Day School in Newton, thinking that he deserved a very different early school experience from the one I had known. I am not a particularly religious or observant Jew, nor is Dora, but we strongly identify with Jewish values and culture and wanted Ben to be exposed to Jewish teaching in a way that we could not provide at home. It was a good decision; today he has a strong moral compass that points him to a life of kindness and compassion toward all people.

At Schechter, everyone was Jewish and no one drove a Ford station wagon with wood trim or belonged to a yacht club (except me) or had a flag decal stuck to the rear left window (I had that too, oops). The teachers were loving, caring Jewish mothers, the kind of women you would expect to say, "Darling, have a little more kreplach." I especially loved the school musical productions they put on. In Ben's first year they did *West Side Story*, actually sung in Hebrew, and the following year, *Annie*, also sung in Hebrew. What a difference from my preppy elementary school fifty years earlier! I saw one kid wearing a T-shirt that read, on the front, in big letters: Undefeated—25 Years. Printed across the back was this: Solomon Schechter Football.

There was a sports field at Schechter, yes, but no teams. Even the jokes the kids told were Jewish:

> *Bill Clinton calls his cleaner and asks him to pick up the blue dress and dry clean it. "But, when you finish, call and tell me the results in some kind of code," he says.*
> *So, a few days later the cleaner calls back and sings: "A Mazel Tov, a Mazel Tov, a zemen off, a zemen off."*

From Solomon Schechter, Ben went on to Beaver Country Day School in Brookline, where he met one of those rare teachers, Larry Murphy, who chaired the Science Department and immediately noticed Ben's passion for the subject. As it happened, Beaver was a satellite for the Boston University City Lab. Beaver had a modern biotech lab that was to be used to introduce biotechnology to students from other schools that lacked such equipment. With Ben's sophisticated computer and website skills, he worked with Larry to set up a summer program for advanced high school students that offered hands-on learning in the lab along with a trip to the NIH's Bethesda campus to meet with researchers and see all the specialized equipment. And with that specialized training, there was the possibility of placement in a lab at Harvard or Tufts Medical schools.

I had mentioned to the NIH director that it might be interesting to give a presentation to the advisory committee on the value of early hands-on teaching, the idea being that if you don't get students hooked on science by the end of their high school years, they're lost and our country will lose our ability to compete scientifically at the global level.

As part of this new program for advanced students, Murphy had created what he termed "peer to peer teaching," where he would train students to become teachers, and when completed, each would receive their own freshly pressed white lab coat as a "graduation" present. Students from other Boston-area schools would come to Beaver during the term and the Beaver students, in their lab coats, would conduct the classes. If you can teach a subject, then you really know the subject. I would occasionally come and observe. What a treat to see Ben up there teaching in front of the class.

We flew down to Washington, Larry, Carl Franzblau, Dmitri, and I, plus seven or eight students from the program. We met with Ted Kennedy on the Hill and ran into a few other senators I knew. I introduced the kids as representatives of the next great generation of research scientists. What a thrill.

Walking into that imposing conference room at the NIH, where they were about to speak to the twenty-member council comprised of Nobel laureates, university presidents, and super scientists plus the directors of the various institutes, would frighten anyone, never mind a group of seventeen-year-olds.

I introduced them and explained how these students taught students from other schools that didn't have all the biotech equipment of a real lab. I added that some of the students would like to demonstrate this novel form of teaching by role playing with the council members.

I remember one of the students asking the council something about the use of enzymes in DNA analysis. After one member answered the question, the student followed up with the same question he would have asked his students: "How do you know that?" To which the member answered, "Because I won the Nobel Prize for it."

With that everyone laughed, and the students calmed down noticeably.

Ben talked about his work at the Beth Israel Hospital with the lead investigator of a lab, blocking T-cell receptors to find a way to control rejection following an organ transplant.

He also taught himself computer programming and computer science, since Beaver didn't offer it. If you walked into your kid's room any morning after he left, you'd expect to find a pair of dirty socks and maybe *Harry Potter* or *Charlie and the Chocolate Factory* on the nightstand. But if you walked into Ben's room, you would find the socks, but on the floor at the head of the bed, instead of *Harry Potter*, you would see C++, Java, Pascal, or Pearl, all three-inch thick computer language textbooks.

So, am I *kvelling* over my son Ben? Yup.

Kvelling is a Yiddish idiom, and as usual with Yiddish, there isn't a simple translation. To explain it requires a story.

Example: You want to know the meaning of, say, *schnorrer?*

Somebody says to you, "You want two tickets to opening day at Fenway Park?"

And you answer: "Do you have four?" That's a *schnorrer.*

So, here's the story on *kvelling.*

"So, how's everything with you?" your friend innocently asks.

"Oh, I just can't stop *kvelling* over my son," you answer.

"So, tell me." And now you have sucked the person in and now have a green light to tell her the whole thing. She asked, didn't she?

"You know how he loves computers and how he taught himself to program and got himself a summer job at Harvard Medical School, and how Beaver is letting him take a semester off, with credits no less, to work in a lab at Harvard on a completely new program called Systems Biology, which uses an entirely new computer language called 'Little b.' Well, guess what? Their work was published in a peer-reviewed journal, and Ben is listed as a co-author! He achieved the highest score in his AP Biology, Computer Science, and Math exams. *And* he's been admitted to Columbia." (All true!)

So, *kvelling* is pretty much just boasting, only done with so much love, it doesn't seem obnoxious.

It's easy for a Jewish father to go on and on praising his son for all his marvelous accomplishments: how methodical he is, how calmly he goes about solving problems, his passion for learning, and, best of all, how warm and loving he is. Today, Ben is thirty-three years old, married to an equally wonderful, smart, and kind woman, Anne-Marie. They have two children: Otis (OT), a brilliant, funny little guy with a great personality, who understands the subtleties of everything going on around him and participates in the humor, even though he is not yet three years old. And, most recently, a beautiful, always-laughing baby girl named Seraphina. To complete our joy, they recently moved from New York City and are now living just a few miles away.

Writing and thinking about Ben, I have to add here that working on this book has opened my eyes to Judaism in a new way, and pushed me to want to share what I have learned with my son and with his children. I now see Judaism as a spiritual and intellectual legacy, one that has profoundly influenced Western civilization by contributing a set of moral principles and a blueprint for a just society. The principles contained in the Torah (the five books of Moses) and the Talmud (the laws and their interpretation) actually comprise the principles upon which every moral democratic society is built.

The Torah and the sacred texts encoding Jewish law form the foundation of Jewish life and may be translated as "the Law," "the Way," or "the Book." The Church fathers understood that these texts were the source of Jewish strength and survival through the centuries and therefore banned their use. Jews, possessing the same understanding, have always elevated study above all other pursuits and created their communal life around the pursuit of learning and understanding of the Law.

It turns out that the value of education has been central to Judaism as far back as the period following reconstruction of the Second Temple (516 BCE) in the time of Ezra (480–440 BCE). He established houses of prayer everywhere that Jews lived, where they met, read, and interpreted the teachings of the Torah, and discussed the moral and ethical issues that arose in their daily lives, which later became the basis of the Talmud. These were called "the people's houses"—"synagogues" in Greek.

Originally, the Talmud was not intended to be written down because rabbis and scholars believed that laws need to be flexible in order to reflect social changes over time. But with the destruction of the temple in Jerusalem in 70 CE, they decided it was necessary to codify what had previously been oral tradition. Over the next four centuries, the Talmud was written down by scribes, but consistent with the original intent, it was organized with the original text in the center of each scroll, with subsequent commentary, interpretations, and supplements in the margins. This structure made the Talmud a living document—almost a dialogue between scholars across several centuries.

Ezra encouraged the people of his time to read the Torah every Sabbath (and Mondays and Thursdays as well). The idea was that through constant reading and discussion, Jews would be exposed to moral teachings and begin to live their lives accordingly. In some ways, Ezra was part of an intellectual awakening in his time, living during the same period as Socrates, Plato, and Aristotle. They all shared the belief that intellect—the ability to reason—was the key to humans' highest aspirations and the route by which we are able to live virtuous and just lives.[71]

Even our holy days (holidays) are celebrated to remind us of the importance of ethical behavior and social justice. For example, as each new year begins with Rosh Hashanah (Head of the Year) and Yom Kippur (Day of Atonement), we are asked to examine our behavior to search out where we have treated others unfairly or unkindly during the previous year, and to seek their forgiveness and make amends. We cannot privately confess to a rabbi and say a prayer to redeem ourselves. God cannot forgive us for injustices we have done to our fellow man; those we have harmed must forgive us. In the spring, at Passover, the readings around the seder table remind us of the immorality and cruelty of slavery and of oppression and tyranny of all kinds. This is brought home by the fact that our ancestors were slaves in Egypt. As we retell the story each year, we become part of the suffering of oppressed people everywhere and responsible for the redemption of all people everywhere.

This is what I learned through the process of writing this memoir: that Judaism more than a religion, it is a philosophy of life, and a *mitzvah* (required good deed) to share that philosophy of just behavior and good works with your children and your grandchildren.

Chapter 23

MOVING TOWARD THE TWENTIETH CENTURY

At school I always wished that I could frame a defense of the Jews. But I didn't know enough (actually, I didn't know anything) to be able to rebut the accusations, even while I understood that some of them made no sense and constituted an attack on my religion. Years later, I discovered copies of the great disputations, a series of debates between learned rabbis and priests that began in the early thirteenth century, originated by Catholic clergy who believed exposure to these debates would prove to Jews that Catholicism was the one true religion.

Those debates were argued by learned rabbis, and the three that were transcribed by Jews are preserved today. I came across a copy of the Disputation of Barcelona of 1263, argued by Rabbi Moses ben Nahman, one of the most distinguished rabbis of the time, equal in stature to the better-known Rashi and Maimonides. Reading even the abridged transcript provided me with a deeper level of understanding of Judaism than I'd ever had before. His arguments started me fantasizing that *I* was ben Nahman, sitting around a seminar table in class, able to boldly assert my positions as a learned Jew rather than a profoundly uncomfortable teenager. In my role-playing fantasies, I was so articulate:

Sir, the main idea about a Messiah is that when he comes there will be peace, as Isaiah 2:4 clearly states: "They shall beat their swords into plowshares, and their spears into pruninghooks, and nation shall not lift up sword against nation, neither shall they learn war anymore."

So, Jesus did come to earth, but where is the peace that Isaiah proph-
esied? I don't have to tell you that just fifteen years ago we fought the
Second World War, with seventy to eighty-five million people dead,
another forty million displaced, and Europe, Japan, and Russia in
ruins. And now we are fighting again in Korea. This certainly doesn't
seem like any kind of messianic age to me.

The Jewish concept of the Messiah is quite different from the
Christian version. There's no magical event where all of a sudden,
out of nowhere, a Messiah arrives and, shazam, we have peace. In
Judaism, the thought is that, here on earth, we must all work together to create the condition that will bring about the Messianic
age. The Messiah, or Mashiah, as he is called in the Hebrew Bible,
means "anointed one," as King David was anointed and referred to as
Mashiah David. It does not and has never meant "savior." In fact, the
notion of salvation is not part of our religion at all. Maybe that's one
of the reasons that conversion to Christianity has been a huge leap
for Jews through the centuries.

It's because of our belief that a peace-loving king and a peace-loving people would usher in the Messianic age that Jesus had to claim
to be King of the Jews. The Gospel writers had him make this claim
(although indirectly) in order to reflect the prophecies of the Old
Testament, which is how Christians refer to the Hebrew Bible. However, this claim became a catch-22 trap for the Gospel writers, because it ran right up against the most serious capital offense under
Roman law, which decreed that only the emperor could appoint a
king. This capital crime committed by Jesus made it obvious that
the Romans, and not the Jews, would have demanded his death. Try
claiming you're the president of Russia and see how long it will take
Putin to arrest and execute you. At that time, Pontius Pilate would
have had no authority to pardon such a serious crime, and no interest in avoiding the responsibility for punishing that crime by saying,
as Matthew 27:24 tells it, "I am innocent of the blood of this just
person. See ye to it." (There was no law or practice that allowed the

pardon of one person at Passover, thus allowing Pontius Pilate to wash his hands of the matter, as it says in the Gospels.)

The Gospel writers needed to find a prophecy for many of the events in Jesus's life in order for the new Christian faith to be accepted by the Romans as a religion and not a cult. There is no mention of Jesus Christ in the Old Testament, although every time the name Jesus appeared, Christian authors would claim it was foretelling the arrival of Jesus. But as the rabbi defending Judaism in the Paris disputation remarked, Jesus was a common name, so every Jesus mentioned in the Torah or Talmud is not your Jesus, just as "every Louis is not the king of France."

Writing one hundred to two hundred years after Jesus, the authors of the Gospels needed to be creative, and they were. To foretell the birth of Jesus, they took another passage from Isaiah (7:14–16), where only a word or two needed to be changed to make the text more compatible with their story, not to mention more exciting. The original text reads: "The L-rd, of His own, shall give you a sign. Behold the young woman is with child, and she will bear a son, and you shall call his name Immanu'el."

So, change "young woman" to "virgin," and you've got a miraculous prophecy—except for the fact that the Old Testament context had nothing to do with the birth of Jesus. Isaiah was referring to a contemporaneous military crisis and prophesying that Judea would survive, and all that was 732 years before Christ was even born. Naming a child Immanu'el was merely a metaphor for the promise that God will protect you.

It is said that there are three central pillars of Judaism: Prayer; Charity or good works; and Study, i.e., learning and understanding Jewish Law. It is the notion of living by the law that most differentiates Judaism from Christianity, which of course also includes prayer and charity. In our Sabbath services, when the ark of the covenant is opened and the congregation sees the Torah scrolls standing inside, we all rise, recognizing that the Torah contains the law. After the week's portion is read and blessed, and before the Torah is returned to the ark, the rabbi raises the scroll to his shoulder and carries it around the sanctuary, giving everyone a chance to connect with it (by bringing their prayer shawls to their lips and touching the shawl to the scroll as it passes by. It is Jewish law that regulates our everyday life, just as secular laws determine how members of society must live and behave.

It is hard to imagine that Jesus would have ever considered throwing out the Jewish laws. I'm sure it was not he who replaced them with canon (church) law as the basis for the new laws found in the Code of the Emperor Justinian (*Codex Justinianus*), which provided little fairness, safety, or justice to the Roman citizens of the mid-sixth century. Under this system, there were no juries or judges, and confessions were obtained through torture, setting the precedent for the way the Church would deal with dissidents and heretics for the next fifteen hundred years. It seems to work better when laws are written down, reconsidered, and revised as times and social values evolve. In this way, society becomes kinder, less arbitrary, and increasingly more accepting of the cultural differences among people.

But looking back over our long and tortured history, especially since the reign of Constantine, it is disturbing to realize how few periods there have been when Jews were allowed the freedom to live in peace and safety, with any semblance of just treatment.

We're living in one of those periods of freedom today. It began at the end of World War II, was marked by the establishment of the State of Israel in 1948, and has lasted for seventy years. The previous period of peace for European Jews lasted seventy-eight years, beginning in 1861 with the unification of Italy and defeat of the Papal States, and ending abruptly in 1939 with the German annexation of Austria and invasion of Poland that started the Second World War. Earlier, the year 1789 brought a brief period of peace for the Jews, when we enjoyed the freedoms that came with the French Revolution and the *Declaration of the Rights of Man* along with everyone else. That was a time when the ghetto walls came down and we lived alongside our Christian neighbors. But with Napoleon's defeat in 1814, the Church rebuilt those walls and locked us in again.

Looking all the way back to the period following Constantine, we see that the earliest period of religious freedom for the Jews came in the late fifth century, when an army of Teutons from Germany (the Barbarians), led by Theodoric the Great, invaded Italy and ruled it from 487–526. Theodoric turned out to be considerably less barbaric than his Christian predecessors. He reversed the discriminatory laws governing religious practice, declaring, "We prescribe no religion, for no person can be compelled to profess any faith contrary to his convictions." [72] But with his death, Italy again became vulnerable to foreign invasion. It was then that Justinian recaptured Naples and returned to the practice of systematically persecuting the Jews. The breath of freedom Theodoric gave us lasted less than fifty years.

Given this mercurial history, is there any hope that Jewish-Christian relations can improve? Has there been any significant change in the mindset that erased the lives of tens of millions of Jews who could be living today, but are somehow missing?

The Catholic Church has to come to terms with its own history and dogma and take steps to reform itself. Progress has been made very recently with the election of Pope Francis, but most of the popes of the past century subscribed to the notion of papal infallibility—an idea that has had terrible consequences through the centuries. The once infamous story of Edgardo Mortara is a case in point.

Edgardo, a six-year-old Jewish boy living in Bologna, was taken from his family in 1886 by the papal police. The inquisitor in that district (yes, even as recently as the nineteenth century, the Holy Office of the Inquisition was still going strong) learned that a fourteen-year-old Catholic girl who worked for the Mortara family, fearing that the young boy was ill and dying, had personally undertaken to baptize him.

For me, the historical time frame made the incident even more frightening, as the house we lived in when our own son was six was built the same year Edgardo was kidnapped. At the time he was taken, canon law decreed that having been baptized, Edgardo was officially Catholic and no longer Jewish. Since the Universal Inquisition required that only Christians raise Christian children, it followed that the boy must be removed from his Jewish family and taken to a House of the Catechumens—essentially a house of conversion. Should the baptized boy ever return to Judaism, he would then be sentenced as a heretic.

(This is insane logic. The early Christians threw out Talmudic law and replaced it with canon law, which legalizes kidnapping, torture, and homicide. Where is the world court of justice?)

At that time, Napoleon III (Bonaparte's nephew) and his troops were defending Rome and the pope against the revolutionary armies of Victor Emmanuel and Garibaldi, who were intent on unifying

Left, façade of Collegio dei Neofiti, an institution built by Pope Paul III to house catechumens (would-be and forced converts preparing for baptism)

Italy. Napoleon was outraged by the kidnapping, and with worldwide pressure building to release the Mortara boy and support of the pope by French Catholics declining, Napoleon withdrew his troops, making it possible for Victor Emmanuel to defeat the papal armies and unify the country.

In the face of Napoleon's withdrawal, the pope's decision was shocking. He was willing to sacrifice all his papal territories—over sixteen thousand square miles stretching from the north to the south of Italy—rather than return one Jewish child to his parents. With this decision, the Church found itself with only a few square blocks of land surrounding the Vatican within Vatican City in Rome—the same footprint it controls today. The remnants of its once powerful army now stand in quaint, colorful costumes guarding the tourist entrances to St. Peter's Basilica and the Vatican museums.

Some of the papal policies in my own lifetime have also left me feeling skeptical about achieving meaningful change in the way the Church relates to the Jews. The activities of Popes Pius XI and XII before, during, and after the Second World War tell the story. In his meticulously researched book *God's Banker*, Gerald Posner outlines the financial and political maneuvering in the Vatican during the first half of the twentieth century. But more significantly, he highlights the total lack of moral leadership shown by the Church during this violent and dangerous period.

From the late 1930s and throughout the war came only silence from Rome—a policy extensively recorded in documents sealed in the archives of the Vatican, which the Church has been reluctant to share. From the tenure of Pius XI during the rise of Hitler and Mussolini and the military buildup of the early 1930s to the German invasions of Czechoslovakia, Poland, and Russia and the eventual murder of six million Jews under Pius XII, not a single word of moral outrage was ever issued from Rome.

Because many of the arrests, deportations, and murders occurred in Catholic countries, local priests and bishops were in a prime position to witness the building atrocities and to make daily firsthand reports to the Vatican. Instead, many of the Catholic clergy were complicit in rounding up people deemed undesirable by the Third Reich, and even took leadership roles in running labor, detention, and death camps in Croatia and Slovakia.

Eventually, under enormous internal and external pressure, the pope made a vague Christmas pronouncement, tangentially mentioning "arbitrary attacks on defenseless individuals in the hundreds of thousands who, without any fault of their own, sometimes only by reason of their nationality or race, are marked down for death or gradual extinction." He never once mentioned the words "Jew," "Germany," or "Nazi" in this message. When questioned about the moral ambiguity of the statement, his response was that he had said "everything that needed to be said." Yet, while Pius never showed concern for the crimes and atrocities of the Germans, he became enraged when the allies bombed the cities of Italy in 1943. One bomb struck the Basilica of St. Lawrence not far from the walls of the Vatican. Apparently, that event moved him to tears.[73]

But there were no tears shed by the pope as he could see, right out of his window from the Vatican, real innocent children and their parents waiting to be transported to their death in the camp he knew about so well from his priests and bishops. However, I am sure he knelt in front of the many paintings of the "Massacre of the Innocents" beautifully displayed in the Vatican. Perhaps he shed a tear for that accusation against the Jews written and preached in church and described so vividly in the Gospels.

It may seem unexpected to end my discussion of the Holocaust there with Pope Pius's decision to turn his back on the Jews of Italy. So much has been written about Hitler's "final solution" to the "Jewish problem" and the shocking efficiency with which Germans eliminated half the Jewish population of the world, that nothing I could say would add to the litany of atrocities that took place. But I hope the historical portions of this book show that what we often think of as a singular episode of horror in Western civilization was actually just the most recent episode of horror—the culmination of centuries of such events.

What probably sets the Holocaust apart from other periods of mass murder was our ability to describe, observe, record, and understand it. There are very few firsthand descriptions and images of the Crusades or the Spanish Inquisition, as the printing press had not yet been invented to preserve written evidence for wide swaths of people. And the power of photography and film to sear the worst images of human suffering and degradation into our collective hearts and minds cannot be underestimated.

Although the events of World War II are decades in the past, it's pretty safe to say that, for most Jews alive today, the echoes of the Holocaust have been seared into us both consciously and unconsciously. Many of the Jews living in Germany in 1939 were from families that had been there for three hundred years. Many had fathers and grandfathers who had fought for Germany in World War I. Many were among the most prominent members of academia, the arts, business, and even government. They simply could not believe that their country—the most educated and cultured in Europe—would turn on them. And that leaves Jews in America today with the uncomfortable thought that sometimes, for us, things can turn on a dime, and once again you can find yourself the unwanted "other." So, I will say no more about the Holocaust, or how a civilized and educated society could intentionally perpetrate such crimes and atrocities against other human beings; as I said, this has all been well documented by others. My own contribution is to shed some light on the connection between the way the Gospel writers portrayed and accused us in the New Testament, and the unimaginable violence that has resulted ever since.

Chapter 24

THE SENIOR SPEECH I SHOULD HAVE GIVEN IN 1957

As my thoughts return to my prep school days and to my experience as a Jewish boy in what felt to me like a Christian universe, one event stood out that seemed to sum up the whole dilemma. As part of the curriculum, every student had to present a First Class (senior) talk to the faculty and students of the three upper classes. You could choose any subject, and since I was having a hard time deciding, my mother suggested that I speak about the nationalization and blockade of the Suez Canal, which had recently occurred.

The blockade, imposed by Egyptian president Abdul Nasser, barred Israel's use of its shipping ports—a direct violation of the 1949 armistice. France and England were outraged and, with their support, Israel attacked. In response, the Soviet Union threatened to use military force if Israel and its allies didn't withdraw, and the United States, which feared an escalation of tension with the Soviet Union, also threatened sanctions if Israel, France, and England did not withdraw. With this strong U.S. stance, the consensus at school was firmly anti-Israel.

And *that's* what my mother wanted me to talk about—the survival of Israel? Are you kidding? Here I had lived among my classmates as a secret Jew for six years and now she wanted me to get up and blow my cover by presenting myself as the lone defender of Israel?

No way I was going to do that.

Instead, I gave a speech about rising sea levels resulting from the melting of the polar glaciers, a topic that in retrospect was way ahead of its time. The presentation was very humorous, if I do say so myself, and at least the students laughed all the way through it. I received a pretty good grade. But I knew that, as usual, I had just used humor to hide my insecurity.

But now, six decades later, with thousands of hours of therapy and years of researching Jewish history under my belt, I was ready to give that talk again in front of them all. I thought I might actually do it at my sixtieth-reunion class dinner. But they didn't schedule a dinner with speeches as at previous reunions, so that opportunity evaporated.

But if it *had* been possible, I would have given a completely different talk from the one I gave as an eighteen-year-old, when I didn't have the nerve to share my real feelings and show my authentic self to my classmates. I like to think that this is what I might have said if I could have given my 1957 speech today.

Good morning.

I don't know if you know this, but I am Jewish. I never shared this with any of you before; I kept it a secret at school and through all the years since, although I must admit it eventually struck me that I'm probably the only one who believed it was a secret. [At this point there might be smothered laughter rolling throughout the hall. Embarrassing!]

But now, I've come out of the "J" closet, and I have to tell you that it was no picnic being the only person in the whole school not invited to Ms. Hall's dancing school, or to the cotillions, or your sisters' coming out parties, and the only Jew having to attend Christian services on Wednesdays and Sundays.

Six decades have passed since we were all at school together, and I don't want to stand up here and whine about how I was treated back then, because I never experienced any overt animosity, nor was I ever ignored. You are my friends, and those early friendships are often the strongest, as we see here today, greeting each other with such fondness and sharing our old school memories. I cherish those memories, and it's clear that you do too.

But I also remember that I was excluded from your social events and was rarely invited to your homes. I believe that this more likely came from your parents and grandparents and not you, yourselves. Perhaps even the older generations were in a bind. They could not easily invite a Jewish boy to a club or venue that restricted Jews, or they would be breaking rules that they themselves may not have made (but did agree to).

Times have changed, and those restrictions do not exist today. Those clubs, including the yacht club I belong to, dropped those policies years ago as they conflict with current social norms and acceptance of diversity.

But unfortunately, antisemitism has not entirely disappeared. As I spent those school years in chapel and in the various churches, I heard the Gospels of the New Testament preached over and over again and discovered, much to my amazement, that the portrayal of Jews in the Gospels seems to be the source of the myths and stereotypes Christians have believed about Jews through the centuries. Even to my schoolboy ears, the hateful accusations about the Jews in the Gospels seemed inconsistent with the message of love that Jesus was preaching. Today hate speech and acts of hatred by one group against another are met with public outrage or at least lip service by political leaders who decry and condemn them. But the messages in the Gospels remain and are sometimes cited by the perpetrators of hate crimes as justification for their acts, even today.

All of you, and the Catholic and Protestant friends I have made throughout my life, seem to be loving people, pursuing your lives as "good Christians" are meant to. You accept the loving words Jesus preached in the Sermon on the Mount, and you read in Matthew 22:39, "You shall love the Lord your God with all your heart, soul and mind," and "Love your neighbor as yourself."

But these words and interpretations seem to be at odds with words from the New Testament that repeatedly demean and condemn the Jews for not accepting Jesus as the Messiah. Is it possible that there were multiple writers of each of the Gospels, with all their words attributed to Matthew, Mark, Luke, or John? Surely all four Gospel writers could not have intended to leave us with such contradictory messages.

No, I think what changed must have been what was happening in Rome in the decades when the New Testament was being written. During this period, the new Christians believed they had to distance themselves completely from the laws and practices of the Jews in order to attract followers to the new faith. Perhaps the Gospel writers, plus Paul and other Christian writers, went about this distancing with a little too much vigor in order to establish themselves as the new "chosen people." The Jews who refused to accept Jesus as the savior had to be condemned to assert Christian legitimacy. And this came at a terrible cost to us.

It seems clear to me that the loving God described by Jesus would not encourage or condone centuries of mass slaughter and the alienation and suffering of a whole race of people, carried out so thoroughly as to assure that there are hardly any more Jews living in the world today than lived in the first century—even while the rest of the population has grown by a factor of eighteen.

Those inconsistent messages were inserted into the Gospels one hundred to two hundred years after the crucifixion, and they were largely based on Roman attitudes toward cults versus accepted religions at the time. But we no longer live in those times.

Looking back six decades, I remember that it was shocking to sit there in my pew listening to the visiting ministers, who seemed to be scolding *me, personally*, for killing Christ. "His blood is on your hands," they told us, quoting from the Gospels. Do you want to know whose hands they were talking about? Mine. For good measure they added, "and not only on your hands but on the hands of your children and their children." And those just happen to be my children and grandchildren.

I doubt any of you would have made that connection, but I did, as did millions of faithful Christians who not only heard those negative stories about the Jews from the pulpit, but saw them repeated in art, sculpture, stained glass windows, theater, and literature for two thousand years. And the faithful did not take these condemnations of Jews as Christ-killers lying down.

They responded with the Crusades, four of them, beginning in 1096 and ending with the Children's Crusade of 1204, made up of vicious teenagers. Although it is rarely taught, the crusaders killed thousands upon thousands of defenseless Jews as they marched through Europe on their way to killing Muslims in Jerusalem and in other communities in the Middle East. They murdered most of the Jews of England, France, and Germany. Then, in the mid-fourteenth century, as the Black Plague raged throughout Europe, Christians used the myth that we poisoned the wells and caused the Plague as justification for another mass slaughter, which wiped out the next generation of European Jews. And then came the Spanish Inquisition, with its instruments of torture and burnings at the stake, followed by the expulsion and eventual death by exposure and starvation of all the Jews of Spain in 1492. At the beginning of the sixteenth century, all the Jews of Italy were locked up behind ghetto walls for the next three hundred years. The twentieth century brought widespread pogroms in Russia and Poland, and in our own lifetime, the Holocaust claimed the lives of half of all the Jews living in the world.

From the fourth century, when Christianity rose to become the state religion under Constantine, until the Vatican was defeated and Italy united under Victor Emmanuel in 1870, the number of Jews in the world did not increase at all. St. Augustine's "sentence" was fulfilled in spades. Tens of millions of Jews were murdered century after century—a crime of historical proportions.

But that kind of violence seems to be very much at odds with the kindness you all showed me then and still show me today. In fact, it seems apparent to me that all of my non-Jewish friends and colleagues live their lives according to the values that Jesus expressed in his Sermon on the Mount.

I do see hope even though progress is slow. I believe the world has no choice but to become more united in order to save itself. Martin Luther King Jr. expressed this as he paraphrased the words of nineteenth-century Unitarian minister Theodore Parker when he often reminded us that, "The arc of the moral universe is long, but it bends toward justice."

Other leaders in the twentieth century had a firm grasp of moral courage. In the first chapter of this book, I mentioned Nelson Mandela, who wrote of the tortured relationship between blacks and whites in South Africa and cited the effects of creating a climate of "otherness." Imprisoned on Robben Island for twenty-seven years, he described how apartheid affected both races in terrible and destructive ways. Eventually, he convinced white South Africans to abandon their policy of racial separation and embrace democracy in South Africa, even though by doing so they would lose their grip on power and authority. He summed it up in the final sentence of his autobiography: "The oppressed and the oppressor alike are robbed of their humanity."

This point of view, and the international esteem in which Mandela was held for expressing it, gives me hope for the future, as does the example of Pope Francis. His pronouncements on many social questions seem to reject the rigidity of his predecessors and reflect his belief in a more loving and accepting Church. Since his inauguration (to which many prominent Jewish leaders were invited), Pope Francis has repeatedly met with delegates from Jewish organizations, repeating his belief that a true Christian cannot be antisemitic. He has spoken out against corruption and violence everywhere, including within the Church, and repeatedly expressed his commitment to religious liberty for all peoples.

Another positive sign was the 2019 release of a report, "God's Unfailing Word: Theological & Practical Perspectives on Jewish-Christian Relations," commissioned by Justin Welby, archbishop of Canterbury, on behalf of the Church of England. Prompted by the recent uptick in antisemitic hate crimes across Europe and the U.S., this first-of-its-kind report states that "Christians have in the past repeated and promoted negative stereotypes of Jewish people, thereby contributing to grave suffering and injustice. They have used Christian doctrine in order to justify and persecute Jewish suffering, for instance teaching that Jewish people are suffering and should suffer because they are guilty of the murder of Christ, the divine son of God, or because they have refused to welcome the Messiah. . . . This has fostered attitudes of distrust and hostility among Christians for their Jewish neighbors, in some cases leading to violent attacks, murder and expulsion." [74]

It goes on to say that "Christians cannot . . . reflect on the past honestly until we have felt the cruelty of our history," and concludes that, because "theological ideas have been used to legitimate anti-Semitism," Christians are urged to "repent for the sins of the past against Jews" and to "challenge [our] attitudes and stereotypes." [75] The report represents a welcome shift in the language that Church leaders are using to define Christian-Jewish relations, both in the past and moving forward. And we can hope that the position taken by the Anglican Church will eventually lead the pope to make similar statements on behalf of the world's Catholics.

Zak Ebrahim, in his book *The Terrorist's Son,* describes growing up as a child of terrorists. His father, with others, tried to blow up the World Trade Center in 1993, murdered a rabbi, hated Jews and gays—and yet, he changed. Ebrahim also describes how his mother said to him one day, "I'm so sick of hating people." [76] It takes so much negative energy to hold those emotions inside, Zak continues, that the overwhelming intolerance and the ideology of hatred toward others needs to end for himself and for others. Zak's message today is that he wants to fight for the *victims* of terror.

A similar transition happened to Derek Black, son of the grand wizard of the KKK, who, after meeting Jews for the first time in college, became repulsed by what he had urged others to do.

As someone who developed a deep personal interest in science as a middle-aged adult, it seems to me that the progress of moral thought is quite similar to the progress of science. It continuously builds upon itself and moves at an ever-increasing pace, driven faster and further by communication technology. Recent advances in the understanding of genetics and the current fascination with DNA and extended ancestry will, in themselves, prove to the world that there is only one race—the human race. We may wear different clothing, recite different prayers, read different books, and eat different food. But at the cellular level, we are the same, nearly indistinguishable from one another, all of us the children of God.

So, now I've told you the truth about myself, and my beliefs, and my insecurities as a boy and a man. Maybe you've known it all the whole time.

The bottom line is I'm hoping you won't take offense at anything I've said about Christianity or the Gospels; I've only tried to explain how painfully the words of the Gospels have affected those of us who did not grow up with Jesus. I hope you can appreciate this.

And I trust that we're still friends.

Afterword

It is a Saturday in late April of 2020, and the entire nation has been quarantined since mid-March due to the worldwide pandemic of the novel coronavirus. I have spent most of this period of social isolation making the final changes the editors have suggested before shipping this manuscript off to the publisher.

April in New England can be rainy and cold, but today it is sunny and warm and I am lying out in the backyard of our home with my wife Dora, listening to a live stream presentation by the Metropolitan Opera, which features some of opera's greatest artists performing from their homes around the globe. They are singing from Georgia in the Balkans, Rome and Lake Como in Italy, Switzerland, Berlin, France, and Wales, across the Atlantic to Toronto, down to Connecticut and New York, and finally to Atlanta, Georgia.

Naturally, as the fanatic you now know me to be, my thoughts are drifting to the three hundred years my people spent locked in the dank ghettos of Rome, Venice, and all the Papal States, as if we had some sort of "Jewish virus."

Listening to the magnificent arias expressing the full range of human emotion, from deep love to fear to vengeful hate, I can't help but see a connection to the tragedy Jews have endured for seventeen hundred years.

And I can't help but ask: When will it end? We cannot fail to learn something from this twenty-first century plague as we witness on a daily basis people of every race, color, and religion coming together to help, risking their lives to save others, stepping up to heal the suffering world, *tikkun olam*, made visible on our computer screens and television sets every day.

And, in this time of widespread suffering, I want to ask Church leaders to do more than pay lip service to asking for forgiveness, and to challenge them to take action to neutralize the most damaging accusations against us. Small steps have been taken in this direction. Vatican councils and recent reports from the Anglican Church have begun to question the relationship of biblical texts to centuries of suspicion and hatred. But so much more remains to be done to prevent another generation from internalizing the wrong message.

As a Jew, Jesus would have understood that the task before him, as he traveled throughout Judea and the Galilee, was to heal the world. Both the words he preached and the actions he took focused on activities of the heart: care for the sick, feed the hungry, comfort the bereaved, visit the imprisoned, and, above all, love thy neighbor as thyself. The rest of his story—comprised of details that were imagined and filled in, over the hundred years following his death—is likely untrue and ultimately irrelevant. The true power of Christianity is found in the central message of "love thy neighbor as thyself."

Timeline

BEFORE THE COMMON ERA (BCE)

1600	Abraham
1300–1200	Moses and the Exodus from Egypt
950	Solomon builds the First Temple in Jerusalem
586	Babylonians capture Jerusalem and destroy the First Temple
538	Persians defeat the Babylonians and Jews are permitted to return to Judea
516	The Second Temple is built
333	Alexander the Great makes peace with Judea
170–165	Maccabee war against Greeks leads to a mutual protection agreement with Rome
100–44	Reign of Julius Caesar
63	Roman general, part of triumvirate with Julius Caesar, is asked to settle a dispute between two groups in Judea, leading to control of Judea by Rome
37–4	Herod's rule as king of Judea (until his death)

COMMON ERA (CE)

30	Death of Jesus
40	BCE 60–CE 40 : life of St. Paul (formally Saul of Tarsus)
70	The destruction of Jerusalem and the Second Temple
132	Emperor Hadrian and the Bar Kochba rebellion
212	Emperor Caracalla grants citizenship to the Jews

313	Emperor Constantine converts to Christianity and removes the rights of Jews
360–363	Emperor Julian grants Jews permission to rebuild the temple; with his death the project is stopped by the rise of a Christian emperor
487–526	Theodore the Great (Barbarian) invades Rome; civil rights of Jews restored
638–691	Moslem conquest of Jerusalem; Jews are permitted to return; Al Aqsa Mosque (Dome of the Rock) built in Jerusalem on the site of the Second Temple
1013	Beginning of the golden age for Jews in Spain
1066	Norman conquest of England; first Jews arrive in England
1095–99	First Crusade; massacre of Jews in France and Germany en route to Jerusalem where both Jews and Moslems are massacred
1147–49	Second Crusade; debts to Jews are canceled for Christians who enlist in the crusade
1189–92	Third Crusade, led by Richard the Lionheart
1202–04	Fourth Crusade
1215	Fourth Lateran Council; Jews are required to wear identifying badges
1242	The pope orders Talmuds to be collected and burned
1290	Jews are expelled from England
1306:	Jews are expelled from France
1348	The Black Plague spreads, leading to slaughter of Jews of Europe
1391	Forced conversion of the Jews in Spain
1478	Spanish Inquisition begins
1492	Jews are expelled from Spain
1497	Jews are expelled from Portugal
1516	The Venetian government establishes the first Jewish ghetto

1543	Martin Luther and the Reformation. He pens "The Jews and Their Lies."
1555	Pope orders establishment of Jewish ghettos
1593	The Medici family invites Jews to settle in Leghorn, Italy
1654	First Jews arrive in North America
1655	Jews are permitted to return to England under Cromwell
1796–9	Napoleon frees the Jews from the ghettos
1815	Napoleon's government falls; Pope Pius VIII returns to Rome; Jewish ghetto reestablished
1858	Edgardo Mortara, a Jewish child, is kidnapped by the Church and baptized against his will
1870	Victor Emmanuel unites Italy; the pope loses control; Jews are emancipated and ghettoes abolished
1881	Russian pogroms begin
1933	Hitler rises to power in Germany
1939–1944	The Holocaust and "Final Solution" to the "Jewish problem"
1948	The State of Israel is established

Notes

Preface

i. Harry J. Leon and Carolyn Osiek, *The Jews of Ancient Rome* (Peabody, MA: Hendrickson Publishers, 1995), 1, 257.

ii. *Jewish Virtual Library* (https://www.jewishvirtuallibrary.org), s.v. "Vital Statistics: World Jewish Population."

iii. Ibid.

Introduction

iv. Nelson Mandela, *Long Walk to Freedom* (New York: Little, Brown & Company, 2013), 624.

v. Roy P. Balser, ed., *The Collected Works of Abraham Lincoln* (New Brunswick, NJ: Rutgers University Press, 1953) 2:532.

Chapter 1: Apparently My Family Murdered Their God

1. Raoul McLaughlin, *The Roman Empire and the Silk Routes: The Ancient World Economy & the Empires of Parthia, Central Asia & Han China* (Barnsley, UK: Pen & Sword History, 2016), Kindle edition, chap. 10.

Chapter 3: Wading in Deeper

2. Robert Wallace, *The World of Leonardo: 1452–1519* (New York: Time-Life Books, 1972), 81.

Chapter 4: My Introduction to the New Testament

3. Pope Benedict XVI (Joseph Ratzinger), *Jesus of Nazareth: The Infancy Narratives* (New York: Image, 2012), 62–63.

4. Jacob R. Marcus, *The Jew in the Medieval World: A Source Book, 315–1791* (New York: Union of American Hebrew Congregations, 1938), 103.

5. J. W. Drijvers, "Helena Augusta: Cross and Myth. Some New Reflections," *Millennium 8. Yearbook on the Culture and History of the First Millennium CE*, ed. W. Brandes (Berlin and Boston: De Gruyter Mouton, 2011), 125–174.

6. James Carroll, *Constantine's Sword: The Church and the Jews, A History* (Boston: Houghton Mifflin Harcourt, 2001), 218.

7. Juan Antonio Llorente and Léonard Gallois, *History of the Spanish Inquisition: Abridged from the Original Work Of M. Llorente, Late Secretary Of That Institution (1826)* (Whitefish, MT: Kessinger Publishing, 2010) 13.

Chapter 5: Misappropriating Judaism

8. Paul Johnson, *A History of Christianity* (New York: Atheneum, 1976), 6.

9. James Parkes, *The Conflict of the Church and the Synagogue: A Study in the Origins of Antisemitism* (London: Soncino Press, 1934), 55.

10. Ibid., 96.

Chapter 6: "I Ain't No Judas"

11. Liaquat Ahamed, *Lords of Finance: The Bankers Who Broke the World* (London: Penguin Books, 2009), 368.

12. *Catholic Encyclopedia Online Edition* (https://www.catholic.com), s.v. "Tomas de Torquemada."

Chapter 7: Jewish Life Before Constantine

13. Johnson, *A History of Christianity*, 30.

14. Ibid.

15. Léon Poliakov, *The History of Anti-Semitism*, trans. Richard Howard (Philadelphia: University of Pennsylvania Press, 2003), 1:8.

16. Leon and Osiek, *The Jews of Ancient Rome*, 24.

17. Ibid., 18 (footnote).

18. Ibid., 28.

19. Ibid., 31.

20. Poliakov, *The History of Anti-Semitism*, 1:9.

21. Leon and Osiek, *The Jews of Ancient Rome*, 40.

22. Edward J. Watts, *Mortal Republic: How Rome Fell into Tyranny* (New York: Basic Books, 2018), 175.

23. Johnson, *A History of Christianity*, 74.

Chapter 9: Stereotyped in the Arts

24. Marcus, *The Jew in the Medieval World*, 367, 370–371.

25. Ibid.

26. Ibid.

27. *Encyclopedia Judaica* (Jerusalem: Keter Publishing, 1973), 5:1135.

28. Marcus, *The Jew in the Medieval World*, 370.

29. *Encyclopedia Judaica*, 5:979.

30. Victor Labate, "Banking in the Roman World," *Ancient History Encyclopedia* (https://www.ancient.eu) (November 17, 2016).

Chapter 10: Back in History Class

31. Haim Cohen, *The Trial and Death of Jesus* (Old Saybrook, CT: Konecky & Konecky, 1963), 171–172.

32. Ibid.

33. "The Death of Jesus—Four Gospel Narratives," Boston College School of Theology and Ministry/STM Online: Crossroads Mini-Courses.

https://www.bc.edu/bc-web/schools/stm/sites/crossroads/resources/mini-course/death-of-jesus.html.

Chapter 11: What? We Killed Little Christian Boys?

34. Rudyard Kipling, *Puck of Pook's Hill* (London: Doubleday, Page, 1906), 237.

Chapter 12: Heading Off to College

35. Marcus, *The Jew in the Medieval World*, 367, 43–45.

36. Parkes, *The Conflict of the Church and the Synagogue*, 238.

Chapter 15: The Crusades: Killing Two Infidels with One Stone

37. Johnson, *A History of Christianity*, 191.

38. Abram Leon Sachar, *A History of the Jews: From the Babylonian Exile to the Establishment of Israel* (New York: Alfred A. Knopf, 1966, 1982), 186.

39. *Encyclopedia Judaica*, 5:1135.

40. James Parkes and Morton C. Fierman, *The Jew in the Medieval Community: A Study of His Political and Economic Situation* (London: Hermon Press, 1976), 63.

41. *Encyclopedia Judaica*, 5:1135.

42. Parkes and Fierman, *The Jew in the Medieval Community*, 64.

43. Parkes and Fierman, *The Jew in the Medieval Community*, 66.

44. Sachar, *A History of the Jews*, 189.

45. *Jewish Encyclopedia* online version (http://jewishencyclopedia.com), s.v. "Pastoureaux."

46. George Zabriskie Gray, *The Children's Crusade: An Episode of the Thirteenth Century* (Boston: Houghton, Mifflin & Company, 1898), 224–225. https://hdl.handle.net/2027/loc.ark:/13960/t3dz13c4g?urlappend=%3Bseq=244.

Chapter 16: From the Renaissance to the Ghetto

47. William Deresiewicz, "Why Primo Levi Survives," *The Atlantic* (December 2015).

48. Ibid.

49. Anne Sarzin, "Passion Plays That Inspired Violence in Rome," *University of Sydney News* (February 24, 2000).

Chapter 17: If We Were the Usurers, Where Are Our Palaces?

50. Raymond de Roover, *The Rise and Decline of the Medici Bank: 1397–1494* (Cambridge, MA: Harvard University Press, 1999), 121.

51. Ibid., 122.

52. Parkes and Fierman, *The Jew in the Medieval Community*, 337.

53. Kipling, *Puck of Pook's Hill*, 240.

54. Parkes and Fierman, *The Jew in the Medieval Community* 337.

55. Ibid., 337.

Chapter 18: The Inquisition and the End of Spanish Jewry

56. Jules Isaac, *Jesus and Israel* (New York: Holt, Rinehart & Winston, 1971), 46, 47.

57. Cecil Roth, *The Spanish Inquisition* (New York: W. W. Norton & Company, 1964, 1996), 29.

58. Ibid., 32.

59. Henry Charles Lea, *A History of the Inquisition of Spain* (London: Macmillan, 1907), 111.

60. Ibid., 97.

61. Ibid., 44.

62. Llorente and Gallois, *History of the Spanish Inquisition,* 70–71.

63. Ibid., 79.

64. Roth, *The Spanish Inquisition,* 80–81.

65. Ibid., 179.

66. Sachar, *A History of the Jews,* 216.

67. Roth, *The Spanish Inquisition,* 179.

68. Ibid., 45.

Chapter 19: Shrink #1 Gives Me the Boot

69. Roth, *The History of the Jews of Italy,* 45.

Chapter 21: My Second Career as a Lobbyist

70. National Institutes of Health Office of Budget (https://officeofbudget.od.nih.gov).

Chapter 22: "Kvelling" Over Ben

71. *Encyclopedia Judaica,* 20:46.

Chapter 23: Moving Toward the Twentieth Century

72. *Jewish Encyclopedia,* s.v. "Theodoric the Great: Arianism."

73. Gerald Posner, *God's Bankers: A History of Money and Power at the Vatican* (New York: Simon & Schuster, 2015), 99.

Chapter 24: The Senior Speech I Should Have Given in 1957

74. *God's Unfailing Word: Theological and Practical Perspectives on Christian-Jewish Relations* (London: Church House Publishing, 2019), xiv.

75. Ibid., xi.

76. Zak Ebrahim and Jeff Giles, *The Terrorist's Son: A Story of Choice* (New York: Simon & Schuster/TED, 2014), 84.

Bibliography

Ahamed, Liaquat. *Lords of Finance: The Bankers Who Broke the World*. New York: Penguin Press, 2009.

Boston College School of Theology and Ministry/STM Online: Crossroads Mini-Courses. "The Death of Jesus—Four Gospel Narratives." https://www.bc.edu/bc-web/schools/stm/sites/crossroads/resources/mini-course/death-of-jesus.html.

Carroll, James. *Constantine's Sword: The Church and the Jews, A History*. Boston: Houghton Mifflin Harcourt, 2001.

Catholic Encyclopedia Online Edition (https://www.catholic.com).

Cohen, Haim. *The Trial and Death of Jesus*. Old Saybrook, CT: Konecky & Konecky, 1963.

Deresiewicz, William. "Why Primo Levi Survives." *The Atlantic* (December 2015).

de Roover, Raymond. *The Rise and Decline of the Medici Bank: 1397–1494*. Cambridge, MA: Harvard University Press, 1999.

Drijvers, J. W. "Helena Augusta: Cross and Myth. Some New Reflections," *Millennium 8. Yearbook on the Culture and History of the First Millennium CE*. Edited by W. Brandes. Berlin and Boston: De Gruyter Mouton, 2011.

Ebrahim, Zak and Jeff Giles. *The Terrorist's Son: A Story of Choice*. New York: Simon & Schuster/TED, 2014.

Encyclopedia Judaica. Jerusalem: Keter Publishing, 1973.

Gerber, Jane S. *Jews of Spain: A History of the Sephardic Experience*. London: Free Press, 1994.

God's Unfailing Word: Theological and Practical Perspectives on Christian-Jewish Relations. London: Church House Publishing, 2019.

Gray, George Zabriskie. *The Children's Crusade: An Episode of the Thirteenth Century*, Boston: Houghton, Mifflin & Company, 1898.

Halsall, Paul, ed. *Internet Ancient History Sourcebook*. Fordham University. https://sourcebooks.web.fordham.edu/.

Isaac, Jules. *Jesus and Israel*. New York: Holt, Rinehart & Winston, 1971.

Jewish Encyclopedia online version (http://jewishencyclopedia.com).

Jewish Virtual Library (https://www.jewishvirtuallibrary.org).

Johnson, Paul. *A History of Christianity*. New York: Atheneum, 1976.

Kertzer, David I. *The Popes Against the Jews: The Vatican's Role in the Rise of Modern Anti-Semitism*. London: Knopf Doubleday Publishing Group, 2007.

Kipling, Rudyard. *Puck of Pook's Hill*. London: Doubleday, Page, 1906.

Labate, Victor. "Banking in the Roman World." *Ancient History Encyclopedia* (https://www.ancient.eu) (November 17, 2016).

Lea, Henry Charles. *A History of the Inquisition of Spain*. London: Macmillan, 1907.

Leon, Harry J. and Carolyn Osiek. *The Jews of Ancient Rome*. Peabody, MA: Hendrickson Publishers, 1995.

Levi, Primo. *Survival in Auschwitz: If This Is a Man*. Translated by Stuart J. Woolf. London: Simon & Schuster, 1996.

Balser, Roy P., ed. *The Collected Works of Abraham Lincoln*. New Brunswick, NJ: Rutgers University Press, 1953.

Llorente, Juan Antonio and Léonard Gallois, *History of the Spanish Inquisition: Abridged from the Original Work Of M. Llorente, Late Secretary Of That Institution (1826)*. Whitefish, MT: Kessinger Publishing, 2010.

McLaughlin, Raoul. *The Roman Empire and the Silk Routes: The Ancient World Economy & the Empires of Parthia, Central Asia & Han China*. Barnsley, UK: Pen & Sword History, 2016. Kindle edition.

Mandela, Nelson, *Long Walk to Freedom*. New York: Little, Brown & Company, 2013.

Marcus, Jacob R. *The Jew in the Medieval World: A Source Book, 315–1791*. New York: Union of American Hebrew Congregations, 1938.

National Institutes of Health Office of Budget (https://officeofbudget.od.nih.gov).

Parkes, James, *The Conflict of the Church and the Synagogue: A Study in the Origins of Antisemitism*. London: Soncino Press, 1934.

Parkes, James and Morton C. Fierman. *The Jew in the Medieval Community: A Study of His Political and Economic Situation*. London: Hermon Press, 1976.

Poliakov, Léon. *The History of Anti-Semitism*. Vol. 1. Translated by Richard Howard. Philadelphia: University of Pennsylvania Press, 2003.

Posner, Gerald. *God's Bankers: A History of Money and Power at the Vatican*. New York: Simon & Schuster, 2015.

Pope Benedict XVI (Joseph Ratzinger). *Jesus of Nazareth: The Infancy Narratives*. New York: Image, 2012.

Roth, Cecil. *The History of the Jews of Italy*. Philadelphia: Jewish Publication Society, 1946.

Roth, Cecil. *The Spanish Inquisition*. New York: W. W. Norton & Company, 1964, 1996.

Sachar, Abram Leon. *A History of the Jews: From the Babylonian Exile to the Establishment of Israel*. New York: Alfred A. Knopf, 1966, 1982.

Sarzin, Anne. "Passion Plays That Inspired Violence in Rome." *University of Sydney News* (February 24, 2000).

Starr, Bernard. *Jesus, Jews, and Anti-Semitism in Art*. 2nd ed. New York: Bernard Starr, 2016. Kindle edition.

Vogelstein, Hermann. *History of Jews in Rome*. Philadelphia: The Jewish Publication Society of America, 1940.

Wallace, Robert. *The World of Leonardo, 1452–1519*. New York: Time-Life Books, 1972.

Watts, Edward J. *Mortal Republic: How Rome Fell into Tyranny*. New York: Basic Books, 2018.

———*The Final Pagan Generation: Rome's Unexpected Path to Christianity*. Berkeley, CA: University of California Press, 2015.

Wistrich, Robert S. *Antisemitism: The Longest Hatred*. New York: Schocken Books, 1994.

Picture Credits:

Acknowledgments

Like many books by first-time authors, this one has been through numerous drafts since I began researching it over thirty years ago. I am indebted to the many friends, family members, and even the occasional strangers who patiently listened to me think out loud on my subject matter through all that time. I'm pretty sure none of them were convinced it would ever be completed, let alone published.

Though he is no longer alive to read this, I owe much to Father Robert Bullock, the Catholic priest who shared his insights about the political agenda of the Gospel writers as we stood together on Mount Scopus in Israel. His words not only surprised me, but lifted a long-held weight from my shoulders and launched me on the path to discover the real roots of anti-Jewish feeling in the world.

I also have to acknowledge the role of literary agent Lane Zachary, who read several very early drafts when the book was organized more as a travel guide to European sites with significance in Jewish history. Lane was honest enough to warn me that histories are best written by historians with academic credentials and suggest that I consider turning my manuscript into a memoir. It turns out that the ensuing process of examining and recording the events and choices of my life, while occasionally painful and difficult, has proved to be a great blessing.

Thanks to my cousin (who is more like a brother) Fred Sherman, who read a recent draft and boosted my morale considerably by declaring that he couldn't put it down. Thanks also to other early readers, including my niece Rachel Samuels, my sister-in-law Rhoda Nudik, *The Tablet* Editor-in-Chief Alana Newhouse, and my friends Richard

Wolman and Barry Schrage. Their encouraging comments were the first evidence I had that other people might find the work interesting and provocative and not merely an exercise in self-indulgence. I'm especially grateful to Barry for his guidance about spreading the word about the book to Jewish groups throughout New England and the United States, and for contributing the foreword to this book.

Thank you to the two professional readers and editors, Carrie Cantor and Beth Bruno, who went through the book with a fine-tooth comb and made useful suggestions and thoughtful remarks throughout.

Thanks to Mary Ann Faughnan, the Bauhan Publishing editor who read this book, found it compelling, and was the first person to say, "Yes!" I am grateful also to Sarah Bauhan, Henry James, and Jane Eklund for their efforts to turn a manuscript and a handful of images and photographs into a beautiful finished product of which I can be proud. They made the entire process easier than I expected and were a delight to work with, start to finish.

I am particularly indebted to Leaf Seligman, who read my manuscript with the "keen eye" her business card promised, and encouraged me to dig deeper, chapter by chapter, into the meaning of my Jewish heritage at all the stages of my life, and helped me to see this entire project as an act of repairing the world.

And I continue to be grateful to Scott Manning and Abby Welhouse for their thorough and tireless efforts to share this book with all its potential audiences, spreading the word about the contribution it makes to the ongoing dialogue between Christians and Jews.

I need to acknowledge, with deep gratitude, the daily efforts of my personal aides, Rita Dirrane, Patecia Denton and Hagar Kyerewaa, who work so hard to care for me and make my life in a wheelchair so much easier to manage. And I can't imagine the past 22 years without the loyal friendship and assistance of Steve Partington, almost a son to me, who makes possible so many of the activities (on and off the water) that add fun to my life.

Very special thanks and love to the people who are dearest to me and whose support has always kept me moving forward: my intelligent, capable, and always insightful wife, Dora; my son Ben, whose career and accomplishments are a constant source of pride; Ben's wife, Anne-Marie, who has been such a wonderful addition to our family; and, though they can't yet read this, my precious grandchildren, Otis and Seraphina. It is ultimately for them and the generations to follow that I have reconstructed the memories and experiences of my life and placed them in the context of "Growing Up Jewish in a Christian World." I hope this book will help them understand the courage and perseverance of the people they come from, and their own place in our history.

Lastly, my deepest thanks to my close collaborator of twenty-five years, Leslie Rosoff Kenney. Throughout the 1990s and early 2000s, she was invaluable in helping to refine the thousands of pages of speeches, testimony, journal articles, and position papers we produced in our efforts to increase federal funding for medical research. As this book moved toward its final form, she challenged me to show myself authentically, encouraging me to add material in some places, omit material in others. Our regular discussions, debates, and occasional arguments about the text provided the focus I needed to wrap up thirty years of work and bring this book to completion.

Discussion Questions

1. Is there a difference between stereotyping and prejudice when it comes to our impressions of other racial, religious or ethnic groups? Does the former necessarily lead to the latter, or can stereotyping be benign and harmless? If we are honest, what are some of the stereotypes that we tend to believe about Jews, Muslims, African-Americans, White Anglo-Saxon Protestants, homosexuals?

2. So much information about minorities is left out of the historical record perhaps, as has been suggested, because history is written by the victors. How much of the information in this book about the treatment of the Jews were you aware of? Did any of it surprise or shock you?

3. In your own life, have you or your family experienced ethnic prejudice—either as the source (perhaps your family engaged in telling jokes or stories that were denigrating to a specific group) or as the recipient? Were the negative comments you heard intentionally hostile, or did they seem to be spoken out of ignorance? How does it make you feel when you hear such comments, even when they are not directed at your own group? Have you ever spoken up in such circumstances?

4. A 1938 survey found that more than half of Americans agreed with the statement that "The persecution of Jews in Europe by the Nazis is partly their own fault." Eleven percent believed it was "entirely their own fault." What do you think they were basing this belief on?

5. Do you think the Bible—both Old and New Testaments—are the actual 'revealed word of God?' If they were written by human beings, do you think it is important to study the reasons why they told the stories the way they did along with the content? For many years now, bible scholars have questioned their historical accuracy. Is there anything to be gained from digging deeper into the truth of the central texts of Judaism and Christianity?

6. Discuss the human impulse to "blame the victim."